W9-AZJ-021

"PROVOCATIVE ... ELLEN GOODMAN IS ON TO SOMETHING THAT IS AT THE HEART OF THE WAY WE LIVE NOW."

—Publishers Weekly

"A very thoughtful book for anyone concerned about the crazy-quilt patterns developing in the personal lives of people today."

—San Diego Union

"One of the many books from which the full social history of these revolutionary times will be written."

—New York Times Book Review

Ellen Goodman

Turning Points

FAWCETT COLUMBINE • NEW YORK

TURNING POINTS

THIS BOOK CONTAINS THE COMPLETE TEXT OF THE
ORIGINAL HARDCOVER EDITION.

Published by Fawcett Columbine Books, a unit of CBS Publications, the
Consumer Publishing Division of CBS Inc., by arrangement with
Doubleday and Company, Inc.

ISBN: 0-449-90015-0

Printed in the United States of America

First Fawcett Columbine printing: May 1980

10   9   8   7   6   5   4   3   2   1

TO KATIE

Contents

Preface   ix

Acknowledgments   xv

Part I   Beginnings   1

Chapter 1   Turning Points   7

Chapter 2   A Scale of Change   39

Part II   The Shuttle Zone   63

Chapter 3   Change Innovators: The Great Leap   68

Chapter 4   Change Resisters   98

Chapter 5   The New Middleground   126

Part III   Inside Changes   161

Chapter 6   Divorce   165

Chapter 7   The Housewife's New Blues   209

Chapter 8   Choice   249

Epilogue   286

Preface

When I was a kid, I wanted everything to stay the same. I wanted to live in the same house, go to the same school, keep the same friends . . . forever. When I was ten, I used to tell my mother that I would grow up, get married, have children, but never leave home.

The truth was that I didn't have to cope with very much change in my youth. I went from high school to college to marriage to motherhood as if it were all in a contract I'd signed. Through my twenties I defended the predictable life with security plans for the present and insurance programs for the future. I drew up more Five Year Plans than the Kremlin.

Yet, in my thirties, my life and the lives of people around me have been in continual process of change.

Despite my own natural inclination to hold the line, the life plan I had settled on at age ten isn't remotely in operation today. The future we were so sure of during the 1950s has been gutted and renovated again and again on the way to and through the 1970s.

I first began to think seriously about change when I was being buffeted by it. I had just come out of a period of personal crisis—the kind that often comes with divorce. While I am hardly an advocate of Creative Divorce—it's an expression that reminds me of "A Stimulating Breakdown"—it was a time of heightened vulnerability, a time when I was most aware of the weaknesses of my plans and most sensitive about how disruptive change can be.

At the same time, I was, after all, in the business of change. Journalism is the pursuit of "news," of newness. During the 1960s and 1970s, newspapers have breathlessly followed events in a time of dramatic social crises. I have been one of those who chronicle change. As a reporter for the last decade and a half, I have worked in a time of Present Shock, when many people feel as stunned by social change as if they'd driven home to find that the oak tree in front of the house was chopped down.

On assignment, I met the civil rights movement, the peace movement, and the women's movement—the last on an August night in a stuffy meeting house on Charles Street in Boston where I had been sent by the Boston *Globe* to "cover what was happening" to some "strange" women in Boston. I have watched people come into contact with these movements and seen the various ways they've dealt with the changes these movements brought. Some people broke because they couldn't bend—broke ties with families, friends, constituents. Some rode a crest of rhetoric and excitement so far from their origins that they lost connection with their own pasts. Others pulled their roots free, as the song goes, only to become slaves to the wind.

I became an observer to, and then a participant in, change, almost against my will.

But by 1974 I was ready to drop out of my seat at the eye of the hurricane, to see if I could make some sense out of what seemed like chaos. I spent a year as a Nieman Fellow at Harvard, reading everything I could find on the subject of change. I read about Erik Erikson's life-cycle perspective, Peter Marris' social-psychological perspective, Abraham Maslow's self-realization. I read almost everything that had the word "change" connected with it, including a book that turned out to be a history of money.

To some extent, of course, my year of study was a personal search. I believed that if I could get inside the dynamic of change and understand what went on inside people and between people when they confronted something new, I would be able to carve out some guidelines that would help me during some future crisis. I figured that change wouldn't be so scary if we knew what reactions to expect and how long the healing process would take.

But finally I felt that my best source of "research" would be people, not books. Like many journalists, I believe that one way to find answers is to ask questions, and so the way to find out how people change is to talk with some of them.

From 1975 to 1978 I talked with over a hundred and fifty men and women. We focused on the changes in their lives that had come with new perspectives on sex roles in America. We explored the old assumptions of how they would—and should—live as men and women and the new realities and possibilities. We talked about how their lives were different and how they were coping with that difference. I focused on the changes due to new attitudes toward sex roles for two reasons. First was my own interest in a subject that I had reported on for years, and a movement which had affected my own life. Second, as I talked with people I came to see that this change had been the most widespread, that people were eager to talk about it.

What began as an interview often ended up as a conversation, the kind in which you learn a lot about yourself by learning about others. The people I met were "ordinary people." There are few "Big Names" in this book. Most of the people you'll meet are the players, not the stars. As one woman said, "I'm Real People." They range in age from their twenties to their late fifties, and they differ in background from blue-collar to professional, from the East to the West Coast, from single to married to divorced. I interviewed more women than men, because in many ways their lives have changed more. I also chose to talk with people who were neither buffered by enormous wealth nor crippled by desperate poverty. They were people who had choices as well as limitations.

These men and women shared a great deal about the details of their private lives. For that reason I have respected their privacy by changing many details and nearly all the names and by using a few composites. The most difficult decision I faced was choosing which stories to tell—they were all important and added to my general understanding, so, in a sense, they are all part of this book.

With them, I explored how we all yearn to be the agents rather than the victims of change. With them I found a strong hope that seems to me typical of this time—a hope that we will be able to hold on to what is best about the past while moving into a future that in some ways offers us "more." Balanced against this, I found a great fear that we will lose something— perhaps without even knowing it—that is vital to our souls. I also discovered how many other people fight the same internal wars I do, between the part of me that finds change exhilarating and full of hope, and the part of me that fears disruption and loss. By sensing this, by realizing its universality, I can now accept it better.

I think of this book, finally, as a storybook of change, in which many characters tell their own tales. It is written for those who, like me, want to learn about themselves, and about the stresses and pulls, the stop and go signs that alternate inside each of us and between all of us. It's a story of growth and loss, advances and retreats. A tale written for fellow travelers who know that every crisis, as Erik Erikson wrote, is not necessarily a catastrophe. It may be a turning point.

TURNING POINTS

The first people we'll meet aren't predicting any major new thrust in their lives. They all have, as most of us do, a strong set of reasons for defending the status quo. But many will change. Like flood victims, some won't be able to go home again because home has been washed away. Others will find encouragement in new ideas and support in political movements. Still others will slowly feel compelled to resolve a conflict that is too painful to "live with" any longer. These men and women may find one set of choices closed out behind them and a new set open in front of them.

THE SCALE OF CHANGE

I'll try to show why people feel differently about change. Why some of us make changes eagerly and easily, while others find it insurmountably difficult. Why some of us sail through enormous change with a sense of exhilaration, while others can only take a tentative half-step before feeling profoundly disrupted.

We'll see that some people are more daring than others and that some changes cost more. It seems that the same set of events feels different, carries different weights for different people. How we experience it depends on whether we see this change as threatening, or full of promise.

From the stories I heard and will retell here, I came to see that there is a scale of change ranging from the most superficial to the most critical. The heaviest changes, obviously, are those which seem to be inundated with loss. We find change easiest when it is psychologically conservative and hardest when it threatens what we think of as "the meaning of our lives."

At each turning point, listening to the people tell their stories, we can ask along with them: "How does this relate to me? What changes are easy to make and which ones are painful? In short, how do we change?"

Acknowledgments

It is very difficult to draw up a thank-you list of all the people who have helped me while I was writing this book. I have been very lucky in having the support of so many.

My family, from my mother to my aunts and uncles have always had the most unreasonable sort of confidence in me. Jane Holtz Kay was someone I could count on to understand, both as a writer and a sister.

My editor at the Boston *Globe*, Tom Winship, gave me the time to work on this book. When I asked him wryly how he wanted to be remembered in the acknowledgments, he answered, "Just call me Santa Claus."

The Wellesley College Center for Research on Women saved me hours of time with a grant that paid for much of the transcribing. I hope that they will find this book a return on their investment.

I have also been helped by remarkably good friends. Micki Talmadge kept the rest of my home life together during these years. Otile McManus' unflagging concern and high spirits restored me in a dozen ways.

Pat O'Brien spent exorbitant hours on the other end of a long-distance phone line working through ideas and problems with me. As always she helped me keep my sense of perspective and energy.

Finally, Bob Levey has been what everyone needs, a best friend.

To them, and to all the people who shared their lives with me and with the readers, thank you.

Turning Points

Part I
Beginnings

Imagine for just a moment that we are at our high school reunion. The old gymnasium is decorated the way it was for our senior prom. There are crepe paper streamers hanging from the climbing ropes and balloons tied up in bunches, camouflaging the basketball net. But this time, instead of formal "prom" clothes, we are wearing name tags.

Like our classmates, we've been drawn home to this reunion with mixed feelings of nostalgia and curiosity. Our memories of the past and questions about the present all mingle on this red and black marked basketball court.

There, over by the bleachers, dressed in tight jeans and open shirt, and wearing tinted eyeglasses and a deep tan, is Tom, the high school radical who went to California, traded in SDS for soybeans, and made a fortune in natural foods. He is talking to Mandy, of all people, the teen queen, who had sixteen sweaters and more boyfriends. Mandy was the one who said she'd marry and live happily ever after. Now she's divorced and you hear she's become a legal aid lawyer. No one calls her Mandy anymore. On her name tag it says Amanda.

For once "Amanda" isn't the star of the class. That title goes to Maureen, the kid who sat beside us in Spanish class pushing her glasses back on her nose, the one who has turned into a chic and confident woman we read about last fall in *People* magazine, "Top Economist in Washington: Maureen Makes Ends Meet."

Maureen is avoiding some of the others, the celebrity-hungry, and is talking quietly with Hal. Hal is just what he always was, only more so. The class president, who was liked for his humor and spirit, seems to have expanded, according to some master plan. Perhaps he is a bit mellower, but he has carried the same sense of self from high school to the family business, to the reunion.

We circulate around the room, exchanging stories with classmates, reminiscing, remembering, playing catch-up, and watching. On the dance floor, the old-life-of-the-party Pamela is gyrating with her husband, the man who pressed his business card in your hand just a moment ago. Over the punch bowl two or three of the old crowd are refilling their cups with sweet spiked punch while exaggerating their successes. We talk about then and now, before and after.

We are at this reunion really to see how our old classmates have changed and also to see—reflected back in their eyes—how much we have changed. Reunions like this aren't just about the past. They have a lot to say about the present.

The questions that hover in the gymnasium at this or any other reunion are: How did she change? What has happened to him? How are they the same? How are they not? What is the process by which our lives have become different?

When I set out with my tape recorder and cassettes, with notebooks and pens to interview people, I often thought of myself as a kind of class reporter. It was as if I'd been assigned the job of finding out what had happened to a large group of people who had been at least partially formed in the same school, where they had once shared some of the same experiences.

I couldn't just take to the road asking people, "How did you change?" The question is far too general. We all change by age, if nothing else, and by our own individual experiences. We change because of accidents that happen to us and choices we make. We each have a Whole Self Catalogue of alterations.

In any case, as a journalist and commentator I have been most interested in one aspect of change—the effect of social change on people's lives. As a columnist, I've always been hooked on current events but from the perspective of people's lives. I'm curious about how each individual, with his or her own psyche, circumstances, and personal history, interacts with the evolving society.

I think sometimes of a simple insight of Erik Erikson's: "We each live in a body and a world." He meant, of course, that the route our lives take is determined by an enormous number of factors—biology, history, culture, family life, even technology. It is an outgrowth of being born white or black, lame or pretty, in the country or the city, in the first century or the twentieth. In short, we don't grow up in a vacuum, we aren't raised in a psychological isolation tank. We are each different and also part of a web of expectations, traditions and prejudices. We are individuals and yet part of a connecting community called society.

So, the turning points that interest me most are not the ones people experienced simply by aging, by the life cycle. While I'm aware that our lives will all be punctuated by crises, I don't believe those crises are really predictable or universal. The timing and nature stem, in part, from the society we live in. A mid-life crisis, for example, may be triggered by approaching forty—but perhaps only by approaching forty in this culture and at this time. Many of the conflicts we feel and the changes we go through depend as much on the times we live in as on our own personal psychological clock. The nature of a mid-life crisis, in this country and at this time, is significantly different from what it was twenty-five years ago, or what it is today in Africa or Asia.

The great social changes cut across the life cycle. They can affect all of us to one degree or another—whether we are child or grandparent. We may change more in two years than we would have in a decade.

As the class reporter then, I tried to narrow my questions to how people had been affected by the greatest social change of our time—the evolving roles of men and women.

This, after all, is one school we all attended. The people I interviewed have all been taught in one way or another the right behavior and the appropriate life pattern for men and women, society's set of expectations for the sexes. But as people who have been living through a time of vast changes in those roles, they have seen women move into the work force and are aware of the impact this has had on public and private life. They are aware that this phenomenon is a great catalyst for personal change—whether they believe that it is for better or for worse. It is changing the way people live their daily lives—not just the Sundays, but the Mondays and Tuesdays.

I came out of each interview with a different story. As Kierkegaard once wrote, each of us is an exception. Our stories are unique, even though they touch universal experiences and chords of recognition.

But out of these "exceptions" emerge patterns and it is the patterns which I will try to lay down. I want to show the step-by-step process, the feelings that precede and accompany and follow a turning point.

How then do people get from here to there? How do they begin?

Chapter 1 Turning Points

"It's an old story. Most people don't even bat an eyelash . . .
Middle-aged man meets thirty-year-old woman, has affair without wife knowing, wants to get rid of old wife to get young wife.
I had read stories like that. But when it actually happens,
well . . ."

When we first meet them, they are people like the rest of us,
going about their daily lives without a hint that the next day or
the next year may bring a new set of circumstances and choice.
They are Jane, Nicholas, Molly, Lillian, and Paul—people who
aren't predicting a turning point in their lives. People who don't
really want change.

At the beginning they have at least one other thing in common. They have all grown up in a society that gave them a
definition of "normal" behavior, "normal" lives. From the time
they were small and read their first picture books, they have
each known that it was "normal" and natural for men and
women to have separate roles, for girls to grow up and be
mothers and housewives and for boys to grow up and be breadwinners and husbands.

The five of them were formed in many crucial ways by these
powerful expectations. Norms are the "shoulds" of society, the
"normal life" is the one people "should" adopt, and these five
people, like most of us, are well aware of that. They may not live
within the letter of that law, but in one way or another, to quote
Emily Dickinson, they each "tip their hats" to the society in

which they live. They co-exist familiarly with its rules and traditions.

For some, the status quo may be a starting block; for others it may remain a safe haven; for still others it may be a room with no exit. But first: Who are they? Who will change and who will not?

JANE

Jane is a woman in her early thirties, nearly six feet tall. Yet she looks remarkably girlish, with her blond hair swept up into a french twist, wearing a print dress. She lives in a colonial white frame house with traditional blue and white furniture, on a street of houses that all look like different models of the same design. The house is right outside one of the ten most livable cities in America, somewhere between the Midwest and the Far West. It is a conservative city, a town with one Republican newspaper and a bookstore that has a huge Magic Marker sign in the window: GET THE U.S. OUT OF THE U.N.

Jane is married to Rich, a ruddy-complexioned, deep-voiced man who travels a great deal for the company he has been working for since they were first married. She is the mother of three children, who range in age from six to fourteen, and she is living the life that she has always expected, hoped for, worked for.

Life wasn't always as easy for Jane as it is now. The only child of a widowed mother on an isolated farm, she felt keenly that hers had not been a "normal" childhood and, more than anything else, she used to dream about growing up, getting married, and living happily ever after.

She left college early and married in the first chapter of that dream. It wasn't easy at first—she had three children who were sick in their infancy. But now, when she tells you with a special brightness that her family is "disgustingly, typically normal," she isn't saying that smugly but with great relief. She has worked hard to create and sustain that "normal family." If you ask her, she will even run through her "Why I Am Lucky" list, like the one she has posted on the refrigerator door: "1. The kids are healthy. 2. We have enough money. 3. I have some friends. 4. At last, some free time of my own!"

If you ask her, she may, but only sheepishly, run through her list of doubts. She worries about her husband's health—Rich has a bad stomach with two operations behind him. And she worries about their relationship. She wonders why they seem to grow more distant as they grow older. She doesn't seem to be able to read anymore, a pleasure that had sustained her through her childhood. Then, too, she doesn't quite know what to do with her free time. She feels that she should be busier—her mother had always been doing something on the farm.

But Jane is, on the whole, an optimist, trained by a mother who used to admonish her: "Think positively!" Jane thinks that her problems are minor, even self-indulgent. There is, after all, nothing seriously wrong in her life as she looks at it. Nothing to be upset about. Even the problems seem to be, well, "normal."

NICHOLAS

Nicholas would say similar things about his life. Compared to the problems he deals with every day in his practice, his own problems seem remarkably average. Nicholas is a slight and wiry child psychiatrist, the sort who calls himself a shrink, even when he's talking with the patients who come to him from their Georgetown townhouses where they live with fathers who are senators and top government administrators.

Nicholas has a slightly bemused expression that makes him look a bit like Dick Cavett, although his blond air has thinned into a circle surrounding a bald spot.

Nicholas grew up in a home in some ways like that of his patients. His own father was a man who spent his twenties subdividing farmland for housing tracts and spent his forties being important. His mother was a woman who read, and read, and believed in the infallibility of doctors. For Nicholas, psychiatry was a way of being a doctor without being a scientist—and medicine was also a way of winning the stature and the money, the prestige his father had—but by healing people rather than carving up farmland.

In medical school, Nicholas was something of a nonconformist
—wearing Marimekko ties with his white jacket, and criticizing
the "jock" mentality of the surgical residents. But he also followed
the path up the residency ladder, following his mentor and his
own inclination into a busy $100,000-a-year practice.

When you ask Nicholas what he values he will tell you: "My
kids and my work and, of course, Sally." His wife, Sally, is a lis-
tener and his social conscience. When he was against the war, she
picketed for both of them. When he gets irate about South Africa,
she writes letters for both of them.

Approaching forty, he has, in many ways, made it. He is able
to support his family quite well, while managing to work effectively with his patients. He has a certain status in the psychiatric
community. His is a good life, although he works three evenings
and Saturdays to maintain it. Fortunately, he says, Sally has
done a great job with the kids. She takes care of the house and
he takes care of the mortgage payments.

As for the kids, well, he feels you can't be home with them as
much as you might like and still work effectively. But he believes
he's much closer to his kids than his dad was to him. Yes, much
closer. That's important to him. As for his schedule, well, that's
the way it is. That's just the way it is.

MOLLY

The "way it is" is different for Molly. Molly didn't accept the
life she was programmed for in the working-class neighborhood
where she spent her childhood. The rest of the girls, she remembers, only wanted to be mothers, but: "I was always
different. I don't know why, but I always wanted a better life,
more money, respect. Where I lived, everything was absolutely
dead. I told myself that I wasn't going to get stuck. I was going
to get out."

And she did. Today Molly is thirty-seven years old, a pretty
brunette whose photograph appears often in *Forbes* and *Fortune*
stories about women executives. She is usually pictured in an
Anne Klein suit and gold bracelets and pink lipstick. Today she

is a vice-president and mother of three children, living half a continent away from her old neighborhood.

Molly didn't accept a life, she carved one out. She had scholarships to help her get out of the neighborhood; she began as a secretary, and worked her way up the corporate ladder. When she met her husband, Cal, and they moved to this midwestern city, she already was determined that she would have both: babies and a successful career.

Molly did it the only way she felt it was possible, by following the rules, paying some dues to the "normal" way of life. She's done all the "shoulds"—everything a woman "should" do and everything a man "should" do. When her children were young, she was criticized for working ("If they had the measles, it was because I was a working mother"), but she has tried hard to prove that despite her "abnormal" life, she is a real woman.

Meeting Molly, it's clear that she's an accomplished juggler, a woman who makes $60,000 a year as a corporate executive and brings in homemade coffee cake for the Friday board meetings. She plays the woman's role on the board, and "I don't make a fuss over that sort of thing. It's easier for me to do it than the men, and they all like it." She is a successful working woman, yet a wife whose husband is "absolutely the head of the family." She oversees the cooking and housekeeping and housekeepers, he carves the roast. At the first of the month, she hands him her paycheck and he pays the bills. Molly never, ever misses a school play or a PTA meeting. She works very hard to keep all those balls in the air, but she is convinced that "I have the best of both worlds. I really do."

LILLIAN

I suspect that Lillian would be awestruck at Molly's energy and lifestyle. Lillian herself is convinced that she is "almost ready for social security." In fact, when we first meet her, she is fifty-two, overprepared, and often tired. She is attractive ("still attractive," she says), with short curly black hair and a rather soft figure which is "Elizabeth Taylor zaftig, or fat, depending on the way you look at it." The only other way she describes herself is as a "mother with an empty nest," even though her last child went off to college five years ago.

Lillian and Harold were married after World War II. They settled into one of the developments that sprouted in New England during the late 1940s and early '50s. There she raised her children while her husband worked as a salesman. They had the "modern" American marriage of the 1950s. Unlike her immigrant parents, Lillian believed in child psychology books and magazine advice columns, not "old world superstitions." Her father had been authoritarian, but her husband wasn't. She never thinks of him as a traditional man, and never thinks of their marriage as traditional. If they have separate roles, well, that is true of everyone she knows who married during their era.

When Lillian's last child went off to college, she looked around her "empty nest" and thought fleetingly of opening a shop with a friend where they could buy and sell the kind of needlework patterns and yarn that can be so hard to find in a suburban town. She was frightened at the idea, but also exhilarated.

But when she talked it over with her husband, he discouraged her. He thought it was foolish to invest any of the money they had saved for retirement. He believed that the business was too risky, although her friend was already running a successful shop in another town. He questioned whether she really had the energy and ability to make a go of it.

"I didn't feel right going against him on that. My husband said, there are so many other things to do. After all the years of raising children, he told me to relax and enjoy life."

So the next year Lillian went back to Weight Watchers and redecorated the living room. And the year after that she tried Diet Workshop and painting class.

"You know," she told her friends, "I'm middle-aged, I'm post-menopause. Pretty soon—I hope, I hope!—I'll have some grandchildren and that'll be nice."

The rhythm of her days is tied to her husband's business schedule and the tasks she does to make his life run smoothly. Lillian isn't happy, she says, but she most often describes her life in the past tense. "My decisions are all behind me. This is my life."

PAUL

At thirty, Paul is only a little older than Lillian's eldest son and yet he too thinks of so many of his decisions as being "behind" him. He has three children, a wife, a trade, and some fairly set ideas.

At thirty, the big lanky former high school basketball player has a shock of light brown hair, and freckles that make him look younger than he is. On the weekends he still "throws some around with the guys" but during the week he is a printer at a newspaper in California.

Paul followed his dad into this trade, and he hopes to remain in it, "as long as the business holds."

Paul always identified with his father: the family court of appeals, the breadwinner, the protector. The only time Paul saw his father cry was after the newspaper he'd worked for back East closed and he was out of work for fourteen months. Paul had walked into the parlor, seen his father sobbing, and closed the door quietly. In those terrifying months, when Paul was eleven and the oldest of the five kids, his mother had gone to work in the houses of upper-class women. She never, in his memory, complained. She never made her husband feel "like a bum." But, as Paul remembers it, "Every day was Prince spaghetti day back then." It was a tense, painful time.

As soon as he could, Paul graduated from high school, went to work, and married his high school girlfriend, Sandy. By the time he was twenty-two, they had settled down and had two of their three children. Since then life has followed one stable pattern, but the economy has not. Paul works the day shift, eight-thirty to four-thirty, Tuesdays through Saturdays. He makes $17,000— more than he ever thought he'd earn—"but it's worth less than I ever thought."

The oldest of his children is eleven and the youngest will be in kindergarten next fall, and he wants to "do the right thing for these kids. Look, by the time they grow up there won't be many

printer's jobs. I want my kids to go through college. I want them
to be able to be anything they want to be. You know, Sandy and
I started having these kids too young. I don't want them to do
that. I want a better life for my kids."

Paul is a political conservative; he's a man who believes it's his
responsibility to be head of the house and his wife Sandy's job to
take care of the house. "I am a take-charge kind of guy. It's not a
rigid authoritarian type of thing, it's the way it should be. The
man needs the woman to take care of the house and family, the
woman needs the man to go out and make a living. If it's like that,
then everything is okay. Otherwise everything will get all mixed
up. I wouldn't live any other way. Sandy knows that."

Each of these five people has evolved his or her own set of
commitments and comfort zones. Jane's sense of the Happily
Ever After is different from the juggling act which Molly describes as the best of both worlds. Lillian's compromises about
an empty nest are different from the economic compromises that
Paul has begun to sense, or the psychological compromises that
Nicholas has dealt with as a psychiatrist and part-time father.

But their lives reflect in so many ways the expectations of the
society they grew up in. All of them—even Molly—are conscious,
self-conscious you might say, about their behavior as men and
women. They carry with them an ingrained sense of what is appropriate and "normal"—that word again. After all these years it
is very familiar. And familiarity is a very powerful need and
strong reason to avoid change.

THE WEIGHT OF THE FAMILIAR

We all take it for granted that most people will resist change
in their lives. We cling to even the minor routines with an odd
tenacity. We're upset when the waitress who usually brings us
coffee in the breakfast shop near the office suddenly quits, and
are disoriented if the drugstore or the cleaner's in the neighborhood closes. We follow a certain habitual pattern for no other
reason than because we are "used to it." The fact that "I have

always done it this way" becomes a reason for continuing to do it that way.

We each have a litany of holiday rituals and everyday habits that we hold on to, and we often greet radical innovation with the enthusiasm of a baby meeting a new sitter. We defend against it and—not always, but often enough—reject it. Slowly we adjust, but only if we have to.

If we resist changes in routine, think how much more tenaciously we cling to the deeper psychological routines and the familiar sense of what is the right way to be and act. The need for social traditions and patterns, a sense of order, is universal, because as Tevye sang in *Fiddler on the Roof*, "Without tradition our lives are as shaky as a fiddler on the roof."

Imagine what life would be like if we couldn't take anything for granted! We would be as insecure as a man without a memory. Every day that man must learn everything all over again. He has to discover his bed, his coffee pot, his street. He has to decide whether and how to shave his face and if he likes soft-boiled eggs. He must figure out anew how to behave in ways that are appropriate to the situation. A life of never-ending discovery, a continual assault of "newness," daily culture shock would be the most exhausting life in the world. Without a pattern of reliable expectations, we could do nothing except cope breathlessly from one moment to the next.

In this way, a wide variety of traditional assumptions simplify our lives and conserve our energy. We hold on to them, not just because they are a piece of continuity with the past, but because they seem to offer some protection for the future. They make our lives more predictable.

Traditions are the guideposts driven deep into our subconscious minds. The most powerful ones are those we can't even describe, aren't even aware of.

In America, of course, we've undergone many transformations, and our traditions are constantly being redefined or updated. Some of them are very short-lived. I was amused at one sign I saw on a restaurant that read: "A Seattle Tradition since 1974."

But social traditions are part of each generation's childhood vision of the way things are, the way things should be, whether it's

a Christmas celebration or a national goal. And this is especially
true for something as crucial as sex roles.

Each of the five people we've been introduced to—from fifty-
two-year-old Lillian to thirty-year-old Paul—grew up learning the traditional rules, how far they could be bent and
stretched, and what the consequences were for breaking them.
Four of them lived well within the old limits. Even Molly, working mother and corporate executive, modified the traditional role
with very careful respect for its power.

Through the process of their daily lives, they have each put
time and energy—the commitment of years—into the creation of
the individual status quo in which they now seem to be living.
By now, they have an investment in their way of life and that investment is a strong reason to fear change. In this sense, all five
are conservatives.

WE'RE ALL CONSERVATIVES

One of the words I had to deal with most in studying change
was the word "conservative." It's a term that comes ladened with
political overtones and, in fact, we often consider political conservatives to be change resisters. But in talking with people, I
found a strain of what I can only call personal conservatism,
among those who are political radicals and moderates as well
as reactionaries. I think now that the best definition of "conservative" is a psychological one used by sociologist Peter Marris
in a book called *Change and Loss.* The five people we're
talking about share with us all one fundamentally conservative
streak; they seek to conserve "the meaning" of their lives. This is
something so basic and so simple that we often overlook it, and
yet it is crucial in terms of trying to understand why one person
changes and another doesn't, why we may accept one change
and reject another.

People are almost always trying to conserve the meaning *of*
and the meaning *in* their lives. What is "meaning"? I think that
Marris described it when he wrote that meaning "in everyday
language can include a sense of attachment as well as under-

standing, as when we say that something 'means' a great deal to someone."

What "means something to us" may be another person, a moral value, an abstract principle, or even a place. "The meaning of life" for each of us is a complicated web of ideas and relationships. It's a commitment—to people, to pieces of our own self-image, and a value system.

So, the five we've met aren't all rigid or reactionaries. Nor have they resisted every change. They just try to avoid those changes that might threaten the meaning of their lives. They are each protecting some investment they have made, the skills they've learned, the relationships they care most about, the course of their history, and the consistency of their values.

FIVE CONSERVATIVES

Lillian is a good example of a "conservative." It's easy to understand the investment a fifty-two-year-old homemaker has in the decisions that had determined her whole adult life. She had, by the time we met her, spent a lifetime taking care of her family. Over time, she had learned a great deal about child-raising and decorating a house. She had become an expert in her field, and she believed in her husband, Harold.

Lillian never did make the one change she flirted with, opening that shop. When her husband disapproved, she dropped the idea. The conflict she saw was not just between them, but within her. It was, in some ways, easiest to follow the familiar course of their relationship. The part of her that was Harold's wife won out over the part of her that was a separate person.

"I just couldn't go against his wishes. That wouldn't have been me. To be fair, I don't think I even let him know how much I'd thought of it. The minute I heard how he felt, I just dropped that whole idea and my friend went ahead without me. I didn't feel that I had any choice."

To have decided otherwise, she believed, would have been to contradict too much of her own past and threaten her future.

But it isn't just a woman of Lillian's age who is conservative. The meaning of Paul's life is already firmly located in his role as provider and father. The printer, who still remembers his father's own shaky time of employment, looks at his job primarily as a "meal ticket." His role as the protector and defender of the family—like his father's before him—is crucial to his sense of identity.

Paul thinks of himself as the strong one. The way he is supposed to be, the way men are supposed to be. It is important to him that he never go through the hard times he witnessed—the time when his mother had to work. He believes that if a wife goes to work, it's because the husband hasn't been able to take care of the family. It's because the husband is sick or out of a job. It is, in short, because the husband has failed painfully. On the whole, Paul wants his life to move along the same path he laid out when he first graduated from high school. A path much like his father's.

But what about Molly, who already lived a relatively nontraditional life? Molly has already bent the rules and her juggling act is very different from the expected pattern of a life she knew in her childhood. But an apparent innovator of change, like Molly, someone who seems to have been on the cutting edge of change, may also be a psychological conservative. At the beginning of this story, Molly has arrived at a status quo that was hard won. It means a great deal to her to be the one woman, the one exception, who can do it all. The sheer difficulty of reaching and maintaining her lifestyle has become a reason to avoid change. She has learned to do it all, the way Lillian learned to do homemaking and child-raising. Molly has worked harder than most of the men in the office, dressed better than the other women. She has developed a style that is carefully nonthreatening to her co-workers, to their wives, to her husband's associates, and certainly to her husband.

"I think I have proven that you don't have to be a hard-bitten career woman and that you can be a wife and mother. I certainly am not a castrating woman, or any of those things. I'm the executive at work, but Cal is the executive at home and it works out best that way for us."

Molly still has a sense of fragility about the life she constructed and she devotes herself to the business of maintaining it, unchanged. "Do you know how few women have a husband who accepts all this?" she asks one moment, and later adds another question, "Do you know how few women ever get this kind of job?"

Nicholas, the psychiatrist, and Jane, the mother of three, have also become conservative. They have both been, they believe, rewarded in some ways by following the scripts of what they should do in life. Jane has won the approval and status she wanted, as well as a life of some ease. Nicholas has reaped the money and prestige he'd been promised by the system.

It's obvious that each of them has significant reasons to defend his or her way of life. And each one of us could list reasons too. Marriage, job, family history, friendships, the comfort of routines —all are figured in to a cost-accounting system. It is easiest in many ways to stick to the charted path.

Why, then, would anyone change? What makes people leave the status quo, a plateau, and embark on something new? Which of these five people changed, and why?

THE FAIT ACCOMPLI

It is always hard to predict change in our own lives or in those around us. Not because we are unperceptive about each other, but because people change most frequently and thoroughly because of the experiences and the accidents that happen to them. The most powerful forces for personal change are often outside our control. An external event may alter the circumstances of our lives so totally that we can only adjust to it, and try to cope. This is what the sociologist Gordon Allport referred to as *the power of the fait accompli.*

The fait accompli may be an economic disaster that strikes a stable family, or a death that wipes out a web of relationships. It may be a flood that sweeps through the valley leaving nothing in its path, or it may be a winning lottery ticket. Or, it may be far less dramatic but equally total. It is, simply, an accomplished fact. As Allport put it, "Most of us do not become converts in advance, rather we are converted by the fait accompli."

A STATISTIC OF CHANGE NAMED LILLIAN

Lillian was just that sort of a convert. At fifty-two, Lillian was kicked out of her traditional place. She became the first of the five people we met to leave the way of life which she had nurtured and been committed to for thirty years.

One day the woman who believed that her decisions were behind her and who was psychologically "ready for social security" became a statistic. Her husband left her for another woman.

"I know, it's an old story," she remembers. "Most people don't even bat an eyelash. It's so horribly typical, almost ordinary. Middle-aged man meets thirty-year-old woman, has affair without wife knowing, wants to get rid of old wife to get young wife." Lillian says this with bitterness. "I had read stories like that. But when it actually happens, well . . . it's the difference between reading about breast cancer and having it.

"There went everything . . . I suppose it's like the man who gets kicked out of the firm after thirty years. Twenty-seven years, my whole adult life, gone. It is still so astonishing to me. He left as if it had been nothing. I stood there while he was packing, saying, "You can't just go . . . you can't just leave." But, of course, he could and he did.

"He wiped out thirty years of me as easily as if he'd had a big eraser in his hand. There I was, a housewife without a husband. There's no such thing as a housewife without a husband, is there? Now the expression is a 'displaced homemaker.' I felt more like a misplaced homemaker, something rather unimportant, something that could be misplaced somewhere or other without upsetting anyone.

"For the first six or seven months after he left, I really thought I was having a breakdown, and in a way I was. I became unsure of everything that I was or had done. All the right things I had done, so many of them well, I thought, how could they have been right when it all came out wrong? I had vertigo just wandering through my house. I'd keep setting the table for two. You know they say that after you have a limb amputated you can still 'feel' it for a long time. It was like that."

Lillian was a *victim of change*. For a long time she was the same woman in a different set of circumstances. Her husband had left, taking with him the part of her that was his wife, leaving her with the house and the alimony check. There were a few times when she thought she would live the rest of her days in a state of mourning, reviewing the list of grievances, hiding from old friends, a housewife without a husband.

"I never had much confidence, really. The only thing I had been sure of was how to run a house and keep a good marriage. Well, it was difficult to believe in *that* anymore. I no longer had any sense of confidence. I was a total failure. And I think I spent a lot of time wallowing in self-pity, putting a great deal of energy into the divorce settlement, and just generally being miserable.

"It was my daughter-in-law who forced me to see something. She is great, but she'll never win any points for tact. She is very, very direct. One day she drove over and said, 'Lillian, you're driving everyone crazy. You're driving yourself crazy. You can stay in this house with a black shawl over your head if you want to. But do you realize you've probably got thirty years of life left? That's a hell of a lot of time to spend looking at the walls.' Well, I went around the house saying, 'Thirty years, thirty years.' I thought, 'Lillian, either you kill yourself on the spot or you find some way out of this.'"

At that moment, Lillian was converted again—this time from a victim to an *agent of change*. She had discovered that even the strongest motivation to avoid risk doesn't always prevent disruption. Her husband had gone, throwing her into a crisis. Now, the effort to find a new meaning of life motivated further change.

"I wasn't one of those women who had to get themselves back together. I had to start *from scratch*. At least I *felt* that way. Now I see some of the strengths that I must have had, way down deep, probably suppressed by my life, the priorities I had, all that.

"Finally, I was lucky. I was lucky in my friends and my family. My friend had opened that needlework shop a few years earlier without me. She offered me a job there." With some trep-

idation, Lillian learned to sell. Then she began to make needlepoint designs herself. Then, slowly, she learned about the running of a mail-order business out of the shop. Within three years,
she and her friend have become partners in a modestly successful enterprise.

She has changed in more ways than she would have believed
possible. Now as we talked, I saw not the woman she described
as zaftig and lethargic, but a woman who is slim and energetic.
"It sounds silly, but I could never lose those twenty extra pounds
while I was married. Now, it's just sheer energy. They're gone. I
feel so much younger. I never had any strength before. Now I
stay up late, I have friends. It's quite remarkable," she says, as
we talk in the house which looks almost like a sample case of her
needlepoint designs.

Recently her daughter had a baby, the first grandchild, and
Lillian says, "I was so pleased. I really was. I went out and
bought a present for my daughter, and for the baby. I went and
visited with them. All the time I was thinking, 'It's lovely that
she has a baby. I look forward to being a grandmother, but not
the way I once would have. I would have been looking then to
the baby for something to do with my own life, some importance, some new place to show off what I knew. It's hard to explain. It's like the only thing I knew was child care and I wanted
a grandchild the way another person might have wanted a job.
Now, I think of myself differently. I am busy, my life is active. I
don't *need* that grandchild."

Lillian has also become active in her community and last year
stood up before the state legislature and testified for the displaced homemaker bill. She was truly an agent for change. "I'm
not ashamed anymore," she says simply. "My daughter-in-law
tells me I'm an independent woman. Well, I feel that I was
forced into independence. I was left. It certainly doesn't feel like
liberation to me. I'm still lonely lots of times and fall into the
doldrums. Yet, I cannot imagine going back to the way I was living before.

"Perhaps this whole thing might never have happened, you
know, in my mother's generation. I can't imagine that my father
would have ever left my mother. It simply wasn't done back

then. But, on the other hand, it's certainly easier to be in my position now, a single older woman, than it was in my mother's time. I'm not trying to say that I'm lucky, but I'm not devastated either."

SEEING ALTERNATIVES, BELIEVING IN CHOICE

Like so many other women in her situation, Lillian had hardly "seen" any way to live other than as a homemaker. Yet, once she was forced, her eyes and her mind opened up, the way a small screen enlarges into Cinerama. That trauma had permanently altered her vision. It took the most powerful catalyst—a painful fait accompli—to encourage Lillian to make new choices.

But ideas can foster change, as events can. A change of mind can precede and, in many ways, force a change of life. There are many people who, somewhere along the way, develop a new perspective about the life they are still leading. A political doctrine, a philosophy, or a religion can be the catalyst that shakes them out of lethargy or off a comfortable plateau. Surely the feminist philosophy was, in this sense, the most sweeping agent of change for a generation of women. Women like Jane.

JANE: A CHANGE OF MIND, A CHANGE OF LIFE

Jane now looks back on her own history with a different point of view. She sees that tall, blond, and girdled woman as "tense, trying so hard to be all the things that I had incorporated into a belief of what I had to be. I see her as denying a lot of reality, determined to be happy, to be perfect, pushing away any sense of discontent."

She sees herself writing not one "Why I Am Lucky" list—like the one she checked off when we first met her—but dozens, convincing herself, pushing down her real uncertainty and confusion.

"Looking back, I can see that for a long time I was in between. The old way wasn't working, but I didn't know a new way. I thought that was what the Catholics meant by limbo."

Once Jane thought that her discontent was selfish, foolish, certainly not something that she could admit in public. In those days, her mother's difficult life as a widow was a reason for appreciating and maintaining the security of her life as a housewife. Now, she sees in her mother's life another lesson, a reason for women to be independent and equal.

"I was sure her experience was a personal tragedy that didn't have any real meaning for my life or for other women. It was something that you could avoid in the normal course of life. It didn't occur to me that women should prepare themselves, should be able to take care of themselves."

It was the women's movement which shifted her perspective, validated her discontent, and then changed her life, and the lives of members of her family.

"I thought maybe I was lazy, ungrateful for everything I had. I was very prone to thinking that way. I'd grown up on a farm and we'd done everything there. So when I was feeling uneasy, I would do more. Can. Sew. I made curtains and slipcovers. I had grown up being told that idle hands were the devil's workshop and so I tried to keep busy. But I know now what I didn't know then: I didn't think much of me. Then, too, I was watching Rich, my husband, change from a very warm person into a cold autonomic man with a backache and a stomach ulcer and all kinds of tension. But I wasn't able to talk with him about things like 'life is too short to do this to yourself.' He was saying, 'I have to provide, it is my duty.'

"I think at some point you say either there's something wrong with me or there's something wrong with this. Which you say can depend on the message you're receiving. For a long, long time I thought it was me."

But gradually the other message was transmitted through the television sets and books and newspapers and that message reached Jane's conservative city.

Suddenly, Jane—a woman who hadn't been able to read a book for years—started to devour feminist literature. She started a book group which in time became a consciousness-raising group.

For the first time, she came to believe that she had choices.

For her, the women's movement transmitted its most important bulletin. "Very simply, what I heard was that it doesn't *have* to be this way. It can be another way."

She heard that she didn't have to be a "girlish six-foot supermom" and that her husband didn't have to climb the corporate ladder, no matter what effects it had on his health. She began to think that the differences in lives of men and women weren't biologically determined, but culturally. And that she could change.

The next chapter of Jane's life was not unusual for the times. It contains a list of changes that runs as long as her "Why I Am Lucky" lists.

She was able slowly to discuss her discontent with her husband, including her yearnings to be closer to him. And he didn't shy away. She began to stop being supermom to her children, and began setting aside time for herself, giving more responsibilities to them.

Once she and her husband began to see choices, and to believe in new possibilities, they took some major risks. Jane went back to college and then to work. Now she runs her state's only program for pregnant teenagers. Rich did what he calls "kicking the ladder"; he quit the corporation and now runs his own business. He began to involve himself more directly with his children and their problems.

Those changes came slowly. They went through the ambivalence of the Shuttle Zone we'll see in Part II. The past years have been difficult as well as exciting, but the woman who thought she had only one acceptable choice now operates with a different perspective. "I guess we both think of our lives as a series of choices now, that we're making together."

They began with one crucial change of mind.

AN OPEN MIND

Alan Watts, the philosopher, once said that the most revolutionary question anyone can ask is, "What do I want?" The question is the essential mind-opener. It implies that there is a choice and that you can make a choice, rather than passively accept the way things are.

Jane was one of the many who were encouraged by the women's movement to ask and then answer that question. She heard about a way of life that she instantly, instinctively believed was "better," at least for her. Whatever difficulties she and her family had in learning to deal with that list, she has never wavered from the belief that she wants a life of role-sharing.

There are many people who only have to hear about another way of life to want it. I have known some for whom change is a relatively uncomplicated desire. They react like a child who sees a toy advertised on television and instantly wants it.

It would have been extremely difficult for Jane to change her mind without then changing her life. The disparity between what she believed and how she lived would have created enormous stress—the stress that comes from conflict.

So, some people, like Lillian, are converted by the fait accompli and others are motivated, like Jane, by a new perspective or ideology. But often the immediate reason they make a move is because they feel uncomfortable standing in place. What was once an easy, familiar status quo becomes a place full of internal battles. Eventually people may change to resolve that conflict, to make a peace in that battleground. This is what finally motivated Nicholas to change.

NICHOLAS: CHANGE TO RESOLVE CONFLICT

When we first met Nicholas, he was secure and settled into his life as a psychiatrist. He was sure that all the trials of medical school and years of residency had paid off in a worthwhile career and a comfortable bank account.

Whatever conflicts he had felt in his youth, he thought were now behind him. "From the time I was twenty-five to the time I was thirty, I was locked into the hierarchical residency system where I worked nights and weekends. It was the kind of life that brought me to the point of exhaustion lots of times, especially when I rotated through the state hospital. I was afraid at times that I didn't have the energy to care for people. But I knew it wasn't forever. You can endure a lot if you think that at the end you will get something for it." Nicholas says this in a soft, direct voice, sitting behind his desk and fiddling with the matchbook he's been carrying since he quit smoking.

"The truth is that medicine is a system, totally competitive, insensitive. Only one in your medical class will get the best internship, only one will get the best residency, only one will butter up the right doctor and get the best hospital affiliations. I was far more locked into it than I believed. I wanted to make money and to make a name for myself and at the same time I wanted to be sensitive, intuitive, and all the rest. I wanted to fill my father's role, but in a way that pleased my mother. She had been scornful of businessmen, after all. I suppose the conflict started to build up in me earlier. I wanted to be tough, competitive, able to push, and yet I was supposed to go through a metamorphosis when I hit the office, shut the door, and be open and caring, kind and selfless.

"Five years ago I started changing my practice to work more with kids. I think, at some level, I was trying to get away from the conflict of dealing with adults. I had become a great deal less sure that I was actually helping them. Perhaps I had an idea that it would be less challenging, personally, to work with children. Which is, of course, absolutely false."

About two years later he began to sense another conflict in his own life.

"A lot of us run away from dealing with healthy people. We justify it by saying that we are dealing with sick people, doing very necessary work. How could your family compete with that? I've seen doctors—as friends and even as patients—who would spend their whole lives doing for everyone but their families and friends. I was the same way, though I didn't know it.

"I was far more available for patients than for my own children. I had prided myself on being a good father, which I defined as being different from my own father. My kids weren't afraid of me. We were close," he says and then smiles. "I thought we were close."

But that year Nicholas was forced to look into a mirror image of his life. The eldest son of the man who had been Nicholas' mentor through medical school and the early years of practice

committed suicide. In the family crisis that followed, one of the
other children came to see Nicholas for professional help. "The
boy was sixteen, and in tough shape. We talked for three hours a
week for several weeks. As we talked, I began to identify with
his father, and to see this boy as my own son in eight or nine
more years. I couldn't help seeing it that way. Talking about this
man who had been my role model and friend, I saw the way in
which he had been so distant with his family. He'd just been ab-
sent, not there. This boy, in some critical ways, was fatherless,
while his father was probably the leading child psychiatrist in
the area. The boy distrusted me for a long time, and I think in
retrospect he was right. I think that his father sent him to me because he believed that I would defend his, the father's, point of
view. That I would represent the father in therapy in some way.

"But what happened was entirely different. The boy made me
face something I knew at some level. That there was something
drastically wrong in the way I was leading my life. That you
couldn't be a sensitive, caring man during work hours and then
be casually negligent about your own family. That there was no
excuse for giving them money instead of giving them yourself.
All of that sounds quite pedestrian, but I just hadn't been able to
acknowledge that as a conflict."

The conflict had never consciously existed for Nicholas before.
But now it became critical, and demanded some resolution.

Nicholas began to test himself slowly. "I went home one afternoon right about the time the boy left my office. I had a canceled
appointment. It was about three, just when my sons came back
from school, and they were having a snack with my wife and I
just walked in. Well, they didn't quite know what to do about
the fact that I was there. My wife thought I was sick. My kids
kind of hung around waiting for me to leave. I was observing all
this and it hit me. I have behaved inappropriately. I had broken
into an operating system, a family that functioned by and large
without me. Which is precisely how I had grown up."

The next six months were a time of great stress for Nicholas,
the stress that came out of his growing sense of contradictions,
both in his self-image and in the ways he was living.

"I had a slow insight into how my father had lived, torn between the sense that he had to make a living, working six and a half days a week and then trying to get back into the family that had simply amputated him, that had closed around what must once have been a serious wound and refused to feel his absence. I realize that he must have been very lonely. I realized that I was lonely. For my family, for my own sense of intimacy. I also had an unbearable recognition that I was not leading the life I thought I was, that I was not the person I thought I was."

Nicholas' problems were not only those of his own self-image. He began to think of the issues in terms of the male role. Role conflict, as Talcott Parsons described it, is "the exposure of the actor to conflicting sets of legitimized role expectations such that the complete fulfillment of both is realistically impossible." To Nicholas that meant a clash between his work role and his fathering role. "There was simply no way to be the supershrink and to have a real relationship with my children. I had been essentially a visiting parent. I didn't have equal input to the kids. I had so little to do with their lives, less than with one of my patients. I didn't take care of them, and unless you are taking care of your children, you aren't a parent. That was how I felt."

Step by step, Nicholas started to make some new decisions. First he moved his office into his home, so he could be there more of the time. Then he realized that he still had to choose between spending the hours with patients and spending them with his family.

"It is extremely unusual in this society to make purposeful decisions to make less money, and this caused me a great deal of stress. I realized that I was very worried about what my wife would feel about this, and in fact she wasn't exactly thrilled. But when we talked about it, she started being re-energized just by entertaining new possibilities of how we might live. At first she only thought of it as threatening—I was trying to cut down the income and cut into her 'territory.' But gradually we talked about what she might want to do, and how I could help her, too."

Now, the children are a few years older and Nicholas spends days but never evenings and rarely weekends working. His wife

went through training and joins him part-time in couple coun-
seling.

"The only problem we have now is getting away from each
other," he laughs.

Nicholas is now, as he is the first to say, less of a high-powered
supershrink than he was. "Sometimes I do miss being on the
boards and in the committees, all that. But I think we may be
able to do some of that later, when the kids are older, in a more
rational way. For now, my relationship with my children is so
much more satisfying. It's worth it. I think the turning point for
me came about when I realized that I had to do this in order to
survive as the person I had always assumed I wanted to be. I am
not, I hope, being dramatic. The conflicts were that intense. I
felt it that acutely."

There were many steps that led to Nicholas' decision. First he
had to see that there was indeed something incompatible between his image and his reality, and between his work and his
family life. Then he had to believe that he had an option, a
choice, that he could change. Then, finally, he had to do it.

"It's hard to describe the ways in which I am a different person. It isn't just the fact that I spend more hours at home and
fewer hours working. It is a change in the way I deal with other
people, my tolerance of differences, a general relaxation which I
believe comes from getting rid of the list of 'musts.' I find that
my mind opens my ears. I hear things that I was deaf to, I feel
things that I never felt before. They are difficult to catalogue,
but I am different."

When I think about Nicholas and the other people I have interviewed and known, I'm aware of the contradictions in every
life, and aware that each conflict doesn't lead to change. We
don't try to resolve them all. We live with many. We all hold a
variety of attitudes and positions that are inconsistent, ideologically or practically. I remember a conference I attended on
aging while I was writing this book. Around me I heard people
who believed on the one hand that older Americans shouldn't be
forced to retire. These same people believed, on the other hand,
that it was crucially important to make room and jobs for

younger people with "fresh ideas" and energy. There wasn't a conflict in their minds, but there was when it came down to filling one job or faculty position. It is often only the specific event or situation that makes us really "feel" a latent conflict.

Similarly, what appear to be incompatible parts of a friend's personality or life—"How can he be a black Republican?" a woman I know asks incredulously about a friend of ours—may not feel that way at all to our friend.

Finally, the motivation to preserve the status quo, "peace" in our lives, may be strong enough to make us ignore contradictions.

This is how I finally understood why Molly and others I know like her didn't change any further.

MOLLY: JUGGLING INSTEAD OF COLLIDING

When I met her, Molly's conflicts seemed more apparent to me than those of Nicholas. Molly was and is an executive at the office and a wife at home. She is a vice-president, but one who brings not only coffee cake but also fresh-ground coffee beans for the corporate board meetings. She pours for the men from her Georg Jensen coffee pot. At home she is a traditional wife and mother who earns more than her husband and never touches the checkbook.

To the outsider, and I was one, these roles seemed at variance with each other. And when I met Molly I was surprised that the dependent and independent, traditional and nontraditional aspects of her life hadn't finally demanded some synthesis.

But in fact Molly is a person who did not change, and I don't think she will. Throughout the years of greatest social change, when more and more mothers chose careers and often feminism, Molly kept her own life in place. The different aspects remained apart, like separate balls. She remained an artful juggler.

Now I realize that in some ways Molly had already departed radically from the traditional expectations of her youth. Like many other "female firsts," her life had been dominated by the fear that women couldn't have both family and work.

In that sense, the changing roles in the outside world had

made her more comfortable as a working mother, but unwilling to move any further: "I find that I am suddenly a role model, and I like it. I feel good about encouraging other women, younger women especially, to go into business and showing them that if I can do it they can do it. I find more people admiring what I do and fewer judging it and that's very nice. It's much more comfortable for me. So that's changed," she says now.

When she travels around the country, she is rewarded in many ways for being the first woman. She is proud of the publicity she receives, and pleased when she sees herself described as an attractive mother of three who also controls the budget of a multimillion-dollar corporation. But when asked by the younger other women in the company or by a reporter why she makes the coffee and why she has the whole responsibility for her home life, Molly puts her legs together, sits up in her Eames office chair behind that Swedish birch desk, and bristles a bit.

"I could go around my office saying, 'No, I won't do this or that,' and demanding to be treated as a man. But that would just make a scene. Everyone would be uncomfortable. The men I work with aren't male chauvinist pigs. But they do like a woman to be feminine. It doesn't bother me if I make coffee or pour for the men. It makes everyone feel good and there's nothing wrong with that.

"As for my home life, I know there are other women who feel that if I'm working, my husband should be sharing the housework with lots of contracts for who does the dishes and all that. I just don't. I could be resentful, but I'm not. I'm actually grateful. I like doing it all."

Then she adds earnestly, "The truth is that if I went home today and said, 'Cal, it's time you started shopping for the children and picking up the house and making the dentist's appointments,' he wouldn't think our marriage was such a great deal anymore. Isn't that what's going around? Frankly I don't see why I should ask my husband to change his ways. I'm the one who wants to live this way. I could quit any day I wanted to. I'm the one who wanted to work. So it's my responsibility to make sure that it all gets done."

As her children have grown older, it has become easier for

Molly to fill her double role. In the past several years, she has had less stress. By now she is unwilling to risk what she has so carefully constructed, for what she considers doubtful rewards.

"I like my life the way it is," she says with a certain finality that she emphasizes by folding her hands on her lap and then, almost as a postscript, she adds, "I suppose it would be different if I lived in New York, or if I were younger and starting out now. Everyone seems to be starting out differently. I expect that my children will have more of a sharing kind of marriage. I know, for example, that my daughters don't think it's fair when they are asked to do something their brother doesn't have to do, and I'm careful about that. I suspect they will all have very different marriages. But . . . well, that's not where I am. I consider myself lucky. For my generation. Very lucky."

No outside, unseen force has come and disrupted the pattern of Molly's life. She has not had to adjust to some powerful fait accompli. She didn't challenge the traditional society, she made her own exceptional way. Molly is used to living with contradictions. She now picks from the new messages of social change those items that support her status quo, that make her more, rather than less, comfortable.

In talking about Molly and Lillian, Nicholas and Jane, I tried to pinpoint one reason why they did or didn't change. I wanted to show one or another of the pivotal steps that may lead to change. But for most people, change is a combination of internal and external events. Like Lillian, we have to deal with a new set of facts, *and*, like Nicholas, we also face a conflict, *and*, like Jane, have a change in perspective. We change, like Lillian, because of choices that are closed, and, like Jane, because of choices that are open.

We change for a combination of reasons. And so did Paul.

PAUL: STEP BY STEP

Paul was in some ways least likely of all five people to change. Paul, after all, once said that a working wife meant a failed husband. In many fundamental ways, the meaning of Paul's life was grafted onto his role as the provider. He was, like his father be-

fore him, a worker, and the reason to work was a simple one: for
the paycheck, for providing. He had been head of only one thing
in his life: his family.

Paul was and is a man who believes that men are stronger and
more able to take care of things. He believes in a hierarchy and
he likes everything and everyone in the "proper" place. Yet, he is
also a realist and a father who is ambitious for his children.

The basic new reality of Paul's life in the past half dozen years
has been economic. To put it simply, the cost of food, gas, utili-
ties, and housing has gone up faster than his paycheck. His children have grown faster than his status. The economic fait accompli of his life finally produced a conflict between his sense of
the male role and his hopes for his family. Paul had always assumed that he could be the sole support of his family, while at
the same time insuring his children's better future, putting college money in the bank, and remaining a member of the middle
class.

"Facts are, to stay dead even, you need the money. You need
more money. I haven't got a Cadillac. I don't vacation in Hawaii.
My savings account is in the roof, you know what I mean? Our
summer vacation was in the garage," says Paul, stuffing his hands
in his pockets. The youthful-looking printer explains this
straightforwardly, sitting in his chair in the living room of their
modest ranch house, outside of Sacramento.

One winter, as he remembers, Paul roamed at night through
the house, worried about money—not money for food but for the
future. The difference between Paul and his father was just that
he wanted more for his kids. His father had struggled just to
keep up; Paul wanted to get ahead.

Paul was the kind of man who made decisions and then presented them. So one night in April he told Sandy that he was
going to start working at a second job at a local print shop.

"Sandy threw a fit," he says, amused at the memory. It was
perhaps the first major argument of their marriage. "I'd never
seen her so mad. The thing is, we've got these three kids and she
doesn't want them growing up with their father as a boarder.
Her dad had been a trucker, and he'd come home out of South
Bend every other week and he'd spend a couple of days dead

drunk and then roll out again. She didn't need me to use the house as a hotel. And, the truth is, I want to spend time at home. I'm not interested in dropping dead at fifty. Anyway, I was real worried. I didn't know whether to take the job and never see the kids, or stay home and forget about helping them with college."

It was Sandy who suggested that his range of choices wasn't quite that narrow. She said that in the fall, when the youngest started kindergarten, she could work. Her sister had gone back to work, after all, and she could freshen up her clerical skills. After nine years at home, she was ready to be out again, at least part-time.

Paul's immediate answer was a flat, "Nooooo way." When Sandy's sister mentioned it, he told her to "butt out." He was silent when Sandy brought it up again. "I think it's ridiculous for you to be moonlighting when I will have six hours a day next year with nothing to do except clean the house, which I hate doing anyway."

The changes in the world around Paul had added another alternative to the list. There was another way to solve the conflict he faced. The idea of a working wife had been linked in his mind to a critical time in his own childhood. But he looked around the plant. He started noticing that many of the other men in the plant had working wives. On coffee breaks and between editions, they told him that it "was working out okay and the money was a help—not that they couldn't do without it—but the money was a help."

Now, he faced a new kind of decision. To solve the problems brought on by an economic fait accompli, he could give up his aspirations for his children's future, or give up his own free time, or give up his investment in being the exclusive family provider.

While all of this information was fed into his decision-making process, ultimately he "let the choice be made for him." He could never have "sent" Sandy to work, but when the hospital in their neighborhood advertised for clerical workers, Sandy talked with them. They would pay her $165 a week to work at the inpatient desk from 7 A.M. to 3 P.M.

It was the first time in their married life that she quietly went about planning a decision on her own. The youngest of her children could go to a neighbor's house after kindergarten from twelve-thirty to three. The two oldest could pick him up on their way home. She would be home by three-thirty.

Paul's choice was reduced to a matter of approval or disapproval. The only thing Paul said was "Well, let's give it a try." But slowly this change resolved their economic crisis—their combined income rose to $25,000. The man continued to believe in the traditional separation of roles but he was less able to live his "beliefs."

Sandy now left before the children were up in the morning. At first she set the table and left the lunch money out. She made sure the night before that they had their own sweaters and homework. But slowly Paul became responsible for the early morning schedule because he was there. Gradually Sandy has had a greater say in their financial life. She no longer asks her husband for money, and if there is something she thinks the kids need, she buys it. Slowly she has become comfortable making daily decisions which once were left to Paul. She still takes care of the running of the house and habitually defers to his opinion in politics. But there has been a definite shift in their positions. Paul is ambivalent about this. He sees it as forced upon him by economics.

He admits this slowly, as he pours another cup of instant coffee, and remarks that this is one of the small ways in which his life has changed. In the mornings now, his wife is out early and he has never learned to use the electric percolator. As he stirs the freeze-dried flakes with his spoon, Paul talks carefully about his life. "It's not what I grew up thinking was the family type of thing. That's first of all. A family to me is the man working and the woman at home. Okay. Now, you can't afford that, and I know it. Then I know that Sandy likes being out of the house, which I'm not sure I understand, but there it is. What bothers me is something different. When I was growing up, everyone looked up to my father. My mother, us kids. Whatever you say, a man likes to be looked up to. Made to feel important. Not in a bad way, not that anyone is afraid of you or anything like that. But looked up to. When the man brought the money in, that was it. But when the woman is bringing in the money too, it changes things. Don't get me wrong. I'm not wearing any apron or anything. It's just not the same."

THINGS ARE NOT THE SAME

Things were not the same for Paul, any more than for Lillian or Nicholas or Jane. At the beginning, I said that they all shared one thing: they had grown up with a set of "normal" expectations for men and women, a set of "shoulds." But gradually they have all become part of something else, the shift in those roles.

None of them, any more than the rest of us, could have given us an advance bulletin on the moment when they would leave their plateau, losing or risking much that was comfortable and familiar in the traditional way. None of them knew the specific nature of the choices they'd be faced with and none knew how they would personally react.

No matter how carefully we can pinpoint the impulses for change, that part remains unpredictable. Like these five first characters, none of us knows precisely when it's our turn, when we come to a turning point. It always remains something of a mystery.

In the last night that I spent with Jane during the course of our interviews, she showed me some old home movies she and Rich had taken when the children were very little. As we sat in her darkened living room, I saw on the screen a woman who looked much like a younger version of the one in front of me, but of course acting for the camera, playing with the boys. Jane, however, was sitting on the edge of her chair, almost holding her breath, her own memories intermingling with her vision. Finally she turned to Rich, sitting in the chair next to her, and started to give a running narrative of the woman in front of her. "Rich, this is so weird. All I can think of is what would I do if I had to spend an evening with her. What would I have to say to her? I have this eerie feeling that I have nothing in common with her. I can see us sitting there with nothing to say to each other. But it's me! It's me!" Then she held her head in her hands and said to me, "You know, I'd almost forgotten just how different I am now."

Chapter 2 A Scale of Change

"I had to face up to the fact that I really didn't want to go back to being a good pastor's wife and that was when I knew that I had changed and had to deal with accepting that . . . In the end I did what I wanted to do . . ."

One day in August, after I had begun interviewing people for this book, I found myself walking along a beach on Lake Michigan in Indiana with a woman my own age. Susan, tall with short curly black hair, was wearing a work shirt that hung loosely over her jeans and as we walked she automatically bent over collecting stones and pieces of glass. Finally we sat down on the sand a hundred yards or so from the wooden walk that led up to the cottage she was sharing with her three children and talked until it turned chilly and dark.

"Have you changed a great deal?" I asked her. She took the stones out of her pocket and played with them like worry beads, as she answered. "Well, I am older. I don't wear Playtex girdles anymore, and I don't wear miniskirts. My kids are growing up. I worry more about money and less about who I am. The world has changed around me, and I've changed too. Certainly other people think that I've changed. They keep telling me, anyway, but I feel more like myself than I ever did when I was younger."

Susan told me then about her old college roommate, a woman who has lived in eight houses in the past eleven years. "She buys a house, moves her family in, fixes it up. I mean, plaster, insulation, the works, down to the curtains, and then, when it's perfect,

she sells it and moves. Her husband, I swear, takes the wrong
train home sometimes. I think she's nuts. I think she's changed
more than anyone I know.

"I couldn't stand that. I'm the kind of person who gets upset
before I go on a trip. I've lived in the same house for ten years.
My kids have the same friends they knew in nursery school. I'm
a squirrel, I have almost every letter, every report card I ever
got. But, on the other hand, I've been through a divorce and two
long relationships that ended. I was the daughter of conservative
midwesterners, but I became a civil rights activist in the 1960s,
and I joined a consciousness-raising group in 1970. I've been a
housewife with three small kids and now I'm told that I'm one of
the twenty most powerful women in Chicago. Well, you tell me
who has changed the most, me or my roommate?"

Susan reminded me that there is a range of change that extends from the shallow to the deep, from the constructive to the
catastrophic.

How do we judge the intensity of change? Is there a scale by
which to measure degrees of change? Did Susan change more
than her friend? How do you weigh these things? Was the sort
of disruption that came from incessant changes of address greater
or less than the change from being a housewife to being a divorced political worker?

Usually we rank change externally. We judge it by outside appearances. It seems to be more upsetting to move from California to Massachusetts than from one suburb to another. It seems
harder to become a radical feminist change agent than simply to
shift some of the housekeeping burdens in an ongoing marriage.
But it may not be.

In the end, I think the only way to measure change in a person's life is by an internal standard. What feelings accompany
that change? Exhilaration? Anxiety? Comfort? Disruption?

I know that each person's capacity to handle change is
different. Some of us are more flexible than others. But each
change is itself different. A psychological scale of change exists—
from the lightest to the heaviest experiences—that can be read
through the responses of the people involved.

THE SCALE OF CHANGE

We say that most people resist change, but it isn't that simple. We don't resist a change of hat or style. We even look forward to some changes; they are as refreshing as a change of scene. We eagerly seek a change that is clearly to our advantage—a raise, or a new refrigerator to replace the broken one.

Nor are we reluctant to make those changes that are actually substitutions—when one thing is exchanged for another. We would, for example, consider it childish and absurd if someone complained because he was not given the model television set on display in the store, but the identical one from the back room.

We often welcome changes that are really elaborations. Our environment, for example, changes as we add furniture to the living room or shrubs to the garden.

Changes like these—at the lightweight end of the scale—involve very little risk, so we don't usually resist them, any more than we resist a change of clothes.

Then, in the middle of the scale of change are those changes which we would label "growth." We graduate from grammar school to high school. We are promoted from assistant manager to manager. These may be unsettling. After all, we have to leave the familiar environment of high school, and perhaps home, in order to go to college. But they often feel like growing experiences and we can accept them and even seek them.

It is, as Peter Marris noted, when change begins to involve some risk that we begin to be hesitant and uncomfortable. We wonder whether it will bring us "more" or "less." Even the changes that offer us growth may threaten us with some loss.

Psychologist Abraham Maslow wrote, "Growth has not only rewards and pleasure, but also many intrinsic pains and always will have. Each step forward is a step into the unfamiliar and is possibly dangerous." It also means giving up something.

So, in the middle of the range of change, we begin to have "mixed feelings."

At the heaviest end of the scale, change may be a crisis that involves a wrenching feeling of loss. The most common crises are those of death, or separation from someone who is loved; they can also include a loss of hope, or of a cherished goal for the future. The hardest changes to make are those which involve a real risk of loss.

In reality, then, we are simply more likely to make changes that seem promising and not threatening to the framework of our lives. I have said before that we are all psychologically conservatives. On this scale of change, we are always more apt to make the alterations that "conserve" meaning in our lives and to avoid those that threaten to disrupt it.

LIGHTWEIGHT CHANGES

The new ideas about men and women which seemed to develop in the late 1960s and early '70s were not, in fact, "new" or startling to everyone. They were already familiar to a core group of people. For them the "change" was not a disruption of ideas but a reaffirmation. In fact, the power of the women's movement and the reason why it was so instantly successful was its familiarity for so many people.

As W. H. Auden once wrote, "I am sure it is everyone's experience as it has been mine that a discovery we make about ourselves or the meaning of life is never like a scientific discovery, a coming upon something entirely new and unsuspected. I think it is rather coming to conscious recognition of something which we really knew all the time, but because we were unwilling or unable to formulate it correctly, we did not hitherto know we knew."

LEWIS: FIRST-WAVE FEMINIST

There were, after all, a core of people, like Lewis, a gray-haired Baltimore physician I interviewed, who had grown up believing, as he says, "Sex roles are rubbish!" Though people like Lewis changed very little themselves, they became crucial models.

Lewis, seventy-two, was a feminist of the first wave. Until the resurgence of interest in new roles, he had been widely regarded as "henpecked" or a man "under petticoat rule." The biggest difference in his life during the last years has not been in the way he and his wife live, but in the way he is seen.

Lewis and Catherine had made a commitment four decades ago when they were both in medical school that they would live an egalitarian marriage. Lewis' own mother had been a suffragist, a Bryn Mawr graduate who had spent years in the libraries of Baltimore or in her private study working. His own father had harumphed around the house, occasionally "trying to lay down the law," but Lewis, his brother and sister, all grew up with a strong conviction for what they called "women's rights."

"In our early years, don't you know, I used to be invited to dinner when Catherine was out of town. By the way, Catherine was not invited to dinner when I was away. Be that as it may . . . when I went, when I accepted these well-meant invitations, invariably someone would sympathize with me. 'Oh, you poor man.' I felt that in return for eating their beef stroganoff, or what have you, I was supposed to complain about my lot in life as the neglected husband. Fortunately, I could laugh about it later with Catherine."

By the 1970s, however, the image of their relationship changed. The younger women at the hospital were pointing him out to their husbands as a "liberated" man and someone invited them both to speak at a conference entitled "New Patterns of Marriage."

"My dear," he said conspiratorially to me the day we met in his office, "I have changed from being henpecked to being avant-garde. Imagine being avant-garde at my age!" and he let out a dry chuckle.

"The conference fell two weeks before our fortieth anniversary. It wasn't exactly a new pattern, of course."

Lewis and Catherine were already leading their lives within their context. What they won from change is prestige and the pleasure of being role models rather than oddballs. On their scale, change is featherweight.

There are others of us who live, even now, on the cutting edge of change quite comfortably because we are sure that we are the avant-garde, and that times will catch up with us, as they did with Lewis. Some of us can live way beyond the social definition of a normal life, if we "feel right," if we are supported by a philosophy and feel committed to an ideal.

RUTH: CHANGE LIGHTLY

Of all the people I met, Ruth had the longest history of political radicalism. Yet she was, in many ways, the perfect example of lightweight change. Her own life has been, in some psychological ways, conservative.

At fifty-one years old, Ruth is at the center of the feminist movement activities in her western city. She works tirelessly to open nontraditional jobs to women, to organize women in labor groups, to keep women's studies courses going at the local center, and to put out a small local newsletter. Dressed in her uniform, a blue shirt and jeans, constantly talking in a rasping low voice that comes from chain-smoking cigarettes, she labels herself comfortably as a radical feminist and a change agent.

Yet Ruth's personal changes are in crucial ways substitutive, elaborative—not at all radical.

Ruth lives in a turn-of-the-century house with her youngest son and three co-workers. In a living room that was worn yet comfortable and full of bright posters and pillows, the phone rang repeatedly with emergency calls, her son banged nails repairing a broken staircase, and the dog ran through the room in solitary pursuit of his ball. But none of this bothered her as she talked easily of her own past with the animated rhythms of a practiced public speaker.

"I tend to think of myself in social terms and not in personal terms," she said. "I started out as the daughter of a Jewish working-class family from Europe. My mother is a social democrat and my father a philosophical anarchist. Both of them are workers. I grew up in an atmosphere where everyone was talking about movements and politics. Of course I grew up a socialist. I was reading Spinoza and Kant when I was still in grade school. By the time I got to high school I was a Trotskyite, philosophically and programmatically. But at the same time I was oriented by my family to go to college and I enrolled at fifteen."

What sounded to me like an extraordinary youth was normal

for her. In fact, in terms of her family expectations, Ruth, the eldest child, was actually a conformist. Like the rest of her family, she realized that her values were at odds with the society around them, but she was committed and she learned to deal with that variance from a very young age. In many ways, her own identity was forged by political radicalism.

It was Ruth's sister who was the "rebel" of the family. Unlike Ruth, she is a suburban mother. "My sister's not a feminist. She's the one in the family who was always the comedienne, the funny lady. She never wanted to have anything to do with politics."

Ruth went into the "family business"—radical politics. Whatever she did, she saw in a political context.

"I got married right after Pearl Harbor. We all got married then. My husband was drafted and got transferred out of town, so I followed. I got a job, I could always get a job, and then I would start trying to organize the workers and I'd get fired," she says with a throaty laugh.

"Actually, that was the pattern of my life. I'm still organizing and getting fired and organizing. My life hasn't changed. Only the cast of characters has changed."

The "cast of characters" has changed, slowly, over many years, from the traditional radical left to the feminist radical left.

The first experience that made Ruth begin to see her life in terms of her sex, and sex role, was having a child. "I really began to understand. I had already been a feminist theoretically. I'd read Engels, my mother belonged to the working circle, a branch named after a socialist of the stripe of Rosa Luxembourg. But, on top of that was imposed some of the Jewish service-to-the-man thing. My father had always told me not to get married. 'Don't give your life to a man, don't get tied down with babies and a family.'"

Ruth coughs again and reaches for another cigarette and glass ashtray. Occasionally she gets up to answer the phone to give advice to one of the women in the midst of an "action" against the local company.

"I had to go through that experience of having a child to really know what it was about. It was a shocker. We were living in a crummy housing project. We didn't have a stove, so we had a hot plate. I had to boil the diapers and trudge with the pails to the laundromat. My husband was on swing shifts and when he was home I was out of the house. He resisted my work and my organizing at first and we had a fight about it. I was stunned. How could he resist that? We both had theoretically had an ideological commitment to equality—God, don't I sound naïve?

"I began to realize what the household drudgery and domesticity was about. The effect it had on my mind! I'd be giving a speech and in the back of my mind it would be, 'Oh, my God, I forgot to make the formula' or 'Oh, no, it's raining and the diapers are out on the line.' My mind would come to a stop. For me it was horrifying. I'm up there talking about the nature of the state in Outer Mongolia or about a strike and there comes all this other stuff."

Ruth remembers all this. Yet at the time, there was no arm of society that was sympathetic. When she even brought up the "woman issue," in the 1950s and early '60s, others told her that she wanted to divide the working class. The men, she says, gave lip service to the issue. "They would find all kinds of ways to clothe their resistance in highfaluting theories. The pogrom against the Uppity Women was that we were too subjective, too personal, careerist."

In many ways, Ruth was kept in the "woman's place" even in the midst of socialist radical movements. A powerful and persuasive woman, she was never "the Leader." But by the middle and late 1960s when her children were growing up and she had been divorced, Ruth made a shift, a lateral move in political philosophy. She took her political knowhow, the knowledge of organizing, the persuasive speaking voice, and devoted it to the pressure for women's rights. She applied much of her ideology about the class structure to women. She essentially substituted one cause for another. She now formed a radical women's caucus and was the mentor to the student protest movement. She has been a cohesive force behind one of the most effective radical women's groups in the country.

In many ways what is most interesting about Ruth's life is this cohesiveness. She is comfortable in a situation where many others would not be—at odds with the mainstream of the society she lives in. She is as invested in changing society as her parents were. While Ruth is a woman who lives in constant touch with change, she herself has been consistently committed to one central set of beliefs, from childhood. She has never really altered them. The women's movement was something of a "promotion" for her personally. Now, in her fifties, Ruth has found a place of leadership which had been denied her in the more traditional movement.

The choices that Ruth made in response to social change were not hard ones. They flowed out of her own history; they required a shift, not an overhaul of her own web of ideals, and she felt very little conflict in making the moves.

THE MIDDLE RANGE OF CHANGE: ROOM TO GROW

What do people want from change? Generally, we are motivated to change our lives because we feel uncomfortable and we hope that change will improve our lives. And one of the things we want more than anything else is room to grow.

There are some people of course who grow in their adult lives as if they were following a graph. They go through life in an orderly fashion, keeping their record intact, becoming a graduate student and then an expert and later, perhaps, a teacher.

But most of us pass through several critical times when we feel a sudden surge of change, an overdose, when growth is disruptive and scary as well as exciting. Faced with a choice of whether or not to make a change—take a new job, even leave a difficult marriage—we calibrate whether the promise is worth the risk. We ask, what is it that we may have to leave behind? How much do we value that part of the past?

I know people who hope that they can grow without relinquishing any of the past. I am not the only one who dreamed as a child of growing up but never leaving home. But we have to let go to grow. As Maslow described it, "We must choose between the delights of safety and growth, dependence and independence."

In this middle range, the scale tips more cautiously as we weigh in the costs of change.

JANINE: GETTING INTO THE HABIT OF CHANGE

Janine was never a person who looked for change. When she contemplated anything new she always said to herself, "Why ask for trouble?" For most of her adult life, until she was forty, she preferred to work in familiar surroundings at tasks she knew well. This black woman had always considered herself lucky to hold a steady job at the New York headquarters of a major corporation, and to be the executive secretary for a man she really liked. Her family had always told her that "security" was the thing. That was what you needed in life. Now, as Janine describes this, she smiles, and flicks her pencil against the side of her palm. She is dressed in conservative yet chic style, in a dark double-knit skirt with a silk blouse, and she is seated in her own private, executive office at the same corporation.

"I had always wanted to be a secretary. I made my mind up very early about that. It just seemed like a nice type of job to have and I always liked it." The first major change in her life came at forty when she decided at last to marry. Then, at forty-one, forty-two, and forty-three she had her children.

"This made a big difference. I was earning at that time about ten thousand, which wasn't too bad a sum, but I had no money left over. Then with the children, money became essential."

But children had made a difference, not only in their economic picture, but also in her own attitude toward working. "In my mind I came from a very old-fashioned family. My mother's concept was that you had children and you stayed home unless you were starving and you had to survive. So I started thinking about the kind of contribution I was making. The thing is that when the children came along, being a secretary didn't seem a good reason for leaving them. I felt that you needed much more of a career than that," she said in a quiet voice that seemed to confide and welcome confidences in return. The changes in her life, as she described them, had changed her mind, and urged her on.

At the same time, her ears were opened to new messages,

about opportunities for blacks and women. Her boss, the corporation vice-president, was also open to those ideas.

"Now a lot of bosses, they just wouldn't want to let you go, anyway. They care for themselves and their routines, and their own comfort. Or they have some kind of problem about women moving up in the world. But this is a good man and he had no hangups about women at all. Anyway, he began to ask me, 'Is this the best job for you?' He asked this, it wasn't that he put a bee in my bonnet or anything. But it was like he pushed me in the direction I knew I should be going."

Janine's own company was involved in affirmative action plans and began moving women up. When there was going to be an opening as assistant manager of personnel, her boss thought that she should have that place. So Janine sat down and thought about it. It was a promotion, it offered her a higher salary and room to grow. With this job came responsibilities and decision-making as well. To make this move, she had to leave what she had known and take a risk.

"Well, I'll tell you, I think it's very hard to decide that you know enough about this job, that being a secretary is no longer meaningful, that you need something else. It's difficult, because you can have a personal attachment for somebody you're working for. At least I did. I had worked with two really fine men, which is one of the hazards of a secretarial job. You may work for truly fine people. You get so identified with them that you don't know that you don't have a career that's your own.

"If you work for a person, as I did, who has some respect for your mind, you're not really an office maid. The personal attachment is there. It's one of the reasons why you like coming to work. And yet, that makes it very difficult to leave. So when I thought about leaving there was something sad in it for me and yet something I wanted."

Finally she was truly gentled into her promotion. Her boss sat down with her and went through a career review process. He first encouraged her to go back and take a management course for women.

"It was like a small risk, a testing thing. I first went back to school and that wasn't too difficult and then when the opportunity opened and he approached me, well, I wasn't too scared. Even so, I was supposed to move in March or April. Well, now this may sound strange to you but Secretaries Week hadn't come yet and I said, I couldn't do it that way, that they couldn't promote me until after Secretaries Week. I wanted to finish up thirty years as a secretary."

It was in June when she was forty-seven that Janine was promoted. Even then, she made sure that she could go back to secretarial work if the promotion didn't work out. "I was afraid and he kept saying that if it doesn't work, you can come back. So I really had it easy."

Still, for the first three or four months in her role, Janine used to come in and hang her coat up in her old office, say hello to her old boss before she went down to her new office.

"He doesn't kind of godfather me anymore. I don't need it anymore. We still talk every once in a while, but I got comfortable in my new role. Now I love it." First she was assistant manager of personnel, and then when the manager was promoted she became full manager and head of the department, doubling her salary. Her old office on the eighteenth floor used to reflect the taste of her boss. Now, her office is full of pictures of her children and a rotating art gallery of their paintings.

Janine is an optimist with both energy and ambition. "Probably I'm overly ambitious. It's like I was let out. I expect to work ten years and to move up five grade levels. Isn't that something coming from me? I never thought before about being anything but a secretary.

"It's the climate now—the climate for women—plus the doing thing. I find that you know as you do. You learn that you can do one thing and then you want to try more. It's like you are encouraged by your own successes. Those successes become a part of you. You feel stronger and you can try out that strength in other ways.

"My mother says I changed so much in two years she doesn't even know me. Well, now, I've never been a person who stood up for herself. My mother had a great tendency to run my life. It's just the last two years I've said, it's mine. I mean, for instance my mother used to come in and rearrange my furniture, then when she was gone, I'd just put it back where it was. My husband would say, 'Why don't you tell her to leave it alone?' and I'd say, 'I can't, she's my mother.' Well, finally I did. The first time I told her, she nearly dropped dead. Now it's okay. But there have been so many changes in my life, you know, sometimes even I look around and say, 'Hey, is this Janine or someone else?'"

One of the things I saw in Janine was the exhilaration that can come with change. Her confidence and excitement were contagious. But I also think that she is and has been very lucky. She had the security of a cushion below her and the encouragement to try for the next rung on the ladder. Janine never faced the choice of sinking or swimming. She was able to build up her self-esteem slowly, and in the same environment she'd been in before. Now, she believed that the future offered her still more and was eager to test herself, stretch further. Loss had been vastly outweighed on the scale of change by growth.

MORE AND LESS

I used to think that "personal growth" was like cake. It was nice, a dessert to the main course of life, but not necessary. Words like "human potential" and "self-fulfillment" smacked to me of Esalen retreats and pop psychology. Now, I see that growth is as vitally nourishing to our lives as bread.

Janine now feels the same way. After any of us sees a new possibility, and gets in the habit of growing, the status quo can feel like a prison. Staying in place may begin to feel like falling behind. There is, for all of us, a point at which not growing means diminishing. A point at which we can only choose between despair or change.

Change may actually seem like the lesser risk.

ELEANOR: RISK TO AVOID LOSS OF SELF-ESTEEM

In many ways, Eleanor became a member of that group of women which pressed most ardently for change in the early '70s:

the college-educated housewives. She was among those who
went through an intense second-growth spurt.

As early as 1949, when Eleanor was just in grade school, a
graduate of one of the seven sister colleges had written to her reunion class, "I have discovered in most of my friends and in myself a feeling of frustration and of having been prepared for
something better than the monotonies of dusting, sweeping,
cooking, and mending."

The truth was that they had been prepared for something better. They were educated on an equal basis with men, educated
for a life that in no way resembled the one that most of them
were living. Like these women, Eleanor too grew up and then
suffered a profound blow to her expectations. She had been
raised in Canada. Her mother had been one of the first women
road engineers and her grandmother had been a pioneer. The elegant, blond, forty-two-year-old woman with high cheekbones,
crystal-blue eyes, and a rather mellow style, says without rancor,
"I grew up with, as Dickens would say, 'great expectations.'"

Her mother sent her to college in the United States because
she wanted to study journalism. All these years later, Eleanor
remembers this ambition and how it was derailed or "rechan-
neled" when she decided to marry a ministry student.

Instead of pursuing journalism, she was convinced by the dean
of students to switch to music. "I still remember talking to the
Dean when I was trying to get into the journalism major. He
said, 'But Eleanor, you're so talented in music. You really should
pursue it. You know, as a minister's wife it would be so useful.'
He said, 'You could play the organ or direct the choir.' I think
the Dean meant to be useful. But why didn't I kick him in the
teeth? I wasn't a passive person. I wasn't a shy wallflower. It
gives you a strong sense of the pressure because I was neither
shy nor stupid but I absorbed the assumption that there were
roles for women and one does what one is supposed to do."

David McClelland has written that the drive for achievement
is formed very early in our lives. To have that drive thwarted,
even reversed, can be a painful, stunting experience.

But women like Eleanor were told that they had room to grow

within the tradition. If being a wife and mother weren't enough, she could, after all, lead the choir.

Talking one afternoon in her comfortably furnished living room in Minnesota, seated on blue-velvet sofas, Eleanor was doing needlework, her delicate manner still suggesting the grace of the minister's wife serving tea. In fact, the china coffee pot on the table and the silver sugar and creamer are the ones she used during the years she poured her energy and commitment into the roles of pastor's wife and of mother.

"At first it was very exciting and fulfilling. But after ten years of being the perfect pastor's wife, the years of being the frugal mother, Caesar's wife, it was simply boring. I was very critical of myself for being bored. Largely, I didn't admit it. I used to say, 'Well, now, you're a college-educated woman, if you're bored it's your own fault. If you're bored go and do something for someone else.' But it was always as the minister's wife, as the children's mother. Always gearing my needs around others."

She now felt "bored," "at a loss." In her own eyes, she was diminished.

The first break for her was when her husband was sent out on a mission to a church in southwest Asia.

"I went over intending to be a wife and mother, and I was coping with four small children. But the local leaders visited me and asked me to help them direct the local school. I remember protesting that as a wife and mother I didn't feel that I could do this, but one of them said to me, 'Mrs. Noland, we understand you have a degree,' and I said, 'Oh yes, I do.' He said, 'But that is a great blessing so that God must intend you to use it.' I said, 'Oh, but American women are often encouraged to have a degree so that they can be a better wife and mother, especially to a pastor or doctor.' And they sat there rather baffled and said, 'But if you have an education, you must use it.' It seemed so clear to them. They didn't let many of their women go for degrees, but once they did, they had great expectations for them. There, I used that expression again, didn't I? Well, anyway, I went to work for four years."

In a way it was easier for Eleanor to step out of the traditional role in Asia. The circumstances were already abnormal and, after all, she told herself, temporary.

But what she derived from the four years she spent running the local school—as a teacher, administrator, and leader—was "this sense of competency. It was a sense of strength, of coming back to my old self. I could identify with the girl I'd been at sixteen, but not the woman I'd been at twenty-eight. I felt like my old self again."

Behaving "abnormally" felt right. She was in many ways her old self. She had made a link back to where the girl had been derailed from her great expectations.

But Eleanor didn't have to confront this until they were ready to go back to the United States.

"I felt that I would have to return to being the good pastor's wife," she says. "I really became ill. I was sent off to a neurologist in Singapore because they really thought I had epilepsy or something. I kept passing out. Finally one doctor said, 'For some reason you are trying to avoid some issue and it's making you ill.' So I had to face up to the fact that I really didn't want to go back to being a good pastor's wife and that was when I knew that I had changed and had to deal with accepting that and with keeping that change in my life."

The conflict she felt was between "herself," the new woman who felt comfortable and expansive, and the good pastor's wife, who felt as if she were doing what was expected. She had to give up one of two things: her commitment to the ideal of the good pastor's wife, or her sense of accomplishment, her pride in growth.

In a sense, Eleanor experienced something typical of the middleweight change: two competing risks, two conflicting losses.

"In the end I did what I wanted to do. I say that carefully, because selfishness was a very evil word in my own language. I could never have gone into an occupation that wasn't in some measure service to other people. But I also chose to do what made me feel good."

With the help of her husband, who was very supportive to her —"I cannot imagine what I would have done if he had been opposed"—she went to graduate school and then became a college administrator, running a continuing education program for older women.

Changes of growth, changes to avoid loss, didn't resolve every conflict in Eleanor's life. She still feels a tug of war between her time with her family and her time on her career. She still feels guilty if she is neglecting either. But on the whole Eleanor is comfortable with the idea that she is "back on her track."

She went through a crisis when her old assumptions came into conflict with her new choices. She went through this turning point without a major loss. In fact, she feels that both her sense of self and her marriage were strengthened by change. They had all grown.

Others are not always able to avoid loss. They're the ones for whom change is a heavyweight experience.

HEAVYWEIGHT CHANGE: THE CRISIS

At some time we have all experienced the most intense kind of change, what we call a crisis. A crisis, according to my dictionary, is "a stage in a sequence of events at which the trend of all future events, especially for better or for worse, is determined." That definition covers everything from wars to Wall Street. But in our own personal lives, the most intense turning points, these crises, always seem to hinge on loss.

One crisis we experience may be the death or departure of someone we've loved and depended on. Another may be the failure to achieve a goal we counted on, or the final frustration of some vital dream. For the politician a crisis may come from the loss of an election, the final defeat of his hopes and his career. For a parent the most fundamental crisis comes with the death or estrangement of a child.

But we also experience crises which are essentially conflicts. Suddenly we are forced to make a hard call, a 51–49 decision. Either way we are threatened with loss, either way is a risk. In that kind of crisis, we try to avoid the greater loss or at least seek the greater gain.

In the mid-1960s, I knew many Catholic couples who went through a crisis because of the conflict between their religion

and their family lives. Raised in the parochial school system
where they were taught that birth control was a sin, many couples I knew came to a moment when they faced a conflict after
three or six children, after rhythm and abstinence and anxiety.
They finally felt that either they had to give up control of their
futures, or give up their religion, a religion ingrained in the daily
and weekly fabric of their lives.

CRISIS OF IDENTITY

What Eleanor experienced in the days before she came back
to America was the kind of internal conflict we label an identity
crisis. Identity, as psychiatrist Robert Coles describes it, is a kind
of confidence in the self, "confidence that somehow in the midst
of change, one is; that is, one has an inner sameness and continuity which others can recognize and which is so certain that it
can be unself-consciously taken for granted."

Eleanor, for example, had once felt that self-confidence, that
inner sameness. Her sense of identity was in being a loving,
other-directed, selfless minister's wife. She was a problem-solver,
a nurturer, a self-sacrificer. Suddenly that image was questioned.
Perhaps, she said to herself, she wasn't selfless. Perhaps her
whole identity wasn't comfortable located in the role of minister's wife. Her confidence became a question—"Who am I?"—a
devastating confusion of self.

But even those crises which come from the fear or actual loss
of a pivotal relationship in life are in some ways a loss of self.
When we lose someone we love, we also lose the part of ourselves
which is attached, even grafted onto the other person. No longer
are we a part of "us." The "us" is gone, leaving behind a diminished "me." When we fear or mourn the end of a relationship, it is often ourselves that we are also mourning, the person we were with that "other."

THE CRISIS OF ROLE CHANGES

For many of us, the changes in sex roles has been a full-scale
crisis. The most common fear for men and women has been of

the loss of a relationship. When I talked with people about their marriages, a pattern emerged. Most often women were the ones who initiated change, especially the most common change in the '60s and '70s from being a full-time mother and housewife to working outside the home. As they worked on jobs and developed a stronger sense of independence, they often became ill at ease with their role as a dependent woman inside the house. They felt different and they wanted that difference to be reflected at home as well as in the office. Of course, a lot of us feel a contrast between the way we behave on the job and the way we behave at home. But sometimes we also feel a conflict between the new person we have become and the old image reflected back to us from a partner or spouse. A partner may inhibit changes which we consider vital to our new sense of identity.

A woman I met who had left her husband after many years once told me: "Being a feminist married to John was like being a pacifist working for Dow Chemical. Either I remained a parody of Edith Bunker or I left. So I left." But I doubt that it was that easy. She left her marriage in order to preserve her sense of self. (This is something I'll talk about more later.) Other women seemed to feel a growing conflict between their desire for independence and growth on the one hand, and on the other, their desire to maintain a relationship built on more traditional roles.

Many of the people I met avoided changing their relationship because they were afraid that change would mean loss. The hardest thing to transform may be a pattern of caring and daily living that has been set up over the years. Sometimes the crisis of change remains with us for months, or years. The conflicts remain at the front of our minds. We rerun them like an old tape, uncertain that we've made the right decision, still reeling from the losses that have ensued. The more equally the losses compete with each other, the more likely it is that the crisis will continue, thorough and devastating for some time.

MARY: EITHER WAY I LOSE

Exactly one year before I met Mary, she faced a crisis from which she was still recovering. A tall woman with brown curly hair, Mary looked like the Los Angeles child she once was, the child who grew up with Shirley Temple ringlets. She had a button nose and cheerleader looks that made her appear to be thirty, rather than forty.

Mary married a college classmate from her small campus in Kansas when she was only nineteen. By the time she was twenty-eight, she had four children and a growing sense of desperation. Sometimes she would release it by sitting in a closet when all the children were napping and letting out a long scream. Then she would come out, wipe her eyes, and go on as if there were nothing wrong.

Rollo May once wrote about reactions like Mary's, saying that "without some new possibility, there is no crisis, there is only despair."

Only slowly did Mary see "some new possibility . . ." At last, she had burst out of her traditional role, accepting enormous strain in the next years in order to make her own life. She went through college while her children were still young, finding babysitters wherever she could, and hurrying home to make dinner and keep the house in some sort of order. Her husband, sometimes approved of her choice and sometimes disapproved, but rarely helped. For a year she became a commuting mother when that was judged harshly, working in government at the state capital some ninety miles away.

"I was guilty and terrified. I think my own need to have something for myself, even when I was feeling guilty and selfish, drove me out of the house every Monday morning to take the car and leave for the capital." Gradually her husband labeled her sick, "diseased with ambition."

Mary felt as if she were growing strong and freer, although there were also losses along the way. "After I started using birth control, I stopped going to church. Yet at the same time when I was in Italy, I went into the Vatican and sat there and cried, and cried. There was a great deal left. I felt, I suppose, deserted by the Church. As if the Church had left me, rather than my leaving it."

She also felt in some conflicted ways that her own growing up had tipped the balance of her relationship with her husband.

While she was expanding, he was contracting. Each time he slipped in business, she felt a panicky need to be able to support the children by herself. Each time she took a step up, he accused her of putting him down. Finally, in her late thirties, they were divorced.

For the next three years, Mary was a competent, caring single mother, supporting her children by a profession that was increasingly rewarding to her. She had won the appreciation of her peers and was now into what she saw as a re-integrative period. "After all those years of anxiety, it was a calm time." Her children were in schools they liked. She was more economically secure than ever in her life. She had fallen in love and was in a relationship with the kind of daily contact and exchange she enjoyed.

She was thirty-nine and content with her life, although her work didn't offer the excitement and open-ended future which she might have wanted. For the moment, it was enough.

Then, almost out of the blue, Mary was offered a job in the new administration in Washington. It was the job she had always wanted. It meant a new city, a federal-level job, a bigger pond. But it also meant uprooting, more change, and putting her relationship in jeopardy.

"Things were very calm before that offer. It's hard to believe, but in most ways that's true. I didn't hate my job. I liked it. The kids were in good shape. There were limits but the limits weren't really bothering me. I was content to see what would develop in this relationship as well.

"But when I got the job offer, I went into a tailspin. I wanted it. I could taste it. Suddenly the new job made me discontent with the job I had. I re-evaluated it. I looked around at all the miserable people ten years older than I. I was forty. It was possible that a job like this just wouldn't happen again. I had worked awfully hard to get into a position where I would be offered this kind of job. Could I turn it down?

"On the other hand, I had uprooted these kids a lot of times. They'd been uprooted from their father, from me during the years I commuted. Did I have a right to do it again? Was I just

being selfish? Wasn't there some way I could do things professionally that were just as good, but without leaving?

"Although I didn't want to hear it, Mike made it clear that if I
left, our relationship would be over. Maybe another man would
have been flexible enough to go into a commuting situation, but
he wasn't.

"What if I took the job, screwed up the kids, hated Washington, lost Mike? On the other hand, what if I stayed and grew
into a dead end?"

In two months of interviewing, the questions became more
and more intense, while the answers became more and more
remote. The answers depended on unknowns. "If I left, the relationship was over. If I stayed there was no guarantee that it
would work out anyway." She thought about the ten years she
had spent breaking out of her traditional life and becoming successful. "Was I going to throw it away for the sake of a man?
Isn't that where I came in? But still, after years of a bad marriage, wasn't something like what we had worth maintaining? If
I said no to the job, would it place terrible pressures on our relationship anyway? If I said yes, that would just be the end." She
was again faced with another new possibility and another crisis.

So, Mary turned down the job. "I felt awful. I felt that I had
said no to everything that I'd worked for. To the kinds of ambitions and goals that had really driven me for ten whole years.
That's a lot to say no to. Finally, I remember I was walking
through a department store and I was really shaky. I can't describe it to you. I hadn't eaten for days. I could hardly think. I
don't know how I did any work then. But I picked up the phone
and called, and asked if the job was still open. They said it was,
and I took it."

In the end, she had gone with her stronger suit, the thing she
had banked on for ten years, her ambitions, her restless energy,
her creative need to expand. "I am a risk-taker, I suspect. I like
to take a flyer. But this was the closest I've ever come to
crashing."

The reverse decision still didn't resolve this crisis. It took six
months before she could say that, on the whole, she thought
she'd done the right thing, "the only thing I could do, anyway."

It took a full year before she would say: "I couldn't have turned it down. I would always have wondered, what if . . . I would always have thought of it as the opportunity I'd worked for my whole life and then just thrown it down the tube. I can't even think of that without shivering.

"You know, if the job hadn't come along, I would probably still be back home. I don't know what would have happened. But it did come along and I can't say, no matter how traumatic the move was, that I'm sorry. I just can't say that."

READING THE SCALE

Change has a different weight for the people in this chapter, as for all of us. The featherweight changes are those which are really familiar, more of the same. The lightweight changes are substitutions, elaborations, and gradual, easy growth. These are the "safe" changes, the ones people are most likely to make and feel comfortable about.

But the scale tips as we load it with loss—fear of loss and actual loss. In the middle range are the changes of growth, those which seem to offer us more room to grow, more fulfillment, advancement, a sense of expansion. Yet these too come with some risk. We often have to let go of what is comfortable and familiar to get to a new place. As the fear grows, as the risk seems to grow heavier, we may hesitate or even turn back. Increasingly we need some strong motivation to make new choices.

Finally, when change feels too heavy we call it a "full-scale" crisis. The most difficult of these crises are weighted with loss and on either side—and the hardest choices to make are those that threaten us with formidable risks.

When I had finished charting this scale of change, I called Mary to see what had happened in her life since we'd last talked. The governor she had worked for in the Midwest had been defeated. Well, she said, she would have been out of a job if she stayed there. On the other hand, one of her children had never made the move successfully to Washington. He had gone home to spend his last two years of high school living with his father, and she missed him terribly. Mary was still figuring out the cost-accounting of a change that had been made a year and a half ago, still dealing with it.

"I have settled in here finally. I've stopped thinking of my old house as home. I'm very happy here. But the costs have still been tremendous, I know that. I don't think I could do it again. Maybe you can only go through that kind of change once or twice before you say, 'No more.'"

We spent a long evening at a rather elegant Washington restaurant while people stopped at the table to say hello to her and talk briefly about the department's new policy. She had just again finally reached out to a new man in her life. She seemed to have more energy and enthusiasm than she had six months ago. When I remarked on this, she tipped her head quizzically and said, "Well, probably. That's probably true. I think for a year I was using up all my energy just staying afloat. I don't want to have to go through that again! It would be great if someone discovered a cure for change. But I think I'd probably settle for a short cut!"

Part II
The Shuttle Zone

If I were given only one word to describe the feelings that accompany any critical change, I would choose the word "ambivalence." Ambivalence is the watchword of the transitional corridor I call the Shuttle Zone.

In the midst of change we all seem to feel this, we all seem to vacillate. As one man said, "It's two steps forward and one step backward." As his wife put it, "It's a kind of zigzag thing."

Changing roles is very much like negotiating a treaty between nations. There is a conflict between the traditional and the nontraditional, the past and the future. Like an ambassador in continual flight between Jerusalem and Cairo, or like an executive working out a contract with firms in New York and Boston, we shuttle from one set of values to another, seeking a comfortable treaty.

Peter Marris describes a typical reaction to a social change this way: "The response to the passing of traditional society was characteristically ambivalent, caught between nostalgia for the past and a desire to pre-empt the future."

CHANGE INNOVATORS AND CHANGE RESISTERS: THE END ZONES

The traditional past is the territory of one end of the Shuttle Zone—the change resister. The nontraditional future is the province of the change innovator.

The change innovator and the change resister will appear at first to have one thing in common: they both seem to have found a short cut—a way to finesse ambivalence, the pain and struggle of change. The change innovators, radical volunteers, believe they can leap over the Shuttle Zone and start a new life. The change resisters, objectors, believe they can refuse to enter a turbulent place. Both hope to avoid a sense of loss.

Often change innovators are people whose investment in the status quo is minimal. Perhaps they are young. Perhaps they are outsiders. Perhaps they are already frustrated in their attempt to live a meaningful life in traditional society. But they are largely people who seek to conserve meaning in their lives through change.

Very often change innovators have or insist upon a totally bleak analysis of the status quo. Times are bad, they say, the situation is desperate or, in any case, intolerable. This belief helps them commit themselves to the future, because they don't believe they have anything to lose from the past. They are, in some ways, like immigrants who began their lives in America with the idea that they would become instant, one-hundred-percent Americans, that there was nothing valuable in the past they left behind on the other side of the ocean. The more radical change innovators often want to uproot themselves, to revolt rather than to evolve.

At the other end of the Shuttle Zone of change, however, are the change resisters. These are often people who see any change as a threat. They hold on to traditions, trying to reassert the values of the past. They see mostly the threat, rather than the promise, in change. Very often they are people who have already made their commitments, invested the meaning of their lives in the status quo, and they see nothing of value for themselves in a future of change.

Eventually, though, many of these people—both innovators and resisters—experience the confusing, disorienting winds of ambivalence.

THE MIDDLEGROUNDERS

It's the men and women in the middle, however, who are most affected—internally buffeted—by their ambivalence. They try to keep some traditional values while acquiring some nontraditional values. They try to embrace those changes that offer growth and rebuff those that threaten loss.

They, like most of us, seek their own place at their own pace. Change now, in this Shuttle Zone, becomes a process of resolving the most painful kinds of ambivalence. From here on, we try to find our way through the Shuttle Zone to a more peaceful plateau.

Chapter 3   Change Innovators: The Great Leap

> She decided that she had to create herself anew, as if she were
> a blank slate . . . She tied her long blond hair up under a cap
> and walked across the campus camouflaged, without makeup, in
> loose-fitting shirts and green pants. She wanted to know if any-
> one would look at her if she weren't pretty. She wanted to know
> if she would feel different if she weren't feminine.
>
> "NIRVANA NOW"—A POSTER, 1970

One fall evening in Cambridge, I went to talk with a woman
named Rachel whom I'd met at a faculty party in Boston some
months earlier. Rachel waved me into her apartment, a long
railroad-style flat, decorated in carefully chosen, secondhand Art
Deco style with a dozen avocado plants, and tables painted in
bright yellows and reds. On the floor near the fireplace were
large lined looseleaf notebooks with various college emblems on
the front, of universities from the East Coast to the Midwest. In
each of them was a year or two of her adult life. They were the
journals that she'd kept for years in college and graduate school,
and now as a teacher.

The woman, who looked chic even in washed-out blue jeans
and a turtle-necked sweater, said that she had been reading
through her past before I came to talk with her.

She had just come to the most extraordinary passages that
she'd written in 1969. As we sat, she read to me:

"Last night, I came home and looked in the mirror. I was surprised because I looked the same, and yet, I am completely different. I've been through a metamorphosis. I feel like Kafka's Gregor Samsa. I feel as if one morning I woke up to find myself completely different. Maybe not as a beetle, like Gregor Samsa, but so changed that everyone would notice and react. I am just not the same person I was three months ago. I look back and cannot believe that I was her. My life has changed totally and forever. I belong to the future. Nothing will ever again be the same." Rachel closed that notebook and we began to talk.

There are some people who change in steps, in carefully graduated phases. They seem to be able to stay in touch with their pasts and to evolve slowly.

But there are others who run away or run toward change, toward some new life, and are determined to make a fresh start. Sometimes the runaways leave in a state of pain, anger, or disillusionment. Sometimes they are carried forward, attracted magnetically toward the future on an ideological high. But, either way, we have all known people who are radical change innovators, who make a commitment to a new society or a new way of living and, as Peter Marris put it, try to "pre-empt the future." They deny any ambivalence, reject vacillation, and grab for certainties. In one way or another, they want to take a short cut through the Shuttle Zone of change.

These change embracers cluster at one end of the Shuttle Zone. As part of the public drama, they articulate the crisis and make society confront it. They represent the future to many in the middleground.

But as part of the private drama of change, they also represent that impulse we all share toward radical change, toward an all-new beginning. Rachel knew that she was one of those innovators.

RACHEL: GOODBYE TO ALL THAT

The first part of Rachel's story, as we pieced it together from her memory and her journals, is in many ways typical of the kind of process of separation that many radical innovators experience. To leave the past, many people have to wipe out any commit-

ment to it, any acknowledgment of its value. To embrace change
without ambivalence, they hold on to the pain, focus on the
worst of the past, as if it were the mantra of escape. In a way,
this denial of ambivalence is also a denial of loss; if there is nothing, *not one thing good*, in the past, then there is nothing to fear
losing. It makes saying goodbye easier, whether it is goodbye to
a marriage, a country, or a sex role.

Rachel was born in 1946, nine months and twelve days from
the day, the Sunday, when her father returned to Boston from
World War II. Her birth seemed, to her family, a reaffirmation
of life. As Jews, they saw her as a survivor of the species. Rachel
was the family baby, the youngest of all the cousins and extraordinarily beautiful.

When her mother walked with her along Blue Hill Avenue in
the late 1940s, the other women, especially the grandmothers,
would stop and pinch her cheeks and tell her mother, "She looks
like a shiksa." She was blond and blue-eyed with long black
eyelashes, an appearance inherited from her German Jewish an-
cestors, many of whom had died in concentration camps.

By the time Rachel was ready for school, the family had
moved up another notch, to a suburb with a contemporary temple which her grandfather liked to call "the Church." Her
mother cooked and hugged and spent hours on the phone with
relatives discussing the details of family problems. Rachel never
thought about her mother as a separate person with her own
needs and ambitions. Nor, in many ways, did her mother. Her
mother was there for her. "It's my pleasure," she used to say,
"you don't have to thank me. I'm your mother."

It was her father who used to watch her "perform," whether it
was in school or in the house, whether it was getting good
grades, or the time she played a major part in *The Importance of
Being Earnest*.

Rachel occupied the center of her family's life, especially after
her brother went away to college. "I was an extraordinarily pampered child. The only condition was that I was supposed to be
happy. That was my side of the deal. My mother has always
insisted that I was the happiest child. To this day, she calls me
her sunshine girl."

In many ways, Rachel's family was her audience as well as her director, producer, costume mistress, script writer. In return, she was a dutiful actress.

She sailed through high school, ironing her long blond hair in the morning, picking something to wear out of her collection of miniskirts, learning how to strike a pose that showed off her figure in a way that was sexy but not "cheap." As a senior, she dated the class president, the boy from the right family and the right crowd who was going to inherit his family's business, and they spent hours necking and petting in his car or her car.

The summer before she was due to go off to the University of Michigan, she got involved with a boy who worked in the kitchen of the camp where she was a counselor. "Just the sort of boy my parents wanted to protect me from."

They started meeting at night in the counselors' hut and making out at the waterfront. The boy didn't know the elaborate rules of sex. In his neighborhood, anyone who would do more than french kiss was fair game.

"One night he just forced his way into me. I didn't know I was being raped. I had grown up believing that you had to be a virgin when you got married. More than that, I'd thought that "going all the way" would be incredible. Terrific. Stars would flash. Instead, it was a grubby struggle. It hurt and I cried and he got furious and started calling me all kinds of names. Now I've heard so many stories like that. But then—good God, you couldn't tell anyone about it. I felt so awful. I was terrified that I was pregnant for about a week, but I was more terrified that I had disappointed my parents and that my mother would know."

When she came home, her mother worried because she looked so haggard, "not like my sunshine girl," but attributed it to the annual bout with hay fever. During the two weeks before school, they picked out "college" clothes and Rachel went off to Michigan with a wardrobe that included twelve skirts and sixteen sweaters. And, the iron for her hair.

It was 1965 when she was a freshman on the Ann Arbor campus. She continued performing in school and got a prescription for birth control pills filled in Detroit. "Since I had already lost

my virginity, I didn't think it mattered if I did or didn't have sex.
If the boy wanted to enough, I did. I was completely passive. I
did what my parents wanted in school and what my dates
wanted in bed. I couldn't tell you what I wanted, I was still trying to be happy for others."

In the summer between her sophomore and junior years, the
summer of '67, she convinced her parents to let her stay in Ann
Arbor in an apartment with friends to take some extra classes.
One day she went into the only delicatessen in town, "Ralph's,"
and began fishing through the large paper bag of bagels im-
ported from Detroit. As she was holding six of them, a graduate
student with a beard and sandals and hair curling down to his
collar looked at the bagels in her hand and asked directly, hos-
tilely, "Are you Jewish or are you trying to pass?"

She didn't answer and he kept pestering her through the
checkout counter. Finally he said, "I know, you're a Jewish
American princess bitch," and she swung around and told him to
go fuck himself. Bob loved it. He was intrigued. He was a boy
whose own grandfather had been a rabbi and whose own parents were dismayed that their only son was a rebel, one of those
"radicals."

Bob found Rachel's name and started sending her notes. The
one she remembers was one saying he would be delighted to cut
her hair for her, the long blond hair she still washed and ironed
every morning.

Finally she went out to dinner with him. "He wore me down.
I suppose I was flattered because he was so persistent."

But the minute she arrived at his house, it turned out that he
had bought food for her to cook. He said he loved to see women
in the kitchen and told her to take off her shoes and cook. "He
literally sent me into the kitchen. I just went and did it. I can't
believe it now. I suppose I was so stunned by someone who
didn't treat me like a special person. I was fascinated by him. He
was fascinated by me. I was his clay. He wanted to see if he
could turn the Jewish American princess into his slave, I suppose. He said he would take over my education if I would cook
for him and screw him. He didn't put it quite that baldly, but
there it was. Marxism and fucking.

"It was a humiliating relationship in so many ways. I still have this wrenching nauseous feeling when I think about it. He also convinced me that I was frigid. He once told a whole roomful of his friends that I looked like a better piece of ass than I was."

She virtually lived in the off-campus house with Bob and his friends for the next year and a half. It was a scary time. "Everything seemed hysterical. I was convinced that Bob was right, that the revolution was just around the corner. Everything, sit-ins, Robert Kennedy getting shot, King getting shot. We knew people who got arrested and we all started getting paranoid. I clung to Bob in the midst of this. He seemed to always know the right thing to say when I felt totally stretched out. Maybe the whole country had a nervous breakdown that year, I don't know.

"The only thing that makes me think maybe I wasn't quite as self-destructive as all that was that in the midst of all this anti-Vietnam, draft-card burning, everything, I filed applications to graduate school and took my Graduate Record Exams. I even went home for a visit, all cleaned up and in one of my mother's favorite outfits and was amazed that I could still fool my family. They all thought of me as this nice little virgin dean's list student who wasn't involved in all that stuff."

She got into the University of Michigan's graduate school in history, and so did one of the other women in the house where they lived. In 1969 Naomi became the first real friend Rachel had had since grade school.

"I had always thought of girls as the people you were with when you couldn't find a boy to be with. But I found myself so at ease with Naomi. We really talked. The whole monitoring system I had with Bob wasn't there. With him, I was always afraid that he was judging and grading whatever I said. Naomi and I just talked."

Naomi was braver than Rachel. "She was probably a feminist before we ever heard the word. She wouldn't let anyone call her a 'chick.' She knew how to get mad. But still, we were the ones who did the dishes while the guys were smoking a joint in the other room after dinner. She was the one who got me to join a women's group with her. She said she didn't want to go by herself. I didn't want to go at all. I thought they were the crazies, the rejects."

In the first meeting, they passed around an article about shit-work and then each woman sitting on the floor in a circle talked about the way her house was organized; who did the housework, who did the cooking, who did the cleaning, who did the typing. Who made policy and who made carbons. The group consisted mostly of women active in the political circle, but there were also two "graduate" wives. As they went around the circle, talk-ing, they slowly shared grievances.

During the next meeting, they threw away the prepared papers and talked directly about their experiences. They talked about their parents and their sex lives and their teachers. They talked about their lives as young women.

"I had never told anyone, not even Naomi, about being raped. In the group, it just came out. It turned out that I wasn't the only one, not at all. We shared all kinds of experiences. Can you imagine that kind of ignorance anymore. I was so angry." Rachel came home from these meetings and lay quietly on the far side of the bed she shared with Bob, wide awake, furious at him, and terrified at her fury.

She started refusing to do things. Refusing to cook. Refusing to clean unless Bob would. Refusing to have sex. She started speaking up, disagreeing with Bob in public, something that enraged him. Each time she said no, Rachel felt flooded with anger and fear and exhilaration. "I felt courageous. I could never have felt that alone, but I was testing out my power. I was pushing."

Finally in March 1969, a month that hardly deserves the word spring, when the campus was gray and the winter boots stained with salt and permanent puddle marks, Rachel made the break. She was faced with a choice.

"Remember the poster, 'Girls say yes to boys who say no,' the anti-Vietnam draft poster? Bob brought it into the house and nailed it up on the wall in the front hall. I came in after school and there it was. I looked at the poster and told him to get it off. He sat in the chair, shaking his leg and telling me that I had no sense of humor. I told him that he was a sick, dominating pig.

That he was no better than Lyndon Johnson or Richard Nixon. I was shaking with rage. We screamed at each other. It was the first time I had ever actually screamed at Bob. I remember hearing my voice as if it were coming from a wall, like a ventriloquist. I finally ripped up the poster and he grabbed me and hit me."

With a coolness that still surprises her, Rachel went to her room and packed, while Bob continued screaming abuse at her, following her from the bureau to the suitcase to the bathroom and downstairs. She stopped at Naomi's room to say goodbye and then walked out of the house and straight to the home of one of the women in her group.

There she stayed in bed for two days examining pieces of her life. She let them up one at a time, tasting one memory, one chunk of pain, and then the next.

"I knew one thing. I had to get out of the patterns I'd been in. I had to get away from the whole past, with my parents, with Bob, everything. I had to change."

It wasn't possible for Rachel, at the moment of crisis, to separate out the good and the bad from her own past. She could only think of the destructive.

She hoped to leave behind the person she had been, with her lover and with her family, the passive, dependent, scared piece of clay, the good little girl, the performer, playing happy. Rachel also felt sure that to survive she had to leave behind her "conditioning," the feminine game she was now certain was disastrous.

"I was furious at my parents. I began to feel that they had never loved me, just their image of me. I had always been afraid to let them know me or, rather, to let them see any part of me that didn't fit their image. I was living my mother's life. She had always wanted to be pretty and popular and she was sure that was what would make her happy. I felt that I had to choose between their 'me' and my 'me.' It was as if I lived in a black hole, with nothing of value. As if everything had been a vicious plot and I had nothing to hold on to in the past."

In the next weeks, Rachel made many changes, some large and

some small. She decided that she had to create herself anew, as
if she were a blank slate. In some ways the physical changes
were the most symbolic. She let the hair on her legs grow for
the first time in eight years. She tied her long blond hair up
under a cap and walked across the campus camouflaged, without
makeup, in loose-fitting shirts and green pants. She wanted to
know if anyone would look at her if she weren't pretty. She
wanted to know if she would feel different if she weren't feminine.

Finally, she decided to go home for the annual Passover family meal. "I knew I had to confront my family. So before I went
I did the most radical thing I could think of, more radical for me
than blowing up a draft office. I stood in front of the mirror with
Naomi sitting on the john, watching in horror, and took the huge
kitchen shears in my hand and started cutting my hair off. I cut
and I cut until I looked like something out of one of those
movies about French collaborators. Then Naomi and I cried and
talked till two in the morning. The next day I got up and went
home, with my no hair and my green pants."

When she got off the plane at Logan Airport, a look of horror
passed across her mother's face. Her father asked directly,
"What have you done to my girl?"

That weekend, she laid out precisely what she had done to ·
their girl. And, more to the point, what they had done to her. In
the name of honesty, she devastated them. She then went, sys-
tematically, to visit her old high school friends and heard them
exclaim, "My God, Rachel, you've changed . . ." They reflected
back an image of an all-new Rachel and, in an odd way, that re-
assured her. She believed at least momentarily that it was possible to come out of the cocoon in a new form. "Even though
they were sure I'd gone in a butterfly and come out a moth, it
was an extraordinary feeling."

In six weeks, she had said goodbye to her family, her lover,
her femininity. This time, she would create herself. She would be
a liberated woman. That was when she wrote in her journal that
she had been through a metamorphosis.

SEPARATION PAPERS

Rachel's violence in rejecting the past, the rhetorical pronouncements that she wrote and spoke over the next months, were full of pain and betrayal. They had the sounds that often accompany divorce. Among many radical innovators there is the sudden permission and need to "speak out rage," to uncap the well of suppressed anger. The power of their former commitment is often counteracted by the power of their rejection.

Like many who are newly "separated"—from some powerful commitment—the first burst of energy is used to leave. They cannot yet afford to feel conflict. Most people, for example, fresh out of a relationship or marriage, refer back endlessly to the bad parts, the arguments, the infidelities. Even the good is seen as a trick; even love is seen as a power trip and commitment as a setup for rejection.

At the beginning of their "separation," many choose to spend time with those who reinforce the black vision of marriage or love and assure them that they are right, that "relationships don't work out," that the past is in fact past and good riddance.

FLIPPING THE COIN

The assumption of many change innovators, like Rachel, is that they can become instant all-new people. That it is possible to make a great leap and start the future now. I have seen many people convinced that they are freeing themselves from their pasts, or from their culture.

They are reacting and rebelling but they are truly unable to start with a clean slate. It is impossible to totally rid ourselves of traditions or to live in a "culture-free" society. Very often the most radical change innovators we know share the same set of values. They are flipping the coin, trying to create a vision that is the opposite, but still connected to the past.

There were, for example, those who believed that if the problem for men and women was the differences in their roles, then the solution was to eliminate those differences—not merely in law, but in nature.

Very often those who advocate the most radical change don't realize how much their future vision is rooted in the past. Sometimes they are driven so hard by terror of the past that they will ensure a different future for themselves at any cost. But not all the change innovators really free themselves from the pain of their personal histories.

ALLYSON'S LIFE INSURANCE

Allyson is one of the women who "insured" a different future for herself by destroying her escape roots, altering her biology. While her experience is hardly common, I saw in her radical decision how and even why a radical innovator may try to eliminate ambivalence, to cut off the past.

She is a slight woman, twenty-eight years old, pale, with light brown hair that parts in the middle and waves slightly to her neck. She has huge blue eyes that can seem eloquent or bitter or even frightened. There is something fragile about her, something elbowy and thin even in the black three-piece suit she wears after coming from work in one of New York's largest banks.

Allyson grew up at the opposite end of the class scale from Rachel. She grew up skinny and runny-nosed with teeth that were never properly cared for as a child. Ten years ago Allyson "escaped," as she called it, her mother, the church, her six sisters and brothers, her predestined future. She was the eldest, the one designated to be the child-carer for the family, the one who took care of her mother when she passed out after an afternoon of drinking; the one who opened the door for her father when he would reappear at will just long enough to plant another child. Every time Allyson saw her mother throw up in the morning, she knew, with a measure of terror, that she, the child, would have more children to take care of.

She grew up believing that she would end up just like her mother. That was the one thing the priest told her teacher: "That one, the eldest, ah, she'll grow up just like the mother if you don't make sure that we see her in church."

Although she loved her younger brothers and sisters, she deeply resented being their "mother" and told herself that when she grew up she would somehow or other get away and never see another diaper, or dish, or pot, or broom again.

"I was saved by one of the sisters, and I mean *saved*," she says nervously. "She found me a place in a parochial high school that was the college prep school, not the one where you ended up learning to type. I was the poorest kid there, the rest were lace-curtain Irish, and I never had a kid come home to my house because my mother would either be drunk or passed out. Anyway, I had to get home to the kids."

Then, August 26, 1970, between semesters at City College, she was walking up from her job as a Wall Street go-fer when she saw women marching. Right in front of her. Thousands of them, holding hands and signs, for Women's Equality Day. One of the women held out a hand to her and said, "Sister, join us," and without precisely knowing why, Allyson joined.

"It was the first sense of power I had ever had. Ever. In my whole life. I was marching up Fifth Avenue with one hundred thousand women. *One hundred thousand!* It was the first time I had ever had a sense that women could do anything. Besides lie around drinking and getting pregnant.

"The biggest shock I had was finding out that I like women. Before I got involved with these women, the only people I could stand were men because they had it figured out. They didn't do the shitwork. They had money. They were in control of their lives. So if I wanted all those things, I had to be like them.

"But the women's movement gave me another sense of the way society worked. They said that it wasn't women's fault that they were in this rotten place they were in. They showed me that it was men who had kept them down by keeping them pregnant."

When Allyson got involved, she soon became a leader. She discovered her voice and tapped her own sense of power. She was the angriest and most daring of the women in her college women's group. She didn't sign protests, she wrote them, and her fury was impressive. When she sat in at the newspaper editor's office, the others went with her; when she ran a campus abortion speak-out, the press covered it thoroughly.

As one woman who knew her at the turn of the 1970s remembers: "Allyson never had any doubt. It was very impressive and somehow comforting. She was a leader because she didn't worry about seeing the other side of things. A lot of us got paralyzed and had trouble acting. But not Allyson. The thing I haven't been able to figure out is whether she hated the system because she wanted to be a part of it so much or whether she just hated it and wanted to tear it down. Now she's a big banker. I suppose that means she just wanted a piece of the pie."

In fact, Allyson lost her leadership role during the days when the women's radical groups were purifying themselves of "leaders." At that point she moved on, enrolled in a business school, and then became a banking manager on the way up. "As far as I'm concerned, a liberated woman is a woman who can stand on her own, and a woman who can stand on her own is a woman with money. I never had any illusions about that. What I want is a room of my own, and thirty thousand a year."

But Allyson took one irreversible step to insure her future. She decided to be sterilized.

She went shopping for a gynecologist who would sterilize a twenty-two-year-old and eventually found one. "It wasn't easy. I must have gone to half a dozen who wouldn't have anything to do with it. They gave me all the old shit. They wanted me to see a psychiatrist. They told me I was denying my femininity and that I'd be·sorry and that no man would marry me. Of course, that was the point. I wasn't going to leave that up to chance. Me with a baby? Finally I convinced one of these guys that I had a rare congenital disease that I would pass on and much as it pained me—pained me, my ass—I had to be sterilized so I wouldn't bring another poor creature into the world. I don't know if he went for it or not, I suspect the bastard just checked to see if I had medical insurance. But I did get my operation.

"I left the hospital, and for the first time in my whole life, I was sure that I wouldn't end up like my mother. I went out and got drunk—I'd never dared before—then I went home and told my mother. She was so horrified, it was unbelievable. She thought I'd go straight to hell. But I never regretted it. I never did understand women who call themselves feminists and then get tied down with a bunch of kids. Eeeyyyug."

A FRESH START

Both Allyson and Rachel made the break at a point in their own lives and in social history when it was easier to believe in a radically different future. They had a greater commitment to the future and less that they feared losing.

But others try to make that great leap after they have already woven webs of commitments and patterns of behavior and relationships.

There are those who shuck not only old ideas but old relationships, believing that they can only be a "new person" in a new environment surrounded by "new people." Some are convinced that it is easier to start fresh than refreshen the old. Some succeed.

Others discover the limits of change. Like Jesse.

JESSE: FINDING HER NEW SELF

There is Jesse I and Jesse II. The difference between Jesse I and Jesse II, or, should we say, Jesse Act I and Jesse Act II, was a consciousness-raising group she was involved with in 1972. She was one of those people who tried to change her identity by changing her scene. Jesse I was a suburban mother of two with a house and a lawn and a dog and cat and a husband who bought her appliances for her birthday. By the time she was thirty, she had a yogurt maker and an ice cream maker, a dishwasher, disposal, clothes washer, and dryer—in all, she once counted, sixteen machines, not counting the vacuum cleaner.

Jesse II, the woman I met, lives in a turn-of-the-century apartment alone in San Francisco with a small refrigerator that frosts up at a hint of humidity and two burners on the counter. The only appliances in the house are her toaster-oven and refrigerator. She lives alone and works as a waitress nights and as an artist days.

"I was this bright, pretty little California housewife who never worked at anything except her tan," said Jesse II. "I could never go back to all that, to the whole middle-class diary-of-a-mad-housewife trip, the little husband and the little kids in the house, all that. We were into the whole California thing. Swimming pool, two cars. I was a chauffeur and a babysitter with all these appliances and my husband sold popcorn. Can you believe that, me married to a man who sells popcorn," Jesse II says, wrinkling her nose in disgust. She is a woman who looks California-faded. She has all the features of a pretty little thing, but one prematurely aging—like a weary forty-five rather than thirty-seven. From her description, Jesse I was a tabula rasa, an empty slate, an inexperienced, naïve woman who first did what her husband told her and then what the women's group told her.

"I was a delayed adolescent. I was in this rich shelter and I needed experience. I was a child like my children. The only thing I had of my own were my paints."

She had joined a consciousness-raising group the day after her thirtieth birthday, searching for something "else." "I was thirty years old with two small children and a box of paints and a new popcorn popper. There was something symbolic about getting that popcorn popper for my birthday from my popcorn-vending husband. I had this vision of me and my hubby popping popcorn down the road of life."

The group of six housewives, only half of whom had been friends before, spent one night a week sharing grievances and trying to reactivate old desires.

"It was the first time in years that anyone had ever asked me, 'What do you want to be when you grow up?' I said I want to be a painter."

Slowly over six months an idea and a plan emerged in her mind. To leave home and become an artist. She began to believe that the only thing that stood between her and fame was her family and her station wagon. All throughout the winter of '72 they talked about what they would do if they ran away. Finally, one of Jesse's friends took off. Just plain left. And Jesse was jealous.

"My husband was getting scared and tightening the screws.

He wanted me to stop going to the group. He wanted me to stop swearing and acting uppity. Then one night I left him with the kids without a babysitter and he threw a fit. He thought we were sitting around and talking about our sex lives—or lack thereof—and he was right. But what we talked about mainly was how to get out. Some of those women are still there talking about the same old thing. Others have done something really 'brave' like taken a part-time job. I knew that to get out, I just had to get going."

One evening, after she had put the two little children to bed and sat there watching them fall asleep with a mixture of guilt and relief, she packed a small bag and took the fifteen hundred dollars scrimped for a "vacation," and she left. Jesse figured she could go "for a while." But once she got to San Francisco she experienced an incredible sense of elation and hope.

"I kept thinking, here I go. This is a beginning. Free at last, lord, free at last. I must have gone around for months with a sign, 'Newly Liberated Housewife,' stamped all over me. I felt so heady." She joined another women's group with women of all ages and experiences, "not just a bunch of carping housewives," and together they learned karate and auto mechanics and how to fix appliances, the appliances she no longer owned. She found an apartment with good light and spent one hundred dollars—more than she'd ever dared before—on paints.

Her new friends didn't know she had a popcorn salesman-husband, and two children. They accepted her as a "single woman."

In some ways it was easy to make the great leap. Jesse believed that she had finessed pain by making one wholesale change, rather than twenty-six incremental steps from A to Z. She thought that she had simply "done it," that the process was over and now she could be Jesse II.

But gradually she discovered that even when you begin with a giant step, you may have to deal with the commitments to the past and the continuing changes of the present.

There was the business of the children. As she talks about that slowly, haltingly, some of the pain seeps through her bravura. "At first it was so exhilarating. To be in the city and to walk down to the grocery store without a baby carriage. To be able to

take a bath by yourself. But every time I would call home, it was
devastating. I couldn't take it. If it hadn't been for the other
women, I would have run home ten times. But gradually I
stopped calling so much. I just couldn't handle it. Now it's five
years and they have their own life. Sometimes they visit me, but
it's hard for them to be comfortable with me and they don't like
my apartment. Sometimes I feel empty, empty, and I wish it
could have been different. But other times I know we're happier
this way. I hope when they're older they'll understand. As for the
popcorn salesman," she says, brightening into a brittle bit of
humor, "he didn't come after me exactly, he divorced me. He
went ahead and got himself a new little bride. Wives are replace-
able, like batteries. One runs down—or runs away—and you go
out and buy a new one."

Jesse was also faced with the reality of working. "I thought I'd
be able to get a job at a museum or an art gallery. I had a naïve
fantasy of working somewhere until I started selling my paintings. Well, it's five years and I've sold two paintings, one to my
landlord in lieu of a quarter of one month's rent."

Her paintings on the walls of her apartment are portraits of
women. They look like female versions of Diego Rivera murals.
"They don't sell because the women are all too strong-looking.
People like portraits of women breast feeding," she said flatly.

Later, however, after tea and ginger biscuits from the health
store down the street, she expressed doubts. "Actually, I don't
know if I'm a good artist or not. I suspect I'm mediocre. I
thought that the only thing that stood between me and Pablo
Picasso was my husband and my kids. Once you're out of that,
though, you have to face yourself in a different way. For instance, I am now a waitress. I tell people I'm an artist, I think of
myself as an artist. But from 2 to 11 P.M., I wear a uniform and
serve food.

"I'm glad I took a risk. I wouldn't want to spend my life in
that little cocoon with the little children and little husband and
the boredom and diapers. But after a while independence isn't as
glamorous. It means hassling by yourself. I have no fantasies left.
I'm thirty-seven. I have many of the same problems I did at
thirty. I took myself along with me to San Francisco. Did I find

myself? Lady, I found myself at the Beef and Ale from two to eleven."

After the Great Leap—was it a dive off a precipice or a flight? —she is back doing the work of adjusting, integrating her life, coping. She is no longer a tabula rasa. Nor is she a happy woman.

AFTER THE FUTURE

Jesse, like many whose first step is a broad jump, discovered some wells of ambivalence. Change innovators, the advance guard of "newness," often discover that their ideal "future" too contains some of the past.

The truth is that we can overhaul our surroundings, renovate our environment, talk a new game, join a new club, far more easily than we can change the way we respond emotionally. It is easier to change behavior than feelings about that behavior. Even when we begin by taking a giant step out of the past, we may still vacillate between our roots and our ideals, trying to find a new comfortable plateau. This was surely true for an emotion as deep as sex, and for a woman like Mara who was a change innovator in sexual politics. She lived her way through an emotional Shuttle Zone.

MARA: THE "NEW" SENSUALIST

Mara's life reads like a textbook exploration of one woman's trip through "the new sexuality." She was one of those explorers who went from Puritanism to the "myth of the vaginal orgasm" to the "sexual alternatives"—from heterosexual promiscuity to celibacy—to what she calls "political lesbianism."

Mara has been teaching in a large university on the West Coast for over ten years. She is forty-five now and her office is still a small one which she refuses to move out of. It has only one window that looks over the sunny campus. Over her desk is a corkboard on which are pinned letters from former students of hers who have gone on to other graduate schools and teaching positions. Her radiator cover is piled high with papers waiting to be corrected.

One spring morning she came rushing in, fifteen minutes late —"I went over in class again"—apologizing and piling more books and papers on her desk. Her long curly auburn hair was pulled back in a pony tail and she was wearing a flowery ruffled blouse over a cotton skirt. The effect was at once girlish and absent-minded. She looked precisely the way a friend and former student described her: "She always reminds me of something out of 'Hansel and Gretel.' She is always scattering little pieces of paper behind her, like bread crumbs on a trail in the forest."

As she talked in her own deep-voiced, hasty way, full of self-amusement, it was obvious that Mara has been through a century's worth of sexual mores.

She was brought up by her grandmother, a woman who always insisted that she wear clean underwear, "in case I was in an accident." Her grandmother had thoroughly indoctrinated her in the double standard.

"Oh God, was I ever a sexual puritan. Everything was 'don't touch.' I've thought about it a lot and it's amazing to me that anyone growing up in that tradition ever had an orgasm. There's been so much written about why Victorian women didn't have orgasms. Well, what amazes me is why any of them did. It must have been the ultimate triumph of body over mind. Can you imagine?"

Mara was a nineteen-year-old virgin when she was married. "I remember my wedding night. I remember saying as we were 'doing it,' well, now I'm a virgin, now I'm not. Big deal."

She was a mother at twenty-one, twenty-three, twenty-five and twenty-six, all the way through her masters and Ph.D. "I was still totally submissive. I was so aggressive at school I suppose I felt I had to be super-passive at home to compensate. You know, to make myself into a normal woman. In any case, my husband didn't know any more than I did, that women could actually like sex. He used to roll over and go to sleep. There's nothing like that kind of relationship to make you uninterested in the whole thing."

She was divorced in the mid-1960s and discovered "the sexual revolution." "When I was married, I once wanted to write a paper called 'Is There Sex After Marriage?' My opinion at the time was no. Then after we were divorced, I wanted to write a second one asking, 'Is There Love After Sex?' At first I was learning a lot. I learned that you didn't have to be married to have sex—don't tell me that wasn't a cosmic revelation, you never met my grandmother. Then I learned that you didn't have to be in love to make love. Then I learned that making love didn't make you in love. I also learned a lot about my own sexuality.

"What happened was that I was seeing this man, the first man after my husband. We'd made love a few times, but I hadn't had an orgasm with him. I said to myself, hey, what's going on here. He isn't even my husband. I began taking some responsibility. See, the tricky thing was that I knew what turned me on, but I was too conditioned to tell a man. He was supposed to know. I finally stopped waiting for him to mysteriously figure out what aroused me.

"After a few disastrous relationships, though, I began to adopt the idea that sex was a biological need like eating or sleeping, and it was something I had to get into my life when I was horny," she said, changing her voice down to a deep baritone.

"I laugh because I think of that now as a very male kind of statement. The way some men can still dissociate their bodies from their feelings. It's tough talk. I still hear a lot of young men talking that way and I tell them, hey, listen to your feelings."

Mara says that in the last half of the '60s she grew increasingly flirtatious and promiscuous.

"I was still looking for Mr. Right and turning up Mr. Wrongs, left and right. I mean left and wrong. Or should I say, wronged and left," she said, laughing a high trill.

Mara got involved in the women's movement early. When it "broke" she was able to give her students an intellectual framework for understanding their experiences in her literature classes. They in turn gave her the right to articulate her anger and sense of outrage.

"It's complicated. I'd been labeled a masochist by three therapists. Three, mind you, that's a whole damn panel of them. But nobody had ever explained why. They always blamed my grand-

mother or something. But now there was a whole movement
explaining why all of us were masochists at some level and that
"someone" had made us that way. Men.

"So I worked through that. You know, 'I'm not a masochist,
men are sadists. I'm a historical victim.' Then, 'Yeah, but you let
yourself be a victim, kiddo.' Then, 'Yes, but my conditioning
made me let myself be a masochist.' It's a feminist chicken-and-
egg story.

"Meanwhile, every time I got near a man, I fell into this ap-
palling, eyelash-batting, cute, sexy thing."

Her own despair at not being able to break out of the past
combined with some of the messages of the movement at that
time. As one pamphleteer wrote: "If the problem is that we are
oppressed by men, then the solution is to get away from men. If
we have lived under men's laws and men's roofs, then we must
devise our own laws and live under our own roofs."

Separatism was one way to break from the male-dominated
past and to identify with women. As the pro-woman Redstock-
ings collective wrote: "We identify with all women. We define
our best interest as that of the poorest, most brutally exploited
women. We repudiate all economic, racial, educational, or status
privilege that divides us from other women. We are determined
to recognize and eliminate any prejudice we may hold against
other women."

Separatism. To some women, it meant self-sufficiency. Women's
bookstores and publishing companies, health collectives and
retreats.

But for a small core of radical women at the end of the '60s
the logical extreme of this was political lesbianism.

Mara was one of the women who read that the true sisterhood,
the true woman-identified woman would be involved sexually
with women as well.

In a piece that Barbara Grizzuti Harrison wrote on Sexual
Chic, she noted this phenomenon. "A group of feminists picketing
Hugh Hefner's Chicago Playboy Club released a statement to
the press declaring that they were all lesbians. In point of fact,
they were not. They were political lesbians, straight women who
'in order to share the oppression of their sisters,' and to forego

male privilege had chosen . . . oh, well, why go on? They made at least as much sense as the young white men who carried signs during the Vietnam protest marches declaring 'No Vietnamese ever called me nigger.'"

As one said to Harrison, "If women who love women carried their thinking to its logical conclusion, they have to become homosexuals."

Mara saw in this political ideology a way to complete her metamorphosis. "I couldn't be with a man without playing the role. I was successful at getting men the way I was successful at getting degrees. You figure out the system and you play it, and lo and behold, it works. It works in the sense that you get the degree, you get the man. But you end up with self-loathing and you end up with Mr. Wrong, who, let me tell you, is worth a lot less than the degree.

"In any case, I honestly didn't see any possibility of breaking the pattern of my life or my personal relationships as long as I was involved with men. I went through a period of celibacy, if you can call it that, for about a year, just me and my vibrator.

"But my own makeup is such that I need touching, body contact. In any case, I met a woman I really cared about. We were friends. We talked as equals. I could talk with her about anything. We were both active in the movement. For the first time I thought, here's a chance to try an equal relationship without role-playing. It may be the only chance we get in this society. Anyway, we became lovers.

"Well, much of it was good. She wasn't Ms. Wrong at least. I learned a great deal from that relationship. I learned that you could be friends after being lovers. I learned how good it was to share with someone else and to be honest in a love relationship. But I also learned lesbianism wasn't a protection from pain—the pain of caring or of losing love. Two women have difficulty living together. I mean, some of the issues between two people exist, whether they are a man and a woman or two women.

"Finally I learned that I was heterosexual. Remember the slogan, 'If sexism is the problem, lesbianism is the solution.' Well, I learned that that was true . . . for lesbians."

Mara had role-played through several "solutions" and finally

discovered in her own way that she at least was not able to be
born again into another body and another pattern of sexual responses. Gradually she began to see that, difficult as it may be,
she will have to change in tune with her own needs.

But her story touches on a deep source of ambivalence within
the whole future-orientation of the change innovators. At the
same time some were seeking to overhaul the present and pre-
empt the future, there grew a yearning and search for roots.
While they were calling for a massive "goodbye" to the traditional role, some feminist innovators simultaneously glorified
many of the values that were a part of the role.

Among those people who seem to be most committed to
change, to embrace its values with the least ambivalence, I have
often seen some unusually poignant nostalgia for the past, for an
idealized version of the traditional.

I remember once sitting in a consciousness-raising group myself in the early 1970s when I was writing a story about it,
and listening to the women telling "war stories" of their child-
hoods. One woman in particular told how bitter and frustrated
her mother was, a professional woman who had retired to home
after her children were born. Yet, in the same evening, this
young woman also spun out idyllic images of a culture and a society in which the "traditional" female principles of love and
mothering were dominant. She too recognized the problems and
the values embodied in traditions.

A KIND OF NOSTALGIA

I saw much more ambivalence among change innovators than
there appeared to be at first. Some called on women to be tough
while exalting the female pacifist spirit. Some insisted that the
females' values were the "right" ones, while breaking out of the
social limits of that role and leading lives that were professionally equal to those of men.

Even among change innovators there was a conversation between the past and future, an argument that raged most fiercely
between the values of nurturing and of achieving. There was

also an extreme reluctance among women to simply wipe out the meaning of their own mothers' lives and in their roots.

They shared, in many ways, a typically ambivalent response to change. I have often met people who worked hard to move from one job to another, or who chose to move to a new city. Often, they express nostalgia for the job they once griped about, and fondness for a place they left eagerly. Similarly, men who fought in World War II often remember that experience years later in terms of their buddies and the camaraderie, not in terms of the mud and the fear. We all have a tendency to glorify the past. And this may be especially true if we have propelled ourselves out of it.

This nostalgia may be an expression of what we feel is missing from the present. The past may not actually have existed as we idealize it. But our "memory" comes from a wellspring of our present needs, our current sense of loss. It also comes from a need for roots, and a history of value.

As a thoughtful woman told me one night after supper during a National Women's Political Caucus Convention: "It sounds like we're splitting hairs, but it's not hairs, it's arteries. I wonder sometimes whether nurturing wasn't grafted onto the mothering thing. That certain softness I like, is that the price of passivity? Are these things, the good and the bad, soldered together, and if so, how are we going to keep the softness and the nurturing and get it unattached from all the negative, self-denying, wasteful stuff. I don't know. It's hard."

The ambivalence of change innovators may be partially rooted in their own relationships with their mothers.

A woman named Joan who runs a woman's bookstore in the Southwest described it to me this way: "My mother is the kind of woman who can listen to your problems until three in the morning. Do you know what I mean? She is the only adult I ever knew who would play Monopoly with us. My father would debate with me, my mother would listen to me. My father would give me a congratulatory handshake if I got a good report card, my mother would give me a rubdown if I was sad or sick. My mother always understood our needs. I mean, here I am a thousand miles away and she'll call me when I'm depressed. It's uncanny, it drives me crazy—how the hell does she know I'm depressed—but it also makes me feel cared for. My mother is a professional carer.

"She's never had enough selfishness. She waited on my father, she waited on us. She enjoyed being a housewife and mother— it's hard for me to believe it but it's true—and then my father died on her last year and the bottom dropped out. She's lonely and sometimes grasping, even from a thousand miles, you can feel it. I feel that she was screwed by a society that told her to put all her marbles in the family basket.

"But on the other hand, goddamn it, she's an incredibly good woman. Objectively I think we should have a whole society of people just like her. I'm afraid to be like her and I'm afraid to be too much unlike her. Do you know what I mean?"

Joan was sorting out her own individual needs—for mothering and men, for control over her life, for security and power—and her own values for society.

When women like Joan began articulating their ambivalence— there were many people who believed that they were retreating from their commitment to change. Commonly people shake their heads, chuckle and assure each other that today's radicals will "grow up" and become conservatives, even change resisters.

But, in fact, this doesn't signal a retreat. Rather, it shows a maturing sense of complexity. These women don't want to wipe out the past, but to incorporate the best of it into the future. They too seek growth without loss.

Many of the most thoughtful innovators eventually have felt the need to link back to their own personal histories, and often to the people in their pasts who embody these values. One of them was Rachel, the woman who had said goodbye to all that, cutting off her roots as she had cut off her long hair.

THE RETURN OF RACHEL

"I had seen my family as shackling me to the past. I'd seen men the same way," says Rachel, that night we searched back through the past in her journals. In 1970 she believed that she was breaking the shackles and liberating herself. Still the old-think lingered on. It was a struggle to believe in herself as "independent." It was a struggle not to fall back into the comfort of the traps she was most familiar with.

"In a sense, the women's group replaced my family. They gave me support and nurturing. I got a new sense of myself reflected back from them. I don't think I could have done it alone. It was the best kind of support in that sense. The support for change."

Yet in the '70s, she came increasingly to feel that the group also imposed some conformity. They supported only a certain kind of dress and a certain kind of relationship. One of the women dropped out because the group was hostile to her marriage. Another woman thought that while they insisted on total loyalty to each other, they spent too much time criticizing each other.

As Rachel began to feel more secure in her own identity and to slowly believe in her ability to take care of herself, she began to feel that she was still missing something.

"I came from a very close family. The people in my family meant something to me. They couldn't really be replaced by my peers. I had to run away from my own sense of pain at seeing these people I loved and was loved by, in a new way.

"When I had gone home for Passover, I had hardly been able to watch my mother making dinner. She had made everything, from soup to the sponge cake. She was exhausted. I wanted to jump up and help her with the meal, as she cleared the dishes and put out the new ones. But I thought, no, I can't do that. If I do that I'm perpetuating the whole system. I saw my brother, whom I'd idolized. He never got out of his chair. My father went through his whole carving number, sharpening the knife and cutting the lamb as if he'd just gone out and killed it.

"All I could see was how fucked up the whole thing was and how oppressed my mother was. She was a woman as smart and aggressive as my father. You could see it in the pictures of her as a young woman. But now, here she was, fifty-six years old, with no kids left at home, spending her days shopping and waiting. She waited for my dad to come home, waited for my sister-in-law to bring over the grandchildren. All I could see in her life was the waste."

The word "waste" was a road sign that stood between herself and her mother. Waste. Waste. In the first year, one of the ideas that kept her going was the powerful rejection of her mother as a role model. "I was terrified of becoming my mother."

Gradually, however, Rachel began to believe that she wouldn't be her mother, that she had somehow changed enough not to fear that relationship.

She learned that "mothering" wasn't necessarily martyring. It could be mutual, the caring that also went on between members of her group.

"It became finally clear to me that taking care of others is 'good' per se—what's bad is being fucked over for it. It's like cooking. Cooking isn't the problem, but being the only cook, being the unpaid only cook, being forced into the role of the unpaid only cook—that's the problem."

As she let the wisps of her blond hair grow back, inch by inch, so she began to relax her defensive posture against the past. Finally, three years after she closed the curtain on her family, she was offered a teaching fellowship in Boston, less than twenty minutes from her parents, and she took it.

"I was afraid of being in that 'magnetic circle.' I was afraid that the minute I got near my home, I'd be reduced to the old dependent, good little sunshine girl role. All my own momentum had been involved in growing strong and independent. For the years at graduate schools I hadn't had the guts to deal with the part of me that wanted to be cuddled and taken care of. That was the no-no. But I suppose when you actually begin to 'feel' powerful, you can take off some of the armor."

She came back to Boston as a teacher and not a student. She came back as a grownup with a salary and not a child with an allowance.

"Don't get me wrong, the issue with my parents isn't over. But I do have some kind of a perspective on it. One of the things that helps is that my sister-in-law has been converted to feminism. She's gone back to work and gotten my brother, the precious son, to dirty his hands on a dish or two. But I'm also more

able to say, 'Hey, that's my parents' lives. Those are their decisions.' I still have a reservoir of anger about my mother's life, but
I can't lay that on her. And I try to remember that she grew up
in different times and made different decisions and to say it's
okay."

As a teacher, she carries with her a sense of strength. Her own
students look up to her and as she encourages them to look at
their lives, she feels more confident about herself.

"Sometimes I worry that I'm less radical than I used to be. I
don't feel the same kind of pain. But then how long can you hold
on to pain without going nuts or becoming bitter. I am still very
aware of how this place [the college] uses women, and I'm still
active on search committees. I've tried to create an old girl network in my field. But I don't spend all of my energy, every minute, on the women's movement. Not anymore . . ."

The most difficult thing for Rachel to feel secure about in her
"change of life" is how it's reflected in her own relationship with
men.

"I was really hurt by my relationship with Bob. Not just by
him, but by my own loss of self-respect. For a long time, I totally
avoided, really rejected, any relationship because I was so sure
that it wouldn't work out. I thought that I would fall back into
the role. I was terrified that I'd want to be loved so much that I
would instantly revert to the dependent little thing that struggled to please.

"On the other hand, I was equally sure that I wouldn't be acceptable as an independent woman. I really believed that no
man would want a woman who didn't devote her life to filling
his needs and bolstering up his ego. I figured that I had just
opted out of the market."

During her first year back in Boston she made small tentative
attempts to get involved with men, "but I kept leaving. I would
get just a little involved and I'd take off. Everything else in my
life was working out, but I still wasn't ready to trust. I thought
that men were interested in me because I was pretty or they
were intrigued with me for being different. I also ran into one
real loser who was into Liberated Women, if you know what I

mean. His idea of a power trip was to make women's libbers. Terrific. Anyway, I certainly didn't expect Alan."

Rachel first noticed Alan at a faculty meeting. He was sleeping through it. "I was so jealous. It was the most boring, godawful meeting about curriculum, and everyone stood up to make their little macho speech so that it dragged on for hours and hours. And there was Alan sleeping. I wished that I had the guts to dose off in the department chairman's face."

As everyone got up to leave, Alan woke with a start. He saw her staring at him and read her mind, and said with a slightly sheepish grin, "You better not do that until you get tenure." Rachel laughed and from then on at meetings they would sit near each other and pass notes like restless kids in class. They became such good friends that she was sure they would never be lovers and so she let him know her.

When he finally stayed with her one night, "It was as easy as anything else. It was the only time I'd ever thought of sex as friendly."

Two years later, they still live separately, though they spend much of their time together. "Alan would like me to make a commitment to live with him. I'm not so sure. It still seems to me that women have a lot more to lose. I'm still concerned about losing even this semblance of independence. I still feel that there's this bottomless well of dependency in me and that if I lived with Alan, I'd be a clinging vine. Marabel Morgan under the skin. On the other hand, I'm afraid that he would push me into some role, that he's a closet chauvinist and he's just being this way till 'he gets me.' I don't feel that consciously but it's there, deep down.

"It's important to me to be in charge of my own life. But on the other hand, I love being close with him. I don't mind that there's a 'we' creeping into my vocabulary. And I do think a lot about wanting to have a sense of family and even a baby."

Rachel stopped and paused for a long minute then, and added: "The problem is that I want to have it all. I want all the good things. I want all the independence and all the closeness. I want the career and the exhilaration at traveling alone and the family and children. I wonder a lot whether our generation will be the one that makes it work. Especially with men and especially in this society.

"These are things I'm still dealing with and it's what? Nine years now since I first got involved in Ann Arbor. I was so sure I'd have it all figured out in a year or two at the most. Now I expect that I'll be dealing with these things for most of my life."

WHAT TIME DOES THE FUTURE START?

When I left Rachel's apartment, I was still thinking of both the public and the private drama of the Shuttle Zone. In public, women like Rachel, the committed change innovators, are the ones who seem to play for the future.

But in private, they follow this zigzag course, like we all do. They glorify their roots, while simultaneously leaping out of old roles.

Typically, their and our internal conflicts have more to do with personal issues than with economic or political ones. They have no ambivalence about wanting equal pay for equal work, or about opening the bars at McSorley's or the doors of the United States Senate.

The most intense conflicts almost always are related to our personal lives. We seem to have the most difficulty sorting out the values of our own private past and finding a place for them in a different future. When we come down to the questions of emotions and identities and personal relationships, few of us are immune to the doubts, the insecurities that accompany major change.

Even those who begin with a great leap forward have some difficulty consolidating change, weighing the profits and debits, the growth and loss involved. The innovators too gradually have to create a sense of continuity for themselves. They stop expecting Nirvana Now.

Chapter 4   Change Resisters

"From what I saw, the women's liberationists were against housewives, against volunteers, and in favor of abortion. I was a housewife, a volunteer, and a Catholic."

Whenever I think of a change resister, I think of my grandmother. Memory, says Freud, is art, and my memories of her are selective; they form a pattern of retrospection. I have a picture of her as a child, sitting seriously with her brothers and sisters, for a photographer on Canal Street, in New York. They are dressed like small uncomfortable adults, layer upon layer of underwear, lace dresses, stockings and shoes. I can only guess how different her childhood was from that of my own daughter who wears blue jeans and assorted T-shirts that boast "Pierce School," and plead, "Be Nice to Me, I've Had a Hard Day."

But I have another picture of her in my mind. She was a woman who incessantly cleaned, was obsessed with neatness, absorbed with scrubbing and scheduling. My father's favorite story of her, his mother-in-law, went back to the days when he was courting my mother. He would leave a small match on the doorframe when he left, and invariably when he returned the next day, it was gone—dusted away like all the other spots in my grandmother's home.

My mother, my aunt, and my uncle all say she was rigid—a woman who regarded any change as a "disruption," a woman who liked the trains of her life to run on time. She planned her meals to the minute. At times her children felt that she regarded them like objects which kept collecting dust.

Yet, when I visited with her, we would go on excursions to the kosher markets—a tour that was as fascinating to me as a trip to a Persian bazaar. She shopped, she pinched, she shook and tested fruits and vegetables as if she were a federal inspector. The meat man never dared give her less than the best.

Once when we came home together, my grandmother cut off both ends of the fresh hot rye bread and gave them to me. I remember telling this to my mother, who was astonished at this "breach" of the rules. My grandmother was a woman who only cut bread from left to right.

Yet she had an extraordinary smile, something worth working for, and a laugh that was sudden and full—one that she saved for me and my sister, and especially for my father, her son-in-law.

I have always thought of her as tragically tied to rituals that were unvaried, the nightly careful unwinding of the two braids she clasped on top of her head, brushing them out and then rebraiding one down her back.

She died when I was in my teens, before I could have bridged the generations and talked with her about her life. So she was locked there in my mind as a change resister, an old-fashioned woman—someone who regarded her role in life as a round of cleaning, cooking.

But then in the summer of 1975, I visited with my great-aunt, Polly, who lives in an apartment on a hill in San Francisco. It was the first time I had been with her in years and my first visit to San Francisco. One night after dinner, we started talking about my grandmother, her sister-in-law. She told me two things that did not jibe with my long-held view of grandmother.

The first was her memory of my grandmother in pre-World War I New York; she worked as a secretary, a daring working woman in a prestigious office job.

The second was the image she carried of her as a stylish young woman, and the clear recollection of her in a bright red dress. The grandmother whom I knew had only worn navy, brown, or black with the inevitable black-laced shoes.

To my great-aunt, she had been the modern woman, something new. She was the second or third generation born in America, while they had been the first. When she married my grandfather—a short, round Santa Claus of a man who demanded service of her as he had of his six sisters—their home had been a refuge for his sisters, a refuge from the restrictions of the Sabbath as it was enforced by their parents, my great-grandparents.

It seems that my grandmother had once been avant-garde compared to other women of her situation and time.

What had happened? Had the times simply changed around her? Is yesterday's modernist inevitably today's traditionalist? The things that my aunt perceived as "radical"—the loosening of the Sabbath ritual—are things I never even thought about.

Or had my grandmother simply grown more conservative over the years? Had the young woman in the red dress, the outgoing secretary, been slowly constrained and maybe even disappointed in life, so that she evolved into a more narrow woman who sought security in routine? Was she afraid of every change, or only those which threatened the meaning of her life? These are some of the questions that I repeated to myself when I looked at the women who most fervently resist a change in their traditional role.

If I had to characterize the change resisters with one sentence, I would say: They are people who value safety and sameness.

Of course, we all seek the comfort of routines. But for most people the attraction of security has a counterpart in the allure of newness, change. For the resisters, however, the fear of loss may be so great that it overwhelms the attraction of newness and may even squelch ambivalence.

There are many different kinds of resister personalities. There are some resisters who are always "careful," the kind of people who warn others continually to watch out. There are others who learn so well how to adjust to the status quo that even an offer of growth threatens them.

If the change innovators at one end of the Shuttle Zone are more likely to be young, the change resisters at the other end are more likely to be older. We expect older people not to embrace change as easily as younger people. But I don't think it's simply a question of hardening of the arteries through which change might flow. It's a matter of investments, in ideas and in relationships. After decades of adjusting and elaborating one series of life choices, people are simply more committed to one course.

The extreme change resisters may feel the simple need to protect their turf.

MIDGE: THE LONG-TERM INVESTOR

I rang the doorbell of Midge's white garrison colonial home in a conservative suburb on the East Coast one morning right on time. But when Midge came to the door to answer the bell, she was surprised to see me. Only later that afternoon did she say that she had expected to meet someone who looked like a "career woman." During our conversation she was surprised that I would call myself a feminist. She said I didn't "look or sound like them."

It wasn't that the fifty-seven-year-old woman was unsophisticated, but rather that a specific image was imprinted in her mind from the first time many years ago she saw "them" on television. What did she hear? "I heard a group of young, blue-jeaned shouting women saying that housewives were slaves and anyone who spent their lives raising children had wasted their lives and the only way to be liberated was to go out into the world and find yourself. I didn't like it at all."

The woman with white hair and bright blue eyes is short and plump and has a peach-fuzz complexion. On this day, she was wearing a blue suit and seated in front of a large picture window that looks out onto the ocean. Surrounded by Early American furniture, including some costly antiques, she obviously lives a very comfortable life with people who are very much like her.

As we talked, I was reminded again of my grandmother, because Midge too was a woman who slowly turned into a change resister. She was born in the 1920s, the first of six children who would come to occupy the house along with a widowed grandmother, an Irish immigrant mother and a father who was a fireman with a grand salary of twenty-six dollars a week.

Her life and identity was built on the solid foundations of

these roots; family and church. As a child, with small features and an upturned nose that looked like a freckled "map of Ireland," she learned that her mother was really the strong one, but her father was a "dear, lovable, really great, great guy who never really understood me." Her father was the one who technically ruled the roost, and her mother the one who quietly conspired with her daughters to work around him.

As a child, Midge was a good student of math and Catholicism. She could rattle off the catechism like the multiplication tables and she was well rewarded by the nuns in her school for being a good child. When she graduated from high school at sixteen, she thought of herself as ambitious, though in those depression days the most she could hope for was a clerical job. "I was a sort of ambitious achiever," says Midge, who kept her hands folded on her lap almost the whole time we talked. "I was terribly conscious of the fact that in order to enjoy the things you wanted in life, you had to work hard and educate yourself. I went to a clerical school really because of my mother's help. My father didn't see why a girl would need that."

She then went looking for work and beat out five hundred applicants for her first job, a twelve-dollar-a-week job entering installment payments in a ledger all day long. She worked at that job, with "rows of girls sitting there and doing the same thing. You couldn't get up from your desk and go to the bathroom without permission from someone."

There was no union in those days and no law against sex discrimination. But Midge believed that she could have control over her life. She set out to do the best she could—just as she had in school—to achieve within the rules.

Like other Irish Catholic girls of the time, she looked to the government. After passing a civil service exam she took a giant step up to a city secretarial post, where she was treated "decently." It was a fine job. A year later she met Buddy, then a law student. But they weren't married right away, because, "I couldn't see this. As Catholics, I thought we'd be likely to have a family right away and that would complicate his career more than mine. I was more concerned that I wouldn't want to interfere in any way with his graduation. So we weren't married until the war."

Midge, early on, transferred her ambitions to those of her husband. She "naturally" went to where his jobs were, following opportunities from Washington to Maine before settling into a pleasant suburb. The only changes in her life were slow cumulative ones that built layer upon layer onto her original commitments. The only variation in her life plans was that they were never able to have children.

"Buddy and I had a lot of time to be together, of course, because we didn't have any children. We wanted to but it just wasn't meant to be. That can do one of two things. It can either divide you because there's a void in your life, or it can bring you closer together because that void has to be filled with common understanding and companionship."

As part of that companionship, Midge worked for ten years as her husband's unpaid secretary. "I didn't feel like I was working for him, but rather with him as a co-worker."

Together they worked, together they were involved with church activities. Together they became involved in politics. Buddy made a bid to become a local politician and Midge became a campaign coordinator. After his unsuccessful campaign, she went on to do volunteer work in the community. In the '60s, she got involved in community work through the Church. Those were the days of Pope John and the local cardinal's interest in civil rights and poverty. Midge was active in Catholic women's organizations, helping to raise money for charities. She and her husband were considered liberal for their ultraconservative community.

Yet, she always considered herself a housewife. "Oh, I had all these activities but that was really my primary duty, to maintain this house and take care of my husband."

For many years, Midge seemed to have integrated her volunteer work, her role as a housewife, her role in the Church. The changes in her life were of a piece. But by the late 1960s she felt the first stirrings of a conflict that would force her to side with the change resisters.

She became concerned over the abortion issue in the League

of Women Voters, an organization she had once led locally. "I was very active in the League. I think it's a great organization. But almost ten years ago, there was a movement to put a study item into the agenda, analyzing the laws concerning contraceptives and abortion. I spoke at one of the congresses and pointed out the fact that I felt this was a volatile issue, that it involved morality, it involved religious beliefs, and I felt very strongly that it would be divisive. My attitude toward abortion is that life has been created and we should never be permitted to take a life."

When the League came out in favor of liberalized abortion laws, Midge left the organization. From then on, she began to identify with those who stood against the changes advocated by the feminists. Slowly she made a series of choices in favor of the most deep-seated commitments of her life: the Church and the family. She chose to side with the traditional women. "I guess I have moved from being a moderate liberal to being a conservative," she says. "From what I saw, the women's liberationists were against housewives, against volunteers, and in favor of abortion. I was a housewife, a volunteer, and a Catholic."

Sometimes I think it is a law of physics that the people advocating change crystallize an opposition. People like Midge who have lived their lives according to the norms of society suddenly find themselves defined as Traditionalists, and even old-fashioned. If they feel personally attacked, they react, of course, defensively.

The radical innovators may declare their first separation by painting the past bleak. It seems to me that the resisters react in two ways. Either they paint that past in ideal colors, looking nostalgically back to the Good Old Days and planning a restoration, or they refuse to listen to criticism of the status quo. They reject a negative analysis and discourage the kind of introspection that may lead to change.

In that way, like so many of the other resisters I met, Midge disapproved of the introspection that feminists call consciousness-raising.

"I think it's destructive. I really do. They have these sessions where women apparently sit around, it's a kind of self-analysis thing. You say, look at yourself and ask if you really are what you want to be, are you really fully satisfied? Well, introspection is not good for most people, especially if you're looking for things you don't like. I feel that the main direction of introspection is to find dissatisfaction." Change resisters on the other hand are likely to deny dissatisfaction.

"I'm tired of having the women's liberation group telling us that we are less than equal to men and that we are not fulfilling ourselves because we're not interested in going out and being independent and getting a job and competing on the open market.

"I don't know why the feminists say that women aren't secure. As far as I can see, they are. Most men have life insurance for their wives, and pensions."

Gradually Midge began to express the fear of what would be lost if women changed out of their roles. A future of new sex roles was vastly different from that of the change innovators I met. She saw a world in which women like her and her friends would be extinct. A world in which she would not be able to live a life of the kinds of choices she had made, the choice to be a part-time volunteer and to be supported by her husband.

"As far as I can see, the women's liberation women will lose these things for the rest of us. I think that they don't realize that they'll end up with a harder life. Now why would anyone want a harder life? I don't understand it. I also think that they will end up alone. It just doesn't seem to me that men will want women who are all for themselves and their careers. They don't seem to want to have families or take care of children. You know, every time we talk about the women's movement we end up talking about marriage, because we feel that the women's movement has threatened marriage more than any other part of our lives.

"These women have made men feel it's okay to leave their wives and children, that they can take care of themselves. I have always tried in my life to protect those who need protection the most. That's why I'm against abortion and against this kind of change. It's the weak women who need to be protected from this. The way of life I grew up with has protected them. I think we have too much to lose. Too much to lose."

By the time I left Midge, I saw her as a long-term investor

protecting her savings economically and emotionally. She was convinced that a change in roles for herself and the people she identified with would mean an upheaval and loss, and she took sides against it. But underlying her defensiveness wasn't bitterness or defeat, but contentment. One of the reasons people resist change may be that they are satisfied with what they had. Life had worked out well, on the whole, for Midge and she saw no reason to alter it.

But that isn't true for all resisters. There are some who are not happy with their lives but still resist change. They resist it passively. Some simply do not believe that they can improve their lot in life. Others settle for security and sameness out of a terror of risk, or simple grit. They may have the sort of tenacity that keeps them committed to their way of life without the belief that they have a right to make changes. Some settle for security. Even the security of inflexibility.

CHARLOTTE, THE PASSIVE RESISTER

Equal rights? Charlotte has never truly believed that she had any rights at all.

Charlotte as a child was seriously responsible, the kind of girl who did chores as required. She was a member of a Mormon family, the daughter who was assigned to kitchen duty with the mothers while her brothers sat in the living room and talked. She was always a woman who thought slowly and deliberately—embarrassed at the teasing of her brothers.

Charlotte lives in a one-story house outside Salt Lake City. Her living room features a wall of old encyclopedias, and a light-blue velvet sofa. There are photographs on the end tables but no pictures on the walls. There is a serious and constrained quality to this woman I met. She was wearing a wash-and-wear shirt, solid cotton knit slacks, and when she spoke, it was with slow painful honesty.

Others might call Charlotte mousy. But she is someone who feels responsibilities acutely and who looks at past choices as obligations to endure. She doesn't really believe that she can make a change in the rules or the regulations of her life. In fact, as we talked, she told me I was the first person to ask her whether she was happy since her father had died.

When Charlotte was nineteen she made some decisions, and she stuck to them for twenty-five years, because in many ways she didn't believe it was right to change the rules in the middle of the game. "Sometimes when I start wondering about my life," she said, "or when I want to complain, I remember that I made these decisions. I knew what I wanted in a husband when we got married. I wanted a man who would be qualified to hold the Mormon priesthood. I wanted a man who was reliable and I got all that. If I'm unhappy, well, I have no right to be." Charlotte's husband is a businessman who talks circles around her. Charlotte mulls things over; he debates. "He's very opinionated. He reads faster than I do. Sometimes I find it quite frustrating. He thinks I'm quite naïve in a lot of ways. In a conversation, I don't think he'd let you say many things that he'd disagree with."

After twenty-five years she doesn't disagree. She doesn't complain. When she is unhappy, she argues away her feelings.

Through our afternoon visit, she argued away her boredom, her sense of being neglected, even her concern that she has no say in financial matters. Her husband has made money and put it into cars and equipment when she would have chosen to pay for the kids' colleges and to have traveled a little. But, she said, "In a way it was my choice. I chose to get married and this is what marriage is."

That same sense pervaded her criticism of other women who were "complaining" about their lot. "The women I know, the women my age, at the time we went to college we chose to be nurses and school teachers and that sort of thing. Now that's the kind of job they have. Well, I don't see how you should call that discrimination. I mean, maybe they wouldn't choose that now, but the decision is made."

So was her decision to be a housewife. "In our home it is my responsibility to take care of the laundry. I haven't got anyone else to help me. If it isn't done, they will criticize me. They say, 'That is your job.' Well, maybe the women's movement would make me think, it doesn't have to be my job! But, after thinking it through, I decided that I really should do the laundry. I shouldn't throw up a women's liberation smokescreen, because that doesn't have anything to do with it. I may not want to do it, but it is my job."

Charlotte, who was never encouraged to grow, seems to have spent her married life being "cut down to size"; she seems to have spent her energy adjusting to the responsibilities she made years ago. The Catch-22 of her life is this: because she is not an independent woman, she has no right to be an independent woman.

Once, however, she almost took a chance. Again and again she mentions this time, several years ago, when she wanted to go back to college. It was a personal landmark in her life.

"When they started the continuing education program, I really got excited about going back to school. I wanted that very much," she says, and I had the sense that it was the only thing she admitted to wanting in years.

"But my husband figured out that it would be half as expensive if I went full-time. I didn't want to go full-time, I wanted to go part-time. I didn't want the burden of a full load after all these years. But on the other hand I couldn't enjoy thinking I was spending twice as much for something as I might have. Especially since I wanted to study history, literature, that sort of thing. My husband felt that if I didn't want to go full-time, these were things I could do on my own." And at home.

Charlotte never took that opportunity to enlarge her world or her sense of self. She was a woman who could only take a small, supported, part-time step, to let the first sprouts of self-confidence grow. She was not a woman who could take a major risk. So the attractions were outweighed by the impulse to safety. She was safe at home.

If Charlotte was unhappy, she wasn't moved to change her role but to do more within it. "In my first ten years in the home I was so needed. But now I have time to do whatever I want. However, justifying it is hard. I am making a Christmas tree skirt now. But sometimes I think there must be something more important for me to do. Or, once I started thinking about a job. I had run a machine at night when my husband was in college, and also I had been a receptionist. But my husband said it's just not economical. If I were very fortunate, I'd be able to get a job as a secretary. I wouldn't increase our income, we'd just move into a different tax bracket. I wasn't happy with that, but I have to say, though, what could I do? I can see my children saying, 'My father is a vice-president and my mother scrubs floors.' Now I try to think of more things to do around the house."

Perhaps underlying her resistance to change—aside from her husband's attitude and her own sense of her options—was that she simply no longer believed in change per se. "I used to want to be a social worker. But now I see people don't change. They have problems and they have problems. They don't change."

With only two children still at home, her routine is unchanged day after day: "I usually get up around seven, fix breakfast, and then I like to have us sit together and have a family prayer. Then the children go off to high school. My husband doesn't leave until nine and I usually have to find his things—I don't like that, sometimes he's like having another child in the house. Anyway, then I clean the kitchen and do something I want to, like sewing, or I might write a letter home, or do a little reading. I do that while the boys are gone, because it irritates them, especially the fourteen-year-old, to see me sitting while he has to do chores.

"I do feel somewhat pampered not to have to work harder. Sometimes I do nothing for two days straight. But even when my husband has a week off, I can't sit down and relax. I feel I should be working in the house."

The last thing she said to me was the most poignant.

"My neighbor says, 'Don't you think you deserve better? Don't you think you deserve this or that?' Personally I don't. I can't think of anything I deserve."

I had a great deal of difficulty even transcribing the tape I had recorded with Charlotte. I wondered whether it was fair to consider her a resister. She hardly had the spirit that word seemed to imply. Yet in the story of change, so many resisters are passive. In our own lives, too, so much of the weight against change is also this passive load. As the poster reads, "Not to Decide Is to Decide." Charlotte was in many ways typical of many resisters I met. A great bulk of the people at one end of the Shuttle Zone are, like Charlotte, those who have called it quits. The constraints of Charlotte's life have laced her in a corset and it seemed to me that only the most irrevocable fait accompli would move her out of a life she was so committed to.

When I look at Charlotte's life, I tend to think of safety and sameness as dull. She seemed to have atrophied in place. But there are other people for whom security is a major and difficult goal. They struggle just to hold on to it. Perhaps their lives have been mined with peril and any status quo looks like peace. There are people who resist change because they have had too much insecurity. The idea of taking a risk looks like an invitation to disaster.

We all know people who yearn for predictability. They long for someone else to depend on—it's the one thing they have never been able to take for granted. More than anything else they want shelter.

Ask someone like Beth to change, to move beyond that shelter, and she will answer simply, "No."

BETH: THE SEARCH FOR SECURITY

The day I met Beth was on her thirtieth birthday. She was sitting on the lawn of her house in San Diego, eating the remains of a pink and white birthday cake. Next to her was her husband, a thirty-three-year-old army major who was off duty that day. Beth was wearing red shorts and a pink ribbed T-shirt. Her brown hair, with a permanent, was suffering from the heat wave, and curled in different directions. She had no particular thoughts to mark this rite of passage, becoming thirty. But then, she was simply not a worrier or a planner. "I just take each day as it comes. I guess I'm pretty calm about things."

If there were two things Beth valued, after her childhood, they were calm and normalcy. She was a woman who suffered through a miserable youth, who sought and found a father in her husband. What some might consider constraints to her life, Beth considered security. She had found a way to be taken care of.

Beth was born to a mother who gradually became an alcoholic. She was the only child, the one who was urged by her mother "not to tell" on her to her father. But she was the one who sided with her long-suffering dad.

Beth's mother gave her a double message. "She always told me to have a fantastic career, to be an architect and go flying off to Paris. She used to say that without my dad she would have been something great." But Beth's mother was home with a bottle.

Her dad offered stability and an ally against the alcoholic mother. "My dad, you know, was the one who would fix it, whatever it was. It was a nice type of security. At least the way I was brought up there are certain things that men do and certain things that women do."

The only thing that was wrong with the deal, in her mind, was that her mother didn't live up to it. She didn't fill the traditional mother and wife role. Beth's family was wealthy and she was sent away to boarding school, the kind of school that siphoned its students into the best eastern colleges. Beth, however, chose nursing school and married halfway through it.

"It was kind of hard, you know, and my husband, well, I knew he was the kind of guy who wouldn't want me to work anyway, so it seemed sort of silly to finish." Instead she married a provider, a man who says that supporting his family is "almost a religious thing with me," a man who wants her to be the "woman and me to be the man." As he puts it, "Otherwise, why should I be married to her? It would be like being married to a man."

They have two small children now, and her life is circumscribed by her husband, children, and their home. Her husband gives her a weekly allowance for the groceries and for incidentals and she in return gives him an accounting. He has never allowed her to have a charge card and he pays the bills. It is only within the last two years that he would leave the car at home for her some days, and then only for car pools. But Beth said, "Oh, I don't mind all that. I like not having to worry about money, and this way we don't argue about it. I just get a certain amount. Also it's nice, like, if we go out for dinner on our anniversary, it's like a date still, kind of romantic."

Beth was aware of her need for a stable home. "Well, it's Kurt really who gave me my first home. The other one, where I grew up, it wasn't like my idea of a home at all." She had been hurt in the war between her parents, and between her mother and the bottle. Indeed, her most vivid memories are of the ritual play her mother enacted, hitting Beth when she was drunk, apologizing and indulging Beth when she was sober. Her father, it seemed, was the only protector she had had before Kurt. But her father, although he lived at home, was out more and more often as the years went on. "I suppose, well, he probably had another woman or something and I can't really blame him."

What she may have wanted was to replay the family scenario and do it over again right. "My idea of a family is that he takes care of you with the money and you take care of him and the kids. I guess I look at my husband mainly as I would my dad . . . as head of the family. I think a husband should be more of what you would call a guide. If you're out more in the world like my husband then I think he generally knows people better than I do. I wouldn't be afraid to ask him for his opinion, and if I really didn't have one of my own, I would take his. He is my husband."

Beth's most ardent hope for the future is that it would be the same: "I guess I'll always live pretty much the way I do. I like it this way. I wouldn't want to work for one thing. I like the idea, you know, that I don't have to get up in the morning and go anywhere if I don't want to. The kids get on me sometimes but other than that I have no complaints. I have what I wanted—kids. I just want them to grow up normal and not get into trouble, like with drugs or anything. I would like to live long enough to see my grandkids."

As for the women's movement: "I don't have any interest in it. I don't think women are equal to men. I'm not interested in that. I'm not Kurt's equal and I don't think I want to be. I think that men are stronger and can take care of women. I haven't read much about the women's lib, but I don't think it's going to affect me one way or another. I think it's a bunch of garbage. The head lady who started it, I have no idea what she looks like, but I can just imagine. I just feel it was started by a couple of frustrated women. I picture this poor frustrated old maid, she's got to get back at the male world somehow for rejecting her."

The women's movement only threatens Beth. She might be pushed out of the nest, forced into equality, into independence. She has chosen carefully to avoid that. Her husband Kurt is the perfect match. As she talked, she kept one eye on him and quoted him continually, "Kurt says . . . Kurt thinks . . ."

Finally Kurt said what he thinks: "Look, if the women's libbers want to be that way, it's okay for them. But I wouldn't be married to it. Beth knew what kind of a guy I was when we got married and that's it. That's the way I am . . ."

Like her husband, Beth shares another characteristic with other change resisters: the belief that the status quo is the immutable Way Things Are. The expression I hear so often among those who resist is: "This is the way things are . . . This is the way I am . . . You can't change human nature . . . It's just a fact of life . . ." They often close their eyes to possibilities, to choices, and prefer to believe that the changes occurring all around them will not touch them.

Yet, even at this end of the Shuttle Zone, the resistance is not on such solid unshakable turf.

AMBIVALENCE OF THE RESISTERS

Only the furthest wing—the ostrich regiment of the resistance —can possibly be blind to change. Only a tiny cohesive minority, like the Amish, can resist it effectively.

I found very few change resisters unaware and unaffected by the new roles for men and women in society. Although they had planted their feet firmly in the status quo, many were attracted by the "excitement" of change, personal growth, achievement which seemed to be offered by this change. The innovators I met were often afraid of losing their traditional roots if they moved out of the old roles. But the resisters I met were often afraid of losing the promise of More, if they remained in the traditional life.

Gradually resisters often find that while change is threatening, it is also attractive. They may dislike the idea that they are pegged as "old-fashioned," and find that they would like to make some changes, the ones that come without risk.

MARABEL MORGAN: THE TOTALLY AMBIVALENT WOMAN

Long before I met her, I had seen Marabel Morgan used as a touchstone of change. Her book, *The Total Woman,* is labeled a backlash or a reaction to women's liberation or even "the bible of the Middle-American Woman." The "Total Woman" is, I have been told, the counterpart of the "Liberated Woman" and I am sure that there isn't a subscriber to *Ms.* enrolled in Marabel Morgan's course.

But after reading her book and going to the exclusive housing development in Miami to interview her, I am convinced that the Total Woman—both the creator and the creation—is successful partly because she is in the resistance, but also because she is an "up-to-date traditionalist," a totally ambivalent woman.

Unconsciously perhaps, Marabel Morgan took some of the aspects of feminism that were most attractive and repackaged them for the traditional woman.

Her book is very different from the work of a real change reactionary like Helen Andelin who instructs her "Fascinating Female," among other things, to stop driving on the highway.

First of all, Morgan's message is directed at women who have been attracted as well as repelled by the message of the women's movement, and who fear that they may lose out on the excitement of the world by staying in a traditional woman's role and relationship. She insists that the Total Woman can be "her own person" *and* a "Queen who never threatens the King." She writes that a woman can be "equal," growing and changing her life, without affecting her traditional role in the home.

When I read her book on the way to Florida, I was struck by the similarities as well as the obvious differences between Morgan's book and a feminist self-help manual. This sentence could have been written by someone advocating change: "There is something about a woman who knows where she's going in life that makes her a very interesting partner . . . There is a great potential within you, undeveloped resources that you've not begun to tap."

Other parts of it sound equally avant-garde: "After your bath tonight, stand before the mirror and look at your body carefully. Say to that girl in the mirror, I accept me as I am." Aside from the use of the word "girl," that could have been lifted from *Our Bodies, Our Selves.*

In other places Morgan seems to adopt the change advocates' analysis of the problems of men and male conditioning: "Your Man, like so many American males, may be an empty cup emotionally. Remember that he grew up in a culture that taught him not to cry when he scratched his leg. Instead of hugging Uncle Jack, he shook hands."

Unlike a change resister like Midge, Marabel Morgan seems to promote introspection, asking all the time, "Who am I?" "Where am I going?"

It is, of course, the other side of her book, the traditional side, which is the more dominant. She directs all the enthusiasm for change toward maintaining the old, feminine, dependent girlish wife status quo. Under the frills, the sexy underwear, the perfumed baths, and beyond the list-making and hints about how to make chores "fun," her changes are those of adjustment. The Total Woman motto after all is "Accept Him, Admire Him, Adapt to Him. Treat Your Man Like a King and He Will Treat You Like a Queen."

But, even before I met her, I thought that it wasn't just the traditional groundwork that made her work so popular.

She offered traditional women the belief that they could have achievement and self-fulfillment along with the security of a dependent marriage. In fact, as I drove from the Miami airport to see her, I thought of one sentence she'd written which said it all: "List your long-term goals . . . the areas in your life that you would like to improve *as a wife and mother.* You can attain your goals, your dream is not impossible." As long as you are dreaming of wifing and mothering.

The woman who welcomed me into her yellow stucco house in an exclusive housing development looked exactly like the lady on the book jacket. She was dressed in a knit pastel pantsuit which seemed to fit her own image of unsophisticated and yet not "old-fashioned." She seemed human and more uncertain than her book might suggest. And as we talked, I realized that she had changed a great deal in order to live a traditional life. She reflected the ambivalence of the Shuttle Zone more than I had expected.

We sat in the living room on a French provincial sofa, on an artificial marble floor, and she told me about her childhood in Ohio. She described herself as the only child of a passive, peace-keeping father and a hostile, dominating mother.

As she put it: "My father was a wonderful man who was willing to have peace at any price. He just crawled into his little shell and stayed there. My mother felt that men are out to do women in. That's about all. She was very hostile. She drummed into my head the idea that men only want one thing. Don't trust them. I heard that all the time I was growing up. I don't think she would go along with the principles in this book at all."

Morgan's own framework of understanding was built from her childhood home. In her own marriage, she would evolve from being a harping "mother" to a peacekeeping "father."

As a child she was ambitious, but not an achiever. "I felt very inferior, but I covered it up. Laughing, acting cool. I had a lot of drive. I was competitive to a fault. I wanted to be the best. Kind of a bully at times. Then in high school, I learned to cover that over with sweetness and light."

Her own home was a place she wanted to leave. "I couldn't wait to leave. It was a very bad experience. I could hardly wait to get out and try to do the things I didn't see happening in my home."

After high school she worked as a hairdresser to save up money for college. She went to college for a year and a half. Then in Miami on a vacation, she met and later married a law student, Charles Morgan. Their early years are described as "disastrous." She was nagging, as she puts it, just like her mother. This attitude is what she calls "Women's Lib."

"I tried to push and shove Charlie into my mold. I guess I was a libber. I felt bogged down with the little ones. I was reading all these magazines. The lib movement was not the lib movement in those days. It was an undercurrent saying, 'If you're home with diapers, you should be dissatisfied.' I was trying to work things out between loving him and being demanding and I was very unstable."

When they came to a crisis, Charlie, unlike her father, was assertive, surprisingly dominating. He told her to shape up and do what he said. Marabel Morgan felt that she had only two options —to continue the squabbling and bitterness that had typified their relationship and that of her parents, or to begin unilaterally to change, to become the peacemaker. She began by working feverishly on her "hangups," as she called them.

But the ultimate goal was the one she describes in her book: "It is only when a woman surrenders her life to her husband, reveres and worships him and is willing to serve him, she becomes really beautiful to him. She becomes a priceless jewel, the glory of femininity, his queen!"

In person she described it somewhat less dramatically. "I gave up all those tactics of pushing him and demanding. I tried the old familiar thing and it worked."

What Morgan meant by "it worked" is very simple: "It spices up marriage. It gets husbands to give you more, open up more, and love more. Gee, Charlie and I are like in a loving contest, who can give more."

In some ways Morgan did understand a tenet of change: when one person changes her behavior, those around her often change theirs. She says that when women change themselves and how they react, and act, in the relationship, their husbands will change too.

But the only Marabel Morgan-approved change is in the direction of the traditional role. "I don't like the word 'traditional,'" said Morgan, reacting to my definition. "It sounds so old-fashioned and stagnant. I wouldn't call it traditional as much as I'd call it common sense." In fact, part of her attraction for other resisters is that she believes you can be in a traditional role without being "old-fashioned."

But the theory of her change-plan is oriented to only one question: "What can be worth having a strained relationship with the one you love and live with?"

Next to that question, all others simply pale for Morgan. Questions of identity, of individual needs (other than those of a peaceful marriage) are put aside. Over and over again she reminds women that they will win love, affection, and a steady stream of appliances, if they adapt, accept.

But she dresses up traditionalism the way she dresses up the Total Woman, in boots or frilly nightgowns. She reassures the traditional woman that she is "in charge" of her life: "A Total Woman is not a slave. She graciously chooses to adapt to her husband's way, even though at times she desperately may not want to."

In that way, Morgan appeals to the ambivalence with which so many women greeted the message of the women's movement: the desire to be "equal," to feel self-confident and in tune with changing times, and the desire to keep peace in a traditional marriage.

A woman with Marabel Morgan's history is surely not a doormat herself. But she believes "through my own experiences," that there is no harmony without order and that the only order is a hierarchy. When I asked her why the woman was the one who had to adjust, she answered obliquely, "That doesn't mean a woman can't be her own person."

Does that mean she can fight as long as she loses? "I don't like the word 'lose.' It implies a power struggle. But let's suppose you want one thing and he wants another and you talk about it and you can't compromise. I think you'd either go along with him or get out. When you get to a point in life where a decision has to be made and there can only be one way, something's got to give. And marriage is a bond, so I'll go his way."

But, I asked, why should the woman always go "his way"? Her bottom line was the code of resistance. "That's the way things are." As for equal relationships, "Well, I think that's great. If they're getting married like that, they're miles ahead of the game. He's aware of what she expects. She's aware of what he expects. However, six years down the line I'd like to talk to her, because she may find, much as she doesn't want to, that he turns out to be a man who says, 'Hey, baby, do it my way.'"

Again and again the ambivalence of the Total Woman

cropped up. Marabel insisted that she was both a leader and under her husband's leadership. As half of a working partnership, she said that she had no antipathy toward other working women, but believed that most women don't want to count on their independence. "No matter how much money she is earning," she said, "I won't put all my eggs in the Total Woman basket." She was more comfortable depending or believing she is depending on her husband.

Similarly she was uncertain about the basic differences between men and women, but certain about the "practical" differences. At one moment, she said, "Men want to be admired and women want to be loved and always will be," and then later told me, "Well, I have a friend who is real brainy and he says that every person, boy or girl, is both with the same characteristics, so I guess it's hard to determine what makes the difference, environment or your mother's preaching."

For an hour, I listened to Marabel tell me stories about women in bad marriages where there was a great deal of fighting and how those marriages improved when the women stopped struggling and started "loving." "Most of the fights in marriages are because there are two egos," she said. But the moral of these stories seemed to be that when the woman gave up her ego, and took a "feminine" and passive role, agreeing, never confronting, her husband, always praising him, those marriages "improved" enormously. She conveyed to me eagerly the sense that only by resisting a change in the biblically ordained order of the family could women have happy marriages. As for women who were changing their roles, "They don't have to get married and have kids if they don't want to. And that's great if that's what they want."

She seemed to be very aware that many women identified personal growth with the changes in their sex roles, but she, and perhaps she alone, was telling them that they could have great heaps of growth without threatening their personal lives at all.

Finally, her husband called from the other room to remind her that it was time to change for dinner and I asked her two last "walking out the door" questions. The first one was about the women's movement directly and her answer was far more gentle than I expected. "I think the women's movement has rocked the boat for a lot of marriages. Women have suddenly given their husbands ultimatums and said, 'I'm going to do thus and so, and if it falls apart, it's your problem.' On the other hand, I think it's done a lot of good. It's opened up choices to women. It's made women who thought they were nobodies find out who they are. They're persons. They have rights to dare to create and accomplish what they want."

The difference between her book, the "Bible" of many resisters, and, say, *Feminine Mystique,* the "Bible" of many feminists is, however, still a basic one. "I haven't read it," said Morgan. "I should. But she meant get out in the world and do something. I realize a lot of women can't, but they can get out within their minds by taking a positive attitude toward these mundane things and making them exciting."

Finally, it seemed to me that even this change resister identified the future with innovation. In talking about her own daughters, she said, "My ambitions for them are the highest. They are lucky to be living in an age when women can do just about everything."

Even the Total Woman lived in the Shuttle Zone.

Many of the most confirmed change resisters have a desire for achievement. They can't help comparing their lives to those of the innovators. Many of them fear loss of achievement or self-esteem if they remain in the traditional roles.

Marabel Morgan tried to deal with that ambivalence. In her book, the Total Woman is encouraged to think of herself as an achieving and self-confident woman.

But, in a way, vacillation in the Shuttle Zone of resistance shows up most acutely when we look at the leadership of the resisters. And especially at the one woman most closely identified with it, Phyllis Schlafly.

I have always been amazed to hear Schlafly supporters tell me with great pride that this woman from Alton, Illinois, is an "anti-libber" *even though* she is a successful woman of the world. Schlafly seems to me in some ways a walking study of the resister in the Shuttle Zone. A political commentator, a writer, a law student and politician, she defends the woman at home. But this woman no longer speaks up publicly against careers, equal pay for equal work. Her message is a different one. "We already have all this," she says and calls for resistance to change in order to protect it.

THE RENOVATED RESISTER

Phyllis Schlafly's appeal is to people who fear that equality will be a step down or a push out. As she put it succinctly, "Why would any woman want to leave her beautiful home and go cook for an army mess." Her women think they have the better end of the bargain than men and see equal responsibility coming with equal rights. They would prefer the pedestal.

I met Phyllis Schlafly the first time in the studio of a television station, accompanied by two older women from the Stop ERA movement in Massachusetts. She was dressed in a rose-colored wool knit dress with ankle-high boots, her hair swept into a french twist and her smile and makeup in place. When I turned on my tape recorder, she turned on hers, and when she talked about her life, it was almost as if her credentials for leading the resistance depended on being equal to the women in the change movement.

"I was brought up to achieve and do well, whatever I did, and I've always been a very industrious worker and very organized. I worked my way through college on the nightshift of the largest ammunition plant in the world. I got through college in three years, Phi Beta Kappa, and got my master's at Harvard and now I'm at law school." She said it all in one breath.

"I feel I'm a good example of how a woman can make her life any way she wants to. There's every type of choice. Full-time wife and mother . . . career woman . . . both at the same time . . . So what's the complaining?"

Both of Schlafly's parents worked throughout her childhood. Her mother was a librarian at the St. Louis Art Museum, her father was a salesman. Her grandmother was the one who cared for her after school. But what she remembers most about that childhood is this: "I happen to come from a family where the women were always treated very well. They got the first pickings. And my husband comes from a family where the women got the first pickings of whatever, whether financial or courtesy. If someone else comes from a family where the man got the first pickings, that's their problem."

Schlafly maintains that she can have all the goodies from the world—more goodies in fact than men—and yet the traditional goodies from family life. "There is no more fun and no more fulfillment than at home. That comes first in my scale of priorities. It is nowhere near as much fun appearing on television or writing books as it is having a baby and the joys of having a fine husband and knowing he comes home at night and seeing a child grow."

The one threatening cloud on women's horizon, Schlafly sees, is the women's movement. "The women's lib movement looks upon marriage as nothing but dirty dishes and dirty diapers. Now there are dirty diapers and dishes in marriage. Any job you go into has drudgery, but you have something to show for it. Over the last few years they've gotten a big percentage of women out of the home and into the work force. Now is that a social good? Do you think they're happier? I don't."

Feminism, as she describes it, hasn't opened up choices— though Schlafly's own daughter now is a student at the newly integrated Princeton University—but rather raised discontent. "The women's studies courses in college—they should be called courses in how to break up marriages. They are breaking marriages left and right. A woman in her forties goes back and takes one of these courses and she's told how oppressed she's been, which she didn't realize until then, and how she's imprisoned and submerged in her husband's identity and if she could just shuffle him off and get out and fulfill herself it would be nicer. Every day I hear about people whose marriages broke up after twenty-five years and immediately after taking one of these courses."

The Schlafly approach is saying that women already have a vast range of choices, and insisting that equal rights would be "less" rather than more. By offering herself as a role model of a Modern Traditionalist, she appeals to those within the resistance camp: those who feel the appeal of a new role but fear risking the security of their dependence.

I think in many ways that Schlafly demonstrates how change has inevitably infiltrated this end zone of resistance.

After talking with others, I wanted to go back again to Midge. This time I wanted to ask this long-term investor, who had chosen sides against change, how she felt about the future. What changes she thought were inevitable, and which ones she approved of and which ones she did not.

MIDGE: RESISTING THE INEVITABLE

Again we sat in the living room, drinking tea and eating some of the brownies that she had made for the church bake sale. The brownies she confessed had come from a mix: "That's my idea of liberation." When we talked again, Midge said, yes, around her she saw women who had to work, women who wanted to expand their roles in a wider world. And she was not, anymore, especially worried about it. Like nearly everyone I met she favored equal pay for equal work because "Why, that's only fair." She saw the changes in the world around her and knew where she stood on the spectrum.

"You know, young people today, they have terrible pressures. Pressures we never had. I truly believe this. There are economic pressures. Everyone wants the best for his family and for himself. I mean, we do want nice things and we do want our children to have the best opportunity available to them."

This time she talked about the pleasure she found in new opportunities available to women. In the Church now she was able to give out communion. "You know, I never knew what it was like to walk up the steps of the altar except when I got married. Women were never allowed there. Now I am an 'extraordinary minister.' The pastor asked me, because of my pro-life work and because I've been so involved with other issues." She described this with pleasure.

Yet again she was not in favor of pressuring the Church for other opportunities for women, especially not the priesthood.

"Well, if you had man and woman priests, well, you'd have all kinds of problems. You would have to have separate facilities, for instance. Then, too, I just can't see men coming to a woman for confessions." Though she responded to one change—the honor of giving communion—she still resisted others on the grounds that "the community isn't ready for it."

In the area she wanted most to defend, Midge had an ideal vision of the family. "I guess my idea of a family is a husband and wife and maybe four kids. That's a comfortable arrangement. I guess they both have had the opportunity to go to college and follow a profession. The wife feels that she has enough time to give to having children and has the understanding of her husband. He's got a good job, but not one with a lot of pressures. She has some help with the children. I guess that would be my ideal." This was a picture she had described before but this time she added, "As I say it, well, I guess I can't see it really happening that way so much."

She has begun to identify her "ideal" as a disappearing possibility.

"Well, now, economically there won't be much choice, will there? The young women either have to work, or seem to want to. And you see so much more cooperation at home from the husbands. Everyone seems to have fewer children than they used to. Why, my nephew shocked me the other day talking about their third child. I hadn't realized that they had been using contraceptives. I was really shocked. Then, too, there's divorce. Oh, you see that the young couples don't believe that marriage is forever. I suppose the comfortable kind of thing we've had, I had, just won't last forever. Women are wanting the things that men have. But I don't think they'll be having an easy life, do you?" As I left Midge she seemed much more relaxed with me as well as the ideas we talked about but unsettled about the future. Nothing could convince her that this change could be for the better. As I got into the car she suddenly perked up and leaned over. She said, "On the other hand, just the other day I got a letter from my niece and she is a college graduate. She said she agreed with me and she wasn't at all happy with what the women's lib people had to say. So there you are. And she's only twenty-eight."

Basically Midge too had come to believe that the future belonged to the change innovators. So the line of resistance moved.

Chapter 5 The New Middleground

"You know, it's kind of hard. Men like me, we just didn't grow up expecting our wives to be, well, like Rose . . .

"Answer this, what would a woman with a master's degree or a Ph.D. want with a guy who isn't going to go much higher up? Will my wife still be my wife if she has a Ph.D.? Answer me that."

Most of us are neither radical change innovators nor hard-core resisters. We are card-carrying members of neither the vanguard nor the rearguard. We don't live in the ends of the Shuttle Zone but rather in that vast territory called the middleground.

But in a time of transition even the middleground is not necessarily a place where people can be protected from buffeting. In many ways the people in the middleground have the most ambivalent feelings about change and are the most harried commuters in the Shuttle Zone.

The people I interviewed for this chapter all identified themselves as "moderates" or middle Americans, although they ranged all the way between the two border lines of the end zones. They were all, however, typical middlegrounders in this sense: they realized that they couldn't and didn't want to avoid change but they did want to control its speed. In one way or another they chose to evolve—rather than revolt—in tune with their own internal conflicts.

What I found in the middleground was both the pull of traditions and the universality of change. I remember a clipping I'd

saved from a *Ladies' Home Journal* in 1976 where the editor
had, I think instinctively, described the new Middleground
Woman. Lenore Hershey had written then:

> Our Woman is a "new traditionalist" seeking the best of all worlds,
> old and new. To her, many of our institutions represent stability
> and coherence. But standards and values seem to mean more now
> than ritual and forms. The past is valuable, nostalgic. But the pres-
> ent is dynamic and adventuresome, full of the promise of excitement
> and growth . . . along with its unhinging perils . . . Our Woman.
> Yes, she is a new traditionalist, facing today's dilemmas with her
> head on straight and her chin held high. The women's movement?
> She may not call herself part of it, but she respects it for upgrad-
> ing women and equality on many fronts . . . She's newly independ-
> ent and self-reliant but she can use the help of life partners, good
> friends, and authoritative guides.

This was a description of ambivalence, of the hope and fear
which permeates the majority of people. The new traditionalists
are a contradiction in terms—they seek the best of both worlds.
They identify the best of the past with stability and security and
identify the best of the changes in roles with excitement and
growth. They are afraid of the "unhinging perils" which many
read in the early messages of the change innovators, but they too
want the goodies that come from moving out into the world. In
short, they want the excitement of independence and the "sameness" of dependence. They want change without risk, growth
without loss. They want it all.

In that sense, the ambivalence I saw in miniature at the ends
of the Shuttle Zone are magnified in the middle. The chief fear
among the radical innovators was that they might lose the roots
of nurturing and the security of family roles and relationships.
The chief fear among the resisters was that they might miss out
on the self-esteem and vitality that came from change. In the
middleground men and women both try to work out a compromise course.

"I'M NOT A FEMINIST, BUT . . ."

The new female traditionalists I met often described themselves in a single code phrase, "I'm not a feminist, but . . ." I couldn't travel anywhere without hearing someone, a movie star, or a waitress, prefacing her remarks with the defusing phrase, "I'm not a feminist, but . . ."

"I'm not a feminist, but I believe in Equal Pay for Equal Work."

"I'm not a feminist, but I don't think it's fair that housewives whose husbands divorce them don't get any social security."

"I'm not a feminist, but I don't think it's fair that a woman has to pay an estate tax on the farm after her husband dies, when her husband wouldn't have to pay a nickel if she died first."

This phrase became so common in the '70s that an editorial writer in the New York *Times*, fantasizing about the first woman President, wrote that her inaugural address would probably begin with a denunciation of uppity women.

It seems to me that this is almost a motto for the middleground. I know that to some degree each of us resists labeling, the kind inherent in saying, "I Am a Feminist." We resist being pigeonholed and having our individuality denied, our complexity reduced to a bumper sticker. But this phrase is more than a reaction against being labeled. I think it is an expression of the central ambivalence of the middlegrounder going through this Shuttle Zone. To understand how they are evolving, I wanted to understand this code phrase.

Both halves of this expression—"I'm Not a Feminist" and "But" —are important. One woman explained it to me this way, "Well, first I say I'm not a feminist. That part means, 'I don't hate men and burn my bra, I'm a real gal.' Then I also say what is bugging me, which may be very women's libby, you know. It's, well, I like what women like Bella Abzug and everyone say, but I don't want to be like them. A lot of things they say are right, but not the way they say them."

When Becky said, "I'm not a feminist, but . . ." to me it was her way of saying, I want change without a loss of love.

In some ways Becky seemed like many of the change innovators. I first saw her, after all, when I was a passenger on the bus she was driving through her adopted city. She was five feet ten inches tall and 160 firm pounds and she grasped the wheel with an unself-conscious authority. As the passengers at my stop got on the bus, the black woman, dressed in one of those unflattering uniforms that are meant to last long rather than fit well, barked them up the stairs. She was both cheerful and noisy, handing out change and directions, with one eye on her rear-view mirror and another eye on some boisterous young boys at the back of the bus. "I won't have none of that on my bus," she yelled at them and, with one look at her, they instantly stopped fooling around.

We met again after work to discuss her life and her childhood in a town in North Carolina.

"Growing up, my daddy taught me to be independent. He used to say, 'Becky, don't take nothing off of nobody.' Now my parents always made me feel I could accomplish anything I wanted, and that, I think, put us in good stead. Now I remember in school when they'd let the boys be book monitors and the girls water the plants. All that dumb stuff. Me? I dissected my first frog when I was in the first grade. The other girls were scared. Not me. I was driving around my daddy's truck when I was thirteen, and now here I am, driving a bus."

Becky leaned over the restaurant table holding her coffee mug in both hands and told me conspiratorially: "I took this job on a dare. I saw an ad in the newspaper. I was working in an office at the time not making the bucks. My brother-in-law told me, you won't make it. But I can do it. I came out number one in seniority on the tests. And I'm liking it fine. I like to drive that bus. Now of course I want to be the first woman instructor. The next time you talk to me, I'm going to be Becky, the first woman instructor. That's my goal."

Then, more quizzically, she added: "I just don't understand

why some woman would be in an office making $150 a week
when she could be down here making $889 a month for starters.
How do you figure them? Just too silly, I guess."

From all appearances, I would have thought of Becky as
avant-garde. Her status as one of twelve women in a twelve-
thousand-man system qualifies her as that. Yet, she sees herself
quite differently. "Noooo. I'm not one of them women's lib types.
I don't take any of that shit. When I got this job, a lot of the
other girls were already hollering about it. I'm not a feminist,"
she says flatly and then adds her explanation like a punchline, "I
still like to be treated delicate-like."

As a bus driver she wants only to be efficient and upwardly
mobile. The nail polish she wears with her uniform is the only
evidence on the job of what she prizes, "my old-fashioned femininity." As for the rest, she wants only to be treated equally with
the men, and to be promoted on a "fair and square basis."

Moreover, she is aware that without the women's movement
she wouldn't have her job. "Well, now you could not have done
it because they would not have let you. Now you have an opportunity. For instance, I always wanted to be an airline stewardess
back in 1959 when I graduated from high school. But there were
no black stewardesses. I could not fight it. Now there are hundreds. Well, it's the same with the bus."

But, in her private life, Becky wants to be, as she puts it,
"regarded as a gentlewoman, if you know what I mean." A feminist, according to Becky, would say that men are for the birds,
and the men would say that she was for the birds. "Now, I don't
feel that way. And I don't want men to think about me that way
neither."

As we sat over coffee I could see how her father's message of
independence conflicted with society's view of women. Her
mother used to clean houses for the white people in her town in
North Carolina and she observed them. She also observed her
parents' relationship: "My dad was always the boss man." And
when she was still quite little, "I knew that to find a man I'd
have to cool my act." For a time she learned to cover her independence with a kind of fluttering girlishness.

She was married at twenty-three and a mother at twenty-four, twenty-five, twenty-six, twenty-seven. For those years she stayed at home taking care of her children, but she was never happy there. Her relationship with her husband became a stormy one as she began to act more in tune with her own sense of self. Now she says, "My marriage was a struggle. My husband says that if he had known what kind of a woman I really was, that I wasn't going to be bossed by him, he never would have married me. Well, now maybe I wasn't fair to him, but I didn't know it then."

Still, she stayed married for twelve years, alternating between trying to adjust to what he wanted and trying to be herself. "He would say, 'You're not doing what I want!' That's what he would say. Well, I wasn't about to do anything anybody told me if I didn't want to. I felt like it was a prison. I was in prison because I was married, I felt like obligated to him, and it made it hard for both of us. Now he's with someone who just says, 'Oh yes, Jesse, yessir, right away, sir.' Can you beat that?"

Her own ambition took off when she got divorced. "Well, now when you're on your own and you got kids to support, you just got to go for the bucks." In that sense, her experience was typical of so many other women. The economic fait accompli simply dominated any other fears or internal conflicts.

But from her new seat, it seemed that the qualities of independence, or ambition, the strengths that qualified her for her job, might always disqualify her in a relationship. So there was a piece of her that still believed that to be successful as a woman, she must be feminine. "I like to go out with a man and have him treat me and take here and there and act like the lady."

NEW DOUBLE STANDARD

In a sense, Becky's assurance that she was not a feminist, but . . . was indicative of the new double standard of the middleground. She believed that the benefits of a personal life—love, a stable family relationship—probably depended on filling a traditional feminine role. On the other hand, the benefits of an independent life demanded a nontraditional role. That is, it seems to me, the conflict at the core of the new middle. Again and again, the middleground women I met sought the safety of traditional relationships and the excitement of new roles in the world. In this Shuttle Zone, they zigzagged between the past and the future, often playing one role at home and another in the world, or one role with men and another with women. They held up a new double standard of behavior.

Because she was single, Becky didn't have to deal every day with this double standard and, in fact, her sense of self was strong and sure. Still, it was interesting to see how reluctant that woman was to give up her psychological link to the traditional stance of women, to hear the sudden sound of reticence in the words of a gutsy bus driver.

But, I was at least as surprised to see the number of more conservative women in the middleground also become, not feminists exactly, *but* . . .

HARRIET: ONE SMALL STEP

When Harriet said, "I'm not a feminist, but . . ." it was the beginning of a limited but important fight for herself.

Harriet was not the sort of person you would expect to make a fuss. The forty-six-year-old woman was on the opposite edge of the middleground from Becky. Yet it is part of the story that she too ended up fighting in public for her "rights."

For the first time in decades, as she herself said, "I'm making waves and it feels terrific." The mother of three had decided to sue a veterans' organization that refused to accept her as a member.

Harriet found it rather odd, but exciting, to be in the spotlight and in the newspaper, especially when she considered herself a conservative woman. "I'm not a radical. I'm feminine, I would say," the graying, curly-haired woman with black rhinestone eyeglasses and a plain white shirt over her blue bermudas told me. "I want to have my cigarette lit by the fellows and the doors opened and all that jazz. That is part of being a lady, I think."

Harriet, it said happily in the newspaper, was no "libber." She liked "Mrs." better than "Ms." and was proud to be a married woman. She just wanted to join the veterans' organization and they wouldn't let her for no reason at all, except that she was a woman.

The Southwest woman talked not about women's rights, but about "fairness." "What's fair is fair," she said. What wasn't fair was that despite her tour of duty during World War II, she couldn't join the group. She wanted her rights, but didn't want to be seen as a women's rightist.

Harriet had become a change agent only when it was safer. A union leader in Michigan described safe-change agents as the kind who only make waves in a bathtub. Harriet was hardly a stormtrooper. But she was one of the hundreds of second- and third-level change agents. She wouldn't have been in this fight if she thought it would cost her what she calls her "femininity."

"I'm not about to say, okay, mister, I'm taking over. I mean there are some women who are antagonistic like that. They really get nasty. If they are trying to push something in that atmosphere, they are not going to get anywhere. Kindness kills. That's what I do and it works."

Down at the local organization where she first got the idea of applying for national membership, she insisted on being treated well. "They all treat me like a lady. If they started cussing me and didn't have any respect for what I was doing, I'd drop it."

There had always been something of a tug-of-war between the side that was traditional and the side that was willing to take on something new, something tough. Harriet was one of the few women in her high school class to ever leave the small eastern town where she grew up, the daughter of a fisherman. She was one of the very few to join the Army during World War II. She always had a fighting streak in her.

For five years the curly-haired energetic mother of three worked as a volunteer with the veterans, and then she decided to take on another fight. She had applied to the national organization with the twenty-dollar bill that her husband had given her, and she had been rejected. Harriet knew it was "discrimination" and, never mind that she didn't like to hear other women fighting for their rights, she decided to fight it.

"Five years ago I wouldn't have done this. No. Not until this whole thing has come about where everything is even-Steven. I still wouldn't have known about the national group unless they were involved in our local hall. They were doing the same thing we were doing, having the same meetings. When I get through with things here at the local, I would like to join them. So my husband says, here is twenty dollars, go and join them. I said, it's all men. He said to try it anyway.

"You see, I am entitled to this. It is an honor to me to have gone into the service. Anybody who served in a wartime period is eligible. But if you are female you are not, and this irritates me. How do you tell someone they are narrow-minded? They just don't see the forest for the trees. One of the guys said, what was I putting up this big hassle for? Well, they can't see the forest for the trees.

"With the women's thing the way it is today, it is equal opportunity. It has brought it all out," she said. In the areas that are safe, accepted, that don't threaten her major decisions of life, she is all for it.

"I remember during the convention in 1972, when I think it was Bella Abzug. Anyway she was saying that it was just equal opportunity for women to run for President. That's where all this started, wasn't it? I started taking notice then. I don't know anybody who thinks this way though. I guess I just heard about it on television. I haven't read about it. My husband brings home *Playgirl* for me—I wouldn't buy it—but that's about all.

"Anyway, the thing I am for is like my mother. She was a widow, the five of us were out of the house. My dad dies and she has nothing. No social security, no benefits at all. She got one fisherman's fund, twelve dollars a month. She had to go out and learn something. She tried for practical nursing and they wouldn't take her because she was too old. No matter what she tried to do, she was too old. Now, she is not the type to sit back and let the world fall over, but she was cleaning houses and things like this. I mean, what has she got? Nothing. Now she has made it okay. Bless her. She went out and scrubbed and worked to try and keep herself above water. But I agree with the women's lib thing in the social security for people like my mother. If my husband died when I was fifty-seven or something and my kids were gone, I wouldn't get anything. This is one thing I would work towards.

"But as far as being a construction worker, going into the man's world, men have always worked in construction or as plumbers. But women, how many women qualify? They are going to tear their insides out."

She thought some of the other things were okay for younger women, but not for her. "My husband," she said as an explanation, "is a very conservative, straight man. No flashy clothes. He still wants the navy blue pants and black shoes. Everything is neat as a pin. But he encouraged me in this. Whatever I want to do, I get a lot of backing from him. He helps by running errands, going to the store, fixing the doors at the Legion Hall, painting."

But they have a very separate, very traditional role-structured marriage. "He is a man and I am a woman. He has his place and I have mine. For twenty-two years we have done a good job at it. We are still together. The kids are very healthy-minded. This is the way my husband is, and this is the way our marriage is. I can see a difference in my daughter, the oldest one. She has a hard-working husband. He will pitch in and do anything. This is a difference. And it's good. I would be a fool not to like that, but this is my marriage."

For Harriet the line was drawn. She had enough. The independent young girl who joined the Army grew into the woman who wanted to join the national veterans' group. But the twenty-two-year-old who didn't hear anything else except, "You grow up, you fall in love, you get married, you have children—you know, the regular," wasn't going to question that. She bought the changes that would help her mother or win her a slot in the organization, but not the part that could upset her marriage, or withdraw the support that comes from her husband. She went only so far into the new middle.

Many women like Harriet take a small step for womankind while ferociously protecting the sanctity of their marriage or their investment in their relationships.

I sat with a woman for hours in a New York restaurant. She pulled out a file folder full of information about her sex discrimination suit, paper after paper, citing case and book on her suit. She was talking in the kind of feminist lingo—movement shorthand—that would turn off most listeners. Words like "capitalist oppression," "male chauvinism," "sex role stereotyping," piled on top of each other.

Suddenly at five-thirty she looked at her watch and her face changed its pallor as if it were the shifting fluid of a kaleroscope. "My God, I have to run," she said, cramming the papers back into her briefcase. "My husband is home at six and I have to be there."

She seemed literally panicked. For a moment it was incongruous that I was taken aback and laughed. Then she turned and with great hostility said, "Don't judge me. This is my husband. He needs me to be his wife and that's all there is to it."

As I left Harriet and compared her to Becky, I began to think about the way in which people deal with their ambivalence. Both of these women—different in almost every other way—were more tentative about changing their private lives than their public ones. The fear of upsetting relationships is the "Go Slow" sign in the Shuttle Zone, while the desire for excitement and growth is the green light.

But this same conflict is obvious in the men of the middleground. I interviewed many of them and often, as a benchmark, asked what they thought of the old joke, "I think every woman should be liberated except my wife." Most of the men gave at least a wry laugh of recognition and half a squirm.

Some of the men in the middleground who fear change in their wives may merely want their socks folded and their shirts ironed and dinner on the table. But others fear not the loss of a housekeeper but the loss of security, of being nurtured, of being needed in the most basic traditional ways. They often, like women in the same place, don't want to be pushed beyond their limits.

I met many men who had once made all the decisions for their families and now were being called on to react to decisions. Many of these men had grown up believing that all women, like their mothers, would "take care of them." It was easier to adjust to change in public life than in their private lives. This was surely true for Jim.

At the AT&T office in a flat, midwestern city, Jim was considered to be very supportive of women. A short, slightly overweight second-generation Italian-American, he talked about "my" affirmative action program, the way his father talked about the small vegetable garden behind his home in California.

"I've a woman on the line out in West Highway. I've got another one moving into middle management, in the Oak Park office, and these four women we hired just last year are coming right along. And by God, these are not tokens. They are competent women." As we walked through the office it was clear that this forty-four-year-old was well liked and respected by both the men and women in the company.

"I've always worked well with women. I don't have any problems," he said. Jim grew up in an activist home. His father, who had left Italy in the early part of the century, had been a community organizer in California in the forties, and Jim remembered the lessons he learned in the garden. Part of his family and personal identity was a sense of doing for others, and doing what was fair.

"Look, these women have been kept out of the good jobs and most of them need the dough. I don't let the guys around here give them trouble. Some of them have husbands who took a walk, they've got a bunch of kids to raise, or some parents to take care of. Hell, nowadays a lot of families need two incomes just to keep up. If a woman's got to work, she should have a fair stake. I'm telling you, I haven't seen one damn thing they can't do around this company."

Jim was fair and a good teacher. He liked being a mentor to the women in the office, and yet he was able to let go and let them grow when they needed to be independent. As we drove around to the various offices in the district, other women testified to that, while he pooh-poohed what he'd done for them. "Doris, for chrissakes, I'm getting every nickel's worth out of you. You

were worth the trouble. If you weren't, I would have dropped
you like a hot potato."

At the end of the afternoon, he invited me home for dinner,
home to the split-level house he shared with his wife and three
of their four children—the fourth was already in college. As he
came in the house, Jim mobilized the kids—in short order, one
turned off the TV set, two scurried off to do chores. He remembered to ask his youngest son how the ball game had gone that
day, and to check whether his girl had done okay on a dreaded
math test. He was a family man, one who clearly got his sense of
self from his home and children and his wife, Rose.

He and Rose had met as college students in California in the
early 1950s. They had married after his graduation and Jim had
gone to work for the telephone company. She had been a teacher
for two years and then she had started having babies, and stayed
home for fifteen years.

Now Rose, forty-two, was a sixth grade school teacher, one of
those women who grow more vital as their children grow older.
She was short and dark-skinned in a knit pantsuit, and a toucher
who casually squeezed and handled her children and her husband even as she served food or collected the dishes.

At the dinner table, Rose served and Jim carved, Rose collected and the children washed and dried, while the adults
drank coffee around the table. Rose had been teaching now for
two years and when I asked if this had changed their marriage
at all, they both quickly said, "No, oh no . . . Not after all these
years."

Then Rose said: "Well now, I guess one thing. It used to be,
when the kids were little and I was at home, that I would be
waiting for Jim to come home, for some relief, a grownup to talk
to. I used to be like a starved person who needed some food
from someone else. That wasn't very good. Now, I bring home
something to talk about. He shares, I share. It isn't a one-way
thing. Even though I work at school, you know, with kids, there
are other teachers there and we talk together."

Rose paused and then, looking carefully at Jim, added, "I also
like making money. Now, Jim, I know what you're going to say,
but I can't help it. I used to feel that it was your money and I

couldn't really say that much about it. I know it wasn't that you made me feel that way; I just did. I used to have some money in an old peanut butter jar so I wouldn't have to ask for something. It was a habit of my mother's, you know; you could always go to my mother, even though my parents were pretty poor, and my mother would have a little money she saved up. Well, I did that too. Now I get a paycheck. Every week. Not that I go on a trip to Europe with it. I cash it at the supermarket. I'm just as careful as I ever was, but I feel differently about it," she said. "Jim won't say this, but he isn't sure he likes that part of it," said Rose. Then she excused herself to go grade papers.

As she left us alone, Jim broke a rather awkward silence to confide about his own conflicts. "Look, it has been different. Good, but different. I mean, now I don't expect my wife to be like my mother. She says I do, but I don't. Who could expect someone to make their own pasta in 1977? My mother didn't have a washing machine until 1958. I was one of nine kids, *nine* kids. My mother was worn-out-looking at Rose's age and she had a four-year-old. Imagine that. That was the way things were, between the Church and being immigrants . . . You want to know something funny? My mother was the one who encouraged Rose to go back to school and be a teacher. When our youngest was ten, my mother came to visit. It was our anniversary present to them, the plane tickets. So my mother and Rose are talking and my mother tells Rose that she's lonely. She loves my father, but all the children are gone, my father still works a full day and she has nothing to do. She also told Rose to plan for her own life, not to think only of her children. Rose was shocked, because my mother had always been a real Italian mother, nothing but doing for the kids in her life, and here she was telling her daughter-in-law to take care, to have something for herself."

According to Jim, that was more important in Rose's mind than anything she could have read in a magazine or a pamphlet about liberated women. Like most people, she listened to the messages that came from those closest to her. Yet, this conversation might never have taken place without the public debate gendered by the women's movement and the consciousness that times were changing, that it would be possible for a daughter-in-law to choose something different.

It was a pivotal experience for Jim, too. "It sounds kind of selfish. I had never thought that maybe my mother wanted something out of life besides taking care of us and my father. I think my brothers and I were all selfish about that. We grew up just thinking that if you were married to a good man, that would be enough. It's a hard thing, it is something hard to think about, that it isn't enough. It makes you feel maybe less loved or something. You grow up with a mother like mine, thinking that if someone loves you they want to take care of you like a mother, then you have to see that it's different. That women want more than that, just like men do." He said this slowly, matter-of-factly, looking down at his hands. "Well, that is still something to think about . . ."

Jim was a man who grappled. There was a gap between his intellectual understanding and his feelings, and he spent the last several years trying to bridge that gap. Especially since Rose went back to work.

"Rose went back two years ago. The youngest had been in school and she'd done some volunteer work. I thought that was good. She should keep her hand in, in case something happened. But now she's gone back full-time and she has some special classes, exceptional kids, what have you. She loves it. I tell you, looking at her, I feel that's doing something for her that I couldn't do. She looks so good, doesn't she? I know, it's a thing with me. I don't know how I'd feel if she earned more money than I do. As it is, most of it, anyway, goes to college for the kids. We don't live off her money, we use it for tuition and for saving for the next tuition. It's not like I feel she's supporting me. I should understand, I guess I do, why she likes the same feeling, the feeling that I'm not supporting her either."

Like many other couples, they have something of an economic conspiracy between them. Jim rejected the idea that it would be impossible to live on his income. "We'd be okay, Rose isn't working because she has to. I earn enough for us to live on."

Yet, he did not earn enough for them to live the way they did. Very often, men like Jim find it difficult to admit that they can't earn enough by themselves to support their family. They make elaborate economic rationales to avoid the idea that they are not able to fulfill their wage-earner expectations. In the case of Jim and Rose, her money went to tuitions, vacations, clothes, dinners out, the "frills." His money went to the rent, the grocery bills, heat and electricity.

It was often easier for Jim to believe that his wife was working for personal fulfillment than for the money.

Jim was proud of Rose the way he was proud of the women in his office. But he was uneasy about her changes—but not those of the women he worked with.

"The thing is, Rose is talking about going to graduate school in this exceptional kid thing. It's a good thing. She's good with kids. She's got patience and she's kind and she's just a good teacher and, Christ, kids like that need all the help they can get . . ." he said, and his voice trailed off.

"You know, it's kind of hard. Men like me, we just didn't grow up expecting our wives to be, well, like Rose, you know? I sometimes have to pinch myself to remember that it's Rose, my Rose. When we were younger she was so pretty and she looked up to me. I was the stronger one. The kids were little and it was good. It's good now, but it was good then too. Now, she wants to go to graduate school. She says she can do it, take some courses part-time. I don't know what to say. I can't say no. I mean, if I said no, she would have to decide anyway. If I said no and she did it anyway, then what? I mean, the fact is that I don't have a say in it . . ." His voice trailed off and then he asked me a direct question:

"Answer this, what would a woman with a master's degree or a Ph.D. want with a telephone company guy, a guy who isn't going to go much higher up, who isn't going to be Mr. AT&T, who isn't going to earn more than twenty thousand? Will my wife still be my wife if she has a Ph.D.? Answer me that."

Jim's wife appeared to him to be moving on a "fast track," just when he felt he'd reached the limit of his career. He had come to terms with the limits of his ambitions. His role as a mentor to the women at the office was very rewarding, but his security in the family had been shaken. Jim had the kind of fear that could only be allayed by time. He seemed to have both the commitment and flexibility to deal with that, but these adjustments come hard.

As I was leaving their home, Rose looked up from the papers she was grading and said to me privately: "Remember one thing about Jim. His father was a socialist at the factory and a patriarch at home. We don't always talk about this, but I know. I know that man."

Although they saw their lives in a very personal, individual way, they were also part of the new mainstream, each trying to adapt. The changes in their roles were initiated by Rose. Jim's response was to some degree a part of his attitude at work. He accepted the basic notions of equal rights for women in the context of his family background and his sense of "fair play." At home, he was aware that he couldn't do less than accept the changes in his wife's life. Yet, it was still new enough and strange enough to make him uneasy. He anticipated disruption, and often feared a loss of status and even love.

Many who travel according to old roles seek incremental adjustments, rather than wholesale reversals. Rose and Jim each grew and held on in various ways. They sought to avoid a crisis.

THE MIDDLE LIFE PATTERN

A variety of modified traditional life patterns and ideals have emerged among the middlegrounders which also show both the persistence of the old and the emergence of new expectations. Many of the people in the middleground grow like Jim and Rose—carrying their ambivalence with them. These new traditionalists change by modifications, not demolitions. They seem to live halfway between what they learned from observing their own parents' lives and what they expect in their children's lives. They make changes step by step. In most of these homes, if women are no longer totally responsible for the house and child care, they are still primarily responsible; if men are no longer the exclusive breadwinners, they are still the primary breadwinners.

There are two life patterns that seem most common in the

middleground which I think reflect this kind of careful adjustment of roles. One of these is a life-cycle pattern.

THE NEW LIFE CYCLE IN THE MIDDLEGROUND

A few years ago, the International Women's Year Committee asked American women to identify their ideal life. More than half of them described a life in which they would work, but drop out of the work force when their children were little and then move back into it. This is still a very common ideal for the middleground. Many women say they would like to be full-time mothers while their children are young and then return to part-time or flexible-time work and then go into full-time work perhaps in their thirties or forties. This ideal fits neatly into the semitraditional model. It seems to allow women to Have It All, stretched out over many decades. I think it's popular because it lets women change without losing their traditional role. It suggests that they can fulfill all the traditional expectations of being a "good mother" and yet also have another built-in period of growth. They don't have to confront the tradition—they can work around it. They can have "the best of both worlds."

Yet, although this ideal seems to finesse the anxieties of change, the middlegrounders who follow it are still subject to a great deal of the stress and vacillation of the Shuttle Zone. The plan has built-in transitions which require a good deal of flexibility and which suggest both the benefits and problems of the new life-cycle pattern.

JOEL AND EVELYN: CHANGING CAREFULLY IN SYNCHRONY

In many ways Joel and Evelyn were the perfect example of a careful timed-in change, a slowly modifying pattern and yet one not without its conflicts and stresses.

When Joel and Evelyn were first married, nineteen years ago, it was against the will of both sets of parents. Joel, a six-foot-tall Irishman with graying black hair and blue eyes, was Catholic, and Evelyn, a slim, vital woman with short hair clipped into a swinging pageboy, was a Methodist. That meant a great deal in

their adjoining hometowns in New Jersey. Joel and Evelyn met
in college, and married, and then moved out to Long Island, to a
house that seemed much farther away from New Jersey than two
hours.

They had moved out of the family orbit. Neither of them was
going to be like their parents. Moving away meant that his parents didn't know if Joel went to church, and he didn't, and
Evelyn's parents didn't know if she went to church, and she
didn't. All their parents blamed it on the marriage.

Joel and Evelyn replaced their families with each other. They
had a kind of life plan, what was called The Dream back in 1959.
It was the house in the suburbs, an old Victorian that Evelyn
could make over into "her house," with a garden like the English
ones she saw in the magazines that she was always reading. Joel
would get a "good job" and they would always do things like
getting dressed up and going into the city for dinner and theater.
It was a good dream. Slowly, they had three children—Beth,
Peter, and Jennifer—and their dream unfolded.

Aside from one really tough year, in 1967 when their son had
open-heart surgery, the McManuses seemed to move right
ahead, easily into their dream. They had a good and growing
sexual attachment to each other and they laughed about it.

"Joel and I had gotten a heavy dose of sin and sex. I don't
know how our sex life survived. I think it was sheer drive. We
got married so we could sleep together—that was the dark ages—
and that's always been something good between us."

But it was also part of the time and caring they devoted to
each other.

Over the first ten years of their marriage they moved three
times. Each time Evelyn nested. She learned to make curtains
with big hems that she could adjust if they moved again, and
learned to make coq au vin from a Julia Child recipe, the one
that started with a chunk of bacon to be blanched and ended
hours later with a spectacular dish. She and Joel learned about
wine together and they were the only couple in the neighborhood who could play tennis without killing each other.

When they argued at all it was about the kids or about his
hours. In the early years, Evelyn felt exhausted and tied to the

house and children. "I always thought the first three years of child-raising felt like twenty, and the next fifteen felt like three. But I also wanted to be there. I couldn't imagine not being the one at home. That's just me, but I did want to be number one with the children. I confess, maybe it isn't the most healthy thing, but I wanted to be the one they called on when they scratched their knees or anything. That was my idea of being a mother."

Evelyn learned child-raising. It was her subject and sometimes she resented Joel's "input," as if anyone who hadn't read Haim Ginott or the women's magazines had a right to deal with children. Joel often felt like he was second in command there, but he didn't feel badly about it.

"Well, it was her job. I wouldn't have wanted her coming to my office and telling me what to do. I understood that."

Though she complained that he wasn't there to help with the children, she also, she admits, found him irritatingly incompetent with the children when they were babies.

In the early years, Evelyn worried over the children incessantly, especially over her son, who had a heart problem from the time he was three; they had to wait to have it operated on.

"In those days, when I look back on it, we were so alone. Joel and I couldn't go to our parents for help and we didn't share as much, I mean, the other mothers. We weren't as honest then as now. Now a young mother can tell her friends that she's going off her gourd without getting 'a look.' Back then, the most you could do was make a joke of it. I felt that my job was to make everything perfect, to do everything totally right. Of course, having my boy sick was a big thing. It was too much for me, but I personally couldn't have let someone else take care of them. Maybe it was guilt, I don't know, but I really felt it was my job. I had taken it on and that was it."

In these years, Joel moved up, working finally as a buyer in a major department store for a vice-president who got manic after the Thursday night closing and kept everyone in the office until the last train. He also worked on Saturdays.

Evelyn was resentful of that, but she said, "It was a lucky thing.

If I didn't have that as an excuse, as a bargaining thing with myself, I might never have gone back to school."

After their son's recovery from his operation, when it was clear that he would lead a normal life, Evelyn took stock.

"That was my year for the grumbles. I was grumbling all the time. I was bored, but I kept telling Joel, 'I'm so boring, how can you stand me?' Even refinishing the furniture, stuff like that, that I'd always enjoyed, started to make me itchy."

This was seven years ago, when the women's movement had just hit, and it had an effect on Evelyn too. "I certainly didn't want to ditch the kids and go run off to a commune," she says. This, for her, would mean being a "women's libber."

"But I couldn't help thinking, you know, how I had assumed this life was it, that I had just taken it for granted that Joel's dreams were mine, that I was part of his life, rather than having a life of my own.

"I started thinking about what was ahead. Here I was grumbling away and the baby was only in kindergarten for three hours a day. The next year I was going to have all three in school until three o'clock in the afternoon. What was I going to do with myself? Clean the house all day?"

She was clearly at a turning point. Evelyn was facing a shift in the self she had invested in being a mother. As she saw it, she had a choice, between adjusting to a more relaxed life, with some pleasure in that—"the idea of reading the paper in the morning, having some leisure"—or filling in that time with "more," something for herself. She could also postpone the decision. But it seemed that change was a more conservative option. The women's movement was one force that made her realize she had a choice to make.

Evelyn decided to go back to college. She'd only finished a year and a half of course work before her marriage. She thought about this decision in the family context. She wanted to be home when the children were home, wanted some flexibility, she wanted to take a step, rather than a leap. Like many other women, she chose to divide her life into part-times to make a temporary adjustment.

"Joel was very good about it. I think he was relieved that I wasn't grumbling. Also, I arranged everything so it wouldn't interfere with our life. I took classes while the kids were in school and studied while they were with a neighbor—I did some sharing with my neighbors. To some degree I did it the way I did the curtains, you know?"

In many ways, this decision was a compromise or a transitional one. As a part-time worker, Evelyn had flexibility. In fact, she had far more flexibility than Joel. On the other hand, she had added pressure to her life. She had changed her life without really changing her role in terms of her family. Joel was still the wage-earner, Evelyn still fundamentally in charge of the home. School was an added extra, her "thing." It didn't interfere with The Dream.

"I think I was really lucky. I could still be at the kids' school if I wanted to be. My vacations were more or less in tune with theirs and if they got sick, I could still stay home. You know, I wanted to be there when the kids came home. Kids aren't kids all that long. Suddenly they are in grade school, then in high school, and now, look, they're almost gone. I didn't want to miss that."

At school Evelyn was drawn to psychology. She became a psychology major, first working in child psychology—"I figured I knew something about that"—and then in adult psychology.

This course dovetailed dramatically with her life. She realized —she even studied it—how much she was growing. School had become something more than "curtain-making." It was the first thing that she wasn't able entirely to share with Joel.

"We were both busy. But I was very involved in psychology and Joel in business. We were lucky, we've always been very close, and Joel would be the first to say, 'Okay, you and I are going out for a long dinner,' whenever we felt that we hadn't seen enough of each other."

Then, just as Evelyn was halfway through her credits, she was shaken again.

"The first thing that happened that year was the Bob and Helen split. They were our closest friends. We used to spend a lot of weekends with them and their kids. Helen and I would talk about things. I knew they had some problems, but nothing I would have called serious. Then suddenly Bob left. He just picked up and moved out."

Like countless other wives, she experienced through Helen the insecurities of being married, and dependent. "Here was Helen, who had been a good wife, not a doormat, but a good wife and mother. That had been the center of her life and, boom, she had nothing. Nothing. I don't mean just that Bob left her, but the whole fabric of her life was based on being Bob's wife. She didn't have two nickels to rub together. She didn't have a job or a husband. I saw firsthand how fragile all this was." Evelyn began to think ahead.

At the same time, Joel had gotten his promotion on the track to being vice-president. The Dream was within reach.

She and Joel were both exhilarated that year. But somewhat separately. Joel was still playing out the dream reel. He was beginning to make money and to have prestige. He talked about how they would have those dinner and theater evenings and perhaps they could start entertaining more and they might think about a larger house, the one with the real English garden.

When Evelyn listened to him rerunning The Dream like an old movie on television she had one panicky insight, "That's not my dream anymore." She harbored that traitorous thought silently. She was still the one in her psychology class who brought up the "man's point of view" when they talked about women's roles. She still ran the home and made the arrangements for dinner parties and she cleared the weekends of studying so that they could play tennis and be with family and friends. But she had begun to dread graduation, because neither she nor Joel had talked about what she would do after.

By this time, the oldest child was in high school. She could see simultaneously either an "empty nest" or "free time" to pursue something new. She had some input from the new friends she had made at school. These women, two of them, had become in many ways her new peer group. They were also women rounding the end of the thirties, also part-time students and part-time mothers. They gave her a new sense of "normalcy" and reflected back the changed image of herself. With them she discussed choices that she rarely would have entertained before, even as fantasies.

One night three weeks before graduation, while Evelyn was finishing a take-home exam, Joel called her impulsively to come to town and join him. He had tickets to *Fiddler*, and a reservation at their favorite restaurant. He figured she would be through with the exam by then. Evelyn said no. It was the first time she'd ever said no. "I felt as if I had said NO in neon, big capital letters, as if I were saying no to what we'd dreamed about. I finished the exam and later I spent a lot of the night crying. Maybe it was the tension, I don't know. But I felt as if I were sticking up for me at the expense of us. I thought, what am I doing to Joel, how I am disappointing him. It wasn't about not having dinner, but about what I knew was happening inside me. I wasn't Wendy Wife anymore."

Still, slowly, Evelyn made more decisions for herself. In a sense, the crisis had passed and she had chosen the path that promised a life for herself, not an empty nest.

By the time I met her, Evelyn had become a social worker on Long Island. By choosing this job she was able to transfer her basic self-image as a "helper," a nurturer, a caretaker, from the private sphere to the public one. "I could never have just gone into a business. I would have been much too guilty. I'm guilty enough as it is. I still feel I'm doing this for me. But at least I can rationalize that I'm helping people who need me in some ways more than my family." But it wasn't that simple. She kept carefully in the middle. Even two years later, as the oldest child was getting ready for college, she overcompensated for every decision. She drove hard bargains with herself. She said, "I will work as long as I can still have dinner parties. I will work as long as the kids don't suffer. I will work as long as I still can give Joel and the kids enough attention."

Her family came first, chronologically and emotionally. Her middle road led from full-time mothering, to part-time mother, and part-time worker. She changed in tune with the demands of her family and her own time. She still largely carried the double role of homemaker and social worker. Although her teenage children did more housework than before, her husband Joel did not. Evelyn was the one who supervised the schedules of the children, planned the meals, and made sure that the cleaning and laundry got done.

"I suppose it isn't right. I know you could say that I should have made my husband help more. But to tell you the truth, I am the one who wanted this change and therefore I can make the adjustments. It's been enough for Joel to adjust to me. I don't always give him the same kind of support that I should, and he is so good to me.

"Also, a lot of times I think, I don't want to let go of my home, my role as mother of the kids, my kitchen. I think of it as my kitchen. I need all that. It's my roots. So I take on the work to keep it. I suppose it's my fall-back position. I can always go home again, so I haven't really let go of my house."

Evelyn and Joel, a friendly and affectionate man who felt lucky to have been successful in his business and in his family, played a duet in which she doubted her ability and he reinforced her.

"Evelyn doesn't know how insightful she is. She is full of doubts about how she's handling her cases and whether she's good at it. I keep telling her how marvelous she is. How well she's handling things. Everything really runs smoothly, the kids are in good shape. We only eat at MacDonald's four times a week . . ." Joel laughed and then quickly denied it.

"No, I am proud of Evelyn. I'd much rather have her doing what she's doing than become one of those menopausal women who play bridge and hang on to their kids. I think it's great that she's found something that keeps her happy."

Actually, Evelyn had grown stronger. She had a sense of professional competency that was reinforced by her co-workers. She was moving to a position where she would head up a training project for new hospital workers. But she and Joel had a deal. She asked for and received his support. She "needed" him. He responded by encouraging her, helping her to believe in herself.

In the middle, this woman changed almost in tune with the modified traditional pattern that has emerged as the new "ideal." She did it, largely by working around the needs of her children and her husband. Her changes were timed cautiously and she maneuvered through them, carefully, managing to avoid loss, by expending her own energy. She bridged the gap between the traditional and nontraditional roles by filling both roles sequentially. Now she filled them concurrently. A working woman and primary homemaker, she was the woman in the middle.

But, in general, this seemed to be only a temporary pattern, an impermanent compromise. Already those of the new middle project different futures for their children, and have different analyses of their own lives.

Was Joel a traditional male chauvinist? "I guess my wife is my credential on that one. I don't feel at all threatened by her working or anything like that. I think it's great," he said.

Evelyn said, "Well, Joel is the kind of guy who could say, 'My wife, I think I'll keep her,' but he wouldn't mean anything by it. He likes to be taken care of, he has a touch of the Irish in him. But he's also just wonderful to me. Do you know how many of my friends' husbands wouldn't even let them work?"

Was Evelyn a feminist? Joel snapped, "Oh hell, no. I don't think you would call her that. She isn't like those women at all. That's one of the things that's great about Evelyn. She can do everything that she wants to do without getting all angry about it. She just went ahead and did it. I admire that."

"Well," she said slowly, "I am for the ERA. I don't think the women's movement is going away. I don't carry any cards. I'm not much of a joiner. I suppose I am part of it, in the sense that I'm doing things my mother wouldn't have done. I think that women should be allowed to have the full range of opportunities that men do. They don't have that now, but I think they will."

As for the children, Joel thought they would be lucky to have a marriage just like his. "They don't come any better than this." Evelyn said: "This is it for me. It's worked for us. But for the girls, I would expect that they would be getting married on more of a partnership basis. That they would be sharing from the first day, sharing with kids, the whole thing."

To me, it was interesting that although Evelyn had lived through the pattern which so many middleground people identify as their ideal, it was no longer her own ideal. Perhaps compromises of this modified pattern become conflicts that push toward another resolution.

Evelyn found this life-cycle pattern to be very demanding in many ways. Even changing sequentially had not made it a great deal less stressful.

What about the other major modified pattern? I call this the Double Shift Pattern. Many people try to avoid loss by simply adding more to their lives. These are the ones Who Do It All at the same time. There are fewer and fewer families like Evelyn and Joel's that can afford to live on one income for even a decade. But women who work all through motherhood may still live with the compromises and fears of the middleground. The woman who does it all retains the primary responsibility for child care—or the supervisions of child care and the home—and has a job. She too avoids confronting the traditional role directly. In theory she too can have "more" without losing. But only at great personal expense in terms of energy.

At the top of the social scale, they are mythical Superwomen, who simultaneously hold prestigious jobs and keep a wonderful home and happy children. These are the elite women featured in magazine stories about "juggling" home and career without letting a hair get out of place.

Very often these Superwomen, the supreme jugglers, feel that the only way they can justify their nontraditional role is by filling the traditional one just as well. They are often reluctant or afraid to ask their husbands to take over more home responsibilities.

But there are tens of thousands of women who never call themselves Superwomen at all. They are not the glamorous career women, but divorced mothers or wives of the working class or the barely middle class. Most often the married working women earn significantly less money than their husbands. It seems to be difficult for them to feel that their jobs are as important as their husbands'. Since their husbands are still the primary wage-earners; they remain the primary homemakers. These are the women who work two shifts—one at the office and the other at home. They often think of themselves as semidependent and don't want to risk their security at home. The working-class woman is especially caught in the middle, with all the pressures of traditional roles and nontraditional roles.

MARIE: WORKING THE DOUBLE SHIFT

Marie's life had also been affected by the emergence of a new "norm." But she had often felt change as a push, an unwanted pressure, rather than a pull.

At forty, she had a routine office job in Chicago taking ads over the telephone and recording them on a piece of paper. She worked downtown from eight-thirty to four-forty, took the El home and then worked again cleaning, making supper, from five o'clock on. It wasn't the life she expected to lead, nor the one she might have chosen.

"I have these kids, three of them. There's one in the sixth grade, one in the fourth, and the baby's only in second. Now they get out of school at three o'clock and on the whole they aren't home much before three-thirty, four. The oldest one runs in, grabs something to eat, and runs out, you know how kids are. So I was at home for about ten years. To tell you the truth, I always enjoyed it at home. When the kids were out of diapers, I had free time and I had my church work, and I never was one to mind doing the housework. I wasn't the kind who scrubbed the floors every day, but I always liked to keep a nice house," said Marie, a short Polish-American woman who was wearing a conservative double-knit pantsuit and flat-heeled shoes.

"Now, here we are and what with inflation and all, we were doing okay, but we weren't keeping up. Then my husband's mother was widowed and there wasn't much of a pension for her, we had to help out, and everything's getting more expensive and my husband is earning about thirteen thousand a year. Well, it wasn't enough. That was all.

"What are you gonna do? Now, in my mother's day, my dad would have gotten a second job. He was always moonlighting one thing or another. Now, you wouldn't feel right about that. I mean, how could I stay at home all day and have my husband moonlighting? It wouldn't be right. It's that I know I can work. I see that just about everyone in the neighborhood is working. I can't let him do that.

"So here I am. It's $165 a week and it makes the difference. But I still worry about the kids. I miss the free time and it seems to be rush, rush, rush and yelling, and what-have-you, at home, and quick meals, and I have to ask the kids to do more than they want to. And I worry leaving them with each other. I hate them to fight or to spend that time watching TV. It isn't a nice family kind of thing as it was with the mother at home, I don't think. Of course, I chose this job so I wouldn't leave them too long. But to be honest, if we could afford it, I'd much rather be in my own house. But what are you going to do?"

In a sense, the new choices open to women also meant that she felt pressured to join the number of women who had gone back to work.

"I don't hate it here. It's a job, you know what I mean. The thing I like is the company. Being with the other women. I've made some friends, and this isn't the kind of job where you have to punch in and punch out. The thing I also like is knowing that I won't end up like my mother-in-law. Now, there she is, sixty-four years old, she never worked, and she can't get a job at all now, and she's being supported by us. This way, God forbid, if Al should die, I have a job, and then, I also will get a pension here. So it isn't all bad."

Basically, however, Marie added more hours to her "work day," and more responsibilities to her life. She changed by tacking a new role onto the old one. She was still the one who ran the house, oversaw the children, made the meals. If the washing machine needed to be repaired, she was the one who missed work to wait for the repairman. If they needed to do marketing, Marie was the one who stopped off on the way home from work, or assigned the task to the oldest child.

"It's like you're sitting at work and your mind wanders to things like, 'Gee, do I have enough for supper? Will Lizzie, my mother-in-law, be eating with us, or does she have church tonight? Did I take the meat out of the freezer?' Now Al doesn't ever think about things like that. He doesn't ever worry about dinner, unless I call him and tell him to pick up something on the way home."

Did Marie ask her husband to do more? "To be honest about it, I don't. Not much. He'll do the dishes with me. That's something that's changed since I went to work. And that's a nice time of day for us. I put on some coffee and we do the dishes and talk. But I don't ask him to do the housekeeping on Saturdays. I don't like to. If he offered it would be fine, believe me, but for me to ask him . . . I don't think I'd like to do that. He comes from a traditional home, and I just don't think he would feel right vacuuming and like that. It would be an embarrassing type of thing for him. You know, he was always the breadwinner kind. I think, he doesn't talk about it much, but I think he feels disappointed in himself that he never earned the kind of money that would have made him a big deal. Now, if I asked him to do the vacuuming, it would make him feel like he was even less of a big deal. It's the ego, the ego. That's men for you. And for me to live with him and not make him unhappy, well, it's okay with me to help his ego."

Marie's experience was rather typical of the middlegrounders. In a *McCall's* study of reader response to the issue of housework, it was reported that the husbands of working wives did only one hour more housework a week than the husbands of wives at home. In Detroit, a study of female doctors showed that 74 percent of them also did their own housework. Superwoman or working mother, some of the women in the new middle evolve by doing it all, filling both roles.

Few of them perhaps consciously make this "decision." But the area of their life which they feel least comfortable changing is their ongoing relationship. In some deeply rooted way, many are convinced that any further change in their relationship would equal disruption. So, the double-shift worker, whether she is working-class or professional, often finesses one fear of change: the fear that by altering their most intimate relationship, they might lose it.

But I also had a sense, at least with many middleground women, that their primary role at home is a fall-back position. "Worst comes to worst, you know, if I hated my job, I could always go home again," Marie told me. When I pressed her on that point she said, "Oh, it would be tight, we've gotten used to living on two incomes, but I could do it." She still feels a certain kind of security in her housewife role.

I asked Marie what she would miss most if she did leave work. "Oh, the money," she said quickly, then added, "When you work, the fact is that you feel different. I know I'm still the one who runs and cooks and stuff, but—and this is awful to say—I would feel like a dumb housewife. I would hate myself if I started watching the soaps again. I did that, I really did."

What, on the other hand, would she like to change most? "I'd like to get more help at home. From the kids and from Al. Honest to God, if I don't do it myself, I might as well. I have to ask and remind and make lists. Everybody still thinks of it as my job. So that if I'm not doing it myself, I'm telling everybody to do it and then I'm saying thank you. I would just like someone else to do something without my even having to think about it.

"It's like my friend Dora said, 'If you're at home awhile and then you go back to work, somehow or other you're the one who has to make all the changes.' The kids are mad at you because now they have to do more work around the house. You feel bad if you can't get to school like you used to. Then, too, the girls you used to hang around with or had time to talk with on the phone and that, their feelings are hurt!" and she continued as if she were making a list: "I don't think it's so much like that if you start out like some of the young couples you know. But if it's like me and Al, well, I really do have to do the two jobs or else we'd end up fighting. And I really do end up worrying about the band costumes for the kids and the laundry. I tell my Susie, when you get married, get one of those contracts, and have it all written out. Isn't that awful?"

Marie too thought of her plateau in the middleground not as an ideal but as a compromise. And perhaps a temporary one.

But the man in the middle also sees some of the flaws in the new patterns. Both patterns leave men still responsible financially and still on a one-track life. There is little flexibility written into the script of the middleground man. He often describes his semitraditional position in terms of the adjustments he's made to his wife's new life, "letting her work," helping with the housework.

But some men, too, see these compromises turn into conflicts in terms of their own lives, and these conflicts move them toward some new innovations.

DAVID: MOVING OUT OF THE MIDDLE

David had grown up in a home with parents who were always saving for the future. His mother collected elastics around the doorknobs, and paper bags behind the refrigerator, and issued warnings whenever he left the house: "Be careful." From the time he first walked to school to the time when, in 1956, at age sixteen, he bought a 1949 Oldsmobile, he never left the house without being told to watch out for something.

From the pictures I saw, he was a handsome kid, with unruly brown hair and legs that had grown out of proportion to his body and only settled together into some reasonable shape when he was a junior at Harvard. That was the year when he had shifted his career aspirations from medicine to journalism "because I just despised Chem 20. I hated the class, I hated the other students. I thought I was going bananas and I had one little article published in the *Crimson,* and so I thought I'd be a journalist. At least you didn't have to dissect things."

David had his career planned quite carefully. He would go to journalism school, then get married, go out to some small-town paper and then come back to New York and become Scotty Reston, while picking up a Pulitzer and a couple of kids along the way.

"The role that I saw for my wife was to be sort of like the Smith graduates of the 1940s or something. Very chic in a tweedy way with a great sense of humor who took care of things for me—including a little typing when I was finishing up a book —and still was really thrilled to be the missus."

He never actually explained this to Sally when they met in journalism school. At that time she had aspirations that were radically different from those of her mother. She wanted a career

too, although perhaps she was willing to work her job around
his, and even to take some time out for children.

What happened was that they graduated from school and
went his way. He got the job in the city room, she was ruled out
by the nepotism clause and got a job in public relations. She
hated it, and partially out of boredom, partially to fill in the rest
of her life plan, they had one child in 1965 and another in 1968.
During those years, she figured that she would free-lance while
the kids were napping. Their life together began really in the
middleground.

"Oh, I did free-lance," said Sally, a blond version of her husband's Smithie dream. "I had one piece in *Mademoiselle* in 1966
and did some stringing for *Cosmopolitan* in 1968. While David
was covering the convention in Chicago and getting tear-gassed
I was green with envy because I was writing about how to pick
up a man in a laundromat. It was terrific."

Slowly, however, things changed for them. David did have a
commitment to his family, and as he saw his friends drifting into
the after-work bar routine, drifting into divorce, as he saw their
wives going crazy, he was receptive to some kind of change.

"We sat down and tried to figure out what we could do to
make life better for her. That was how we both thought of it.
She was the one who had the problem. I was the one who could
'help.' So I 'helped.' I took the kids on Saturday so she could get
in some solid work hours. We arranged for a babysitter three
mornings a week for Tessa, after Sara was in nursery school. We
started to make some adjustments. She was still basically in
charge of the home, but I started to do a lot more.

"Because Sally is so damn smart, it started to come together
for her. She started publishing stuff in the good magazines. She
got a book offer and we both let the household go to hell while
she was writing it.

"Sally was still basically working around the kids. She was the
one who did our time at the nursery school cooperative, usually—
not always, but usually. She brought the kids there and back."

They had grown through many phases of the new middle and
gradually found a greater commitment to change. However, it

was David whose compromises turned into some growing sense of resentment.

"I started feeling that I was the one who was doing the compromising, I was the one who had done all the changing for her, really. I was feeling sort of hemmed in at work. How many riots can you cover before you just have had it? Daily journalism had really lost a lot of glamour for me. They say that you lose your legs at thirty. Well, by thirty-five I needed to do something deeper, something realer. I knew I could get a book contract, but I couldn't figure out how the hell I could do that and support us at the same time.

"You see, neither of us had ever truly considered whether I wanted to be the breadwinner forever. Sally got nervous around men who weren't working. It's true. And the idea of being the one who had to support us, well, it was scary to her. She liked the flexibility, she liked not having to earn the money. Not that she didn't like money, but the idea that it was a little extra, that when she got a check in the mail it was a bonus rather than bread and butter, that was pleasing to her.

"I started to feel that she was living off me. I did," David says again, shaking his head, "I started to feel like I had the worst deal. I am thirty-seven years old and as far as making any kind of professional break-through, I think that I will do it in the next four or five years or I won't at all."

Sally and David have talked about it and talked about it and finally they both querulously agreed. Now it was David's turn. She would take a steady job, the nine-to-five hours, and he would take the "flexible" job working at home while the kids are in school from eight to three, parenting while they are at home.

"It's an enormous change for a guy like me. I had always been a safety-first kind of thinker. I was programmed for that. But all this has taught me that flexibility comes first. I see that life is pretty long and Sally and I have different needs at different times and so do the kids. Now I think in terms of changes, not plans, but keeping more open. I never used to think this way. It's all new for me as well as for Sally. I sometimes think that's what keeps us together. It's kind of interesting."

In many ways the middleground is a vital territory. Here are the people who shuttle between the past and the future and here is where the tug-of-war between the issues of loss and growth go on. It is very often the middleground that determines what changes will stick.

In talking with them, I was impressed with how much time we all need to feel comfortable in new situations. People can't comfortably renovate their society in a day or metamorphose their own lives in a week. We all need links with the values of our own past as well as some sense of purpose and growth.

And in this process we do take the shuttle. We do go back and forth between future visions and nostalgia. The values of the past and the present. We think both of our parents and of our children. The trip through a crisis of change, through any Shuttle Zone isn't a quick one. In fact, I think perhaps the best slogan for the new middleground is the one that the beat generation author Jack Kerouac once wrote: "Walking on Water Wasn't Built in a Day."

Part III
Inside Changes

As I talked with people who were living in the Shuttle Zone of change, they expressed the same feelings again and again. While excited, even elated, at changes which offered a growing sense of satisfaction and achievement, they were anxious, even paralyzed in conflict by the fear that they might have to relinquish attachments to old ideas or relationships which still retained meaning in their lives.

Fear of loss is clearly at the crux of change.

So, I looked hard at three of the issues which seem most pivotal and widespread among those who were ambivalent about change: (1) fear of disruption of the family, (2) fear of submergence in the family, and (3) fear of the uncertainty of the future of change.

When I asked people what concerned them most about the emerging new sex roles in America, the answer almost invariably was "the disruption of the family." Again and again, the men and women I interviewed expressed uncertainty about their own feelings of changing the traditional family. Even those who were still living in households with a father-breadwinner and a mother-homemaker, talked about the traditional family as a thing of the past. On the other hand, even those who had struggled out of the old structure talked about parts of it with nostalgia.

I had expected to hear the most anxiety about children—who would take care of the children if Mother went to work? And in fact there is much concern with that. But when questioned closely, I found that the gut issue, the root fear, isn't anxiety about children at all, but rather about love relationships, marriage. The crucial question for most of the married couples is whether they can alter their own lives, without disrupting the life they have made as partners.

The question for single adults is similarly related to marriage: Can men and women have long-term sustaining relationships as their roles change? Men and women wonder whether their relationships are flexible enough to accommodate change. If one partner changes, it forces the other to change, and what if she or he cannot? They look around and see divorce. They question the connection between the role changes and marital disruption. Is there such a thing as a women's lib divorce? What happened in those marriages which had ended?

The stress of change and the fear of loss among the group which remained in the "traditional role" is different. I found great unease among the dozens of housewives I interviewed. Often housewives feel that recent social changes have undermined their status and security. They feel left out. They fear loss of self-esteem—that they are being disparaged and undervalued, that it is becoming increasingly difficult to "choose" the "traditional" way in this society. In talking with them, I heard their questions: Will the old choice be available, or will the new option close out the old one? Can there be change within the "unchanged" choice?

The other important issue for those in the Shuttle Zone is the future. There is general uncertainty about the direction future changes will take.

This section then is focused on three groups who have felt change acutely and whose lives are really messages for the majority. These are the divorced men and women, the housewives and their husbands, the people living what they are told are New Life Choices.

By looking at these inside changes, one can see the options and conflicts of the continuing process of change. These men and women showed me that a turning point is not a doorway which we pass through in a neat completed motion. It's rather a chain of reactions, a continuing interaction between the individual and society, these people and the times in which they are living.

Chapter 6 Divorce

"Finally, I looked up at my mother and said, . . . 'I am about to break a tradition, God only knows how many hundreds of years old, a family tradition. I am going to break the longest line of martyrdom in Italian history.'"

There was a long time—when was it? before 1970—when Sally Fields used to polish her children's shoes every night. While the kids were taking baths, she'd line up the shoes, left-right, left-right, and take the polish out of the medicine cabinet and strike them white or red. Peculiar, because, of course, they'd get dirty the next day. But the next night she'd polish them again. And again.

There was a long time—when was it? before 1970—when Roger Fields thought that polished shoes were probably a good thing, polishing them a good job for a mother. Himself, he went to work every day in his Ivy League clothes and his Ivy League haircut with his Ivy League education to his family business.

And there was a time when they both figured, well, maybe marriage isn't happy, not really happy, not really what we expected, but it's okay. There was a time when they lived in a house in Wellesley and belonged to the country club and would fantasize about what they would do if the other one died. It was always "move to Cambridge and start all over again." Then, three months ago, Sally and Roger Fields, the couple, died, and did move to Cambridge. Rather, they disintegrated, or, as the lawyers say, separated.

Now Sally, who is the president of the local chapter of the National Organization for Women, lives in a railroad apartment with red burlap stapled on the walls, a mattress on the floor, and a coffee table made of wooden planks on cardboard boxes. Roger lives two or three miles away with the four children, Julie, eight, Jennifer, six, Christopher, three, and Katie, two. In the past three months, he has lost twenty pounds, grown a mustache and a moderate crop of hair and quick-changed into dungarees and turtle-necked sweaters. He has also quit the family business to become a legal aide lawyer at a third of his former salary.

What happened to Roger, whose parents had bused all the kids at his Bar Mitzvah party to a private screening of a movie in Boston? What happened to Sally, whose parents encouraged her to be a debutante in midwestern society? What happened to the couple who eloped in 1961 when she was nineteen and he was twenty-two?

"I credit the women's movement with the whole thing," says Sally.

Several years ago, I wrote those words in the Boston *Globe* about the uncoupling of a husband and wife I've now called Roger and Sally Fields. I received more than fifty letters full of anger and fear, disgust and judgment about this feminist dissolution. One woman wrote, "That is where all this talking about women's rights will get you . . . right into divorce court."

There was a growing terror of a phenomenon that would soon be labeled "Women's Lib Divorce."

That article was followed shortly by others: a *Look* magazine cover story on "Runaway Wives," featuring feminist Wanda Adams on the cover; pieces in *New Yorker* magazine reporting how many women's-movement women were deserting home, hearth, and their husbands for "liberation." These stories tapped a well of anxiety along the spectrum all the way from the Feminist Change Innovators to the Fascinating Female Change Resisters.

The resisters saw in divorce the "proof" that this change in roles would bring only disruption, loss. Feminists who ideologically believed that marriages would be stronger if they were based, not on separate roles, but on shared humanity, also felt uneasy as marriages dissolved in the midst of change.

For a time the feminist leaders played down the reality of divorce.

Betty Friedan was asked at first not to discuss her divorce in public. The woman I've called Sally Fields was herself forced to resign from her post as president of the local NOW chapter because she had publicly associated divorce with feminism. Conversely, it seems at times that the women's movement pushed its married women out front the way the Right to Life organization tends to push forward its non-Catholics. At the National Women's Conference in Houston, I remember watching Bella Abzug as she introduced the members of the International Women's Year Commission. She ended with the beaming announcement that one member was even engaged. Divorce is still a psychological stop sign for the people who are Not Feminists, But . . .

In December 1977 my newspaper ran a story revisiting the members of a local consciousness-raising group six years after they had met. The five women had once all been married. Now, four of them were divorced. Their divorces seemed again to carry more weight with the readers—the weight of fear, the weight against change—than the fact that each of the women described her life as happier and more fulfilling thán it had been in her marriage. The fear of divorce among middlegrounders is, on one level, a simple anxiety about the disruption of their own marriage. But "divorce" is also a code word, even for those who are not married, that describes the anxiety about any male-female relationship surviving the changes in roles on which they were culturally based.

The question for many is the one Betty Friedan posed in her second book: "Can I be me, all that I am, and still love and be loved by a man?" If you are not half of a whole, seeking the other half, can you still find a fitting place? Can men and women be independent and yet interdependent, interrelated?

Now, in these somewhat calmer times, I thought it might be possible to take a deeper look—beyond the neon signs, and the headlines and the scare sheets—at the nature of the relationship between divorce and sex role change.

When I first began to interview divorced men and women, I thought that I would find a pattern of dissolution. I did, after all, choose to talk with those who identified sex role changes as a "cause" of their divorce. I suppose I had in mind a rather simple scenario: woman finds job, leaves husband. Woman becomes Feminist, man leaves woman. But in fact, I found these divorces to be very similar to any other disrupted marriage. The quality of alienation, the sagas of unmet needs, were the same. The cause was, not this change, but change.

DIVORCE AS CHANGE

Every divorce is a story of change. The uncoupling may be slow, or dramatic. It may be more or less traumatic. Divorce may be the final legal acknowledgment of years of battling, or an exit after a brief honeymoon spat.

But each one is a tale of personal change, if only of the gradual refusal of one partner to accept the status quo any longer. This personal change may come as gradually as aging. A lifetime commitment is based on the belief that two people can grow closer together as they grow older. But people don't always develop in the same direction at the same time. How many divorced people have we heard say, "We grew away from each other . . . We didn't have anything in common anymore . . . We both changed . . . He seemed like a stranger . . . I couldn't talk to her anymore . . . We are just different." Two people who were married at nineteen or twenty-two may have shared school and friends, common backgrounds and experience. But as they have new and separate experiences, as they grow in their own ways psychologically, they may not be able to sustain the same kind of marriage. Their relationship may atrophy. And if there is no strong cultural or personal prohibition against divorce, the relationship may be dissolved in court.

As complicated as it is for one person to change, it may be geometrically more complicated for a relationship to change. When one person grows stronger in the course of his or her life, when another is diminished by life, when one becomes cautious or bold, the other has to adjust. One person cannot change without affecting the other. Even those who try to hide the ways in which they have changed, feel a difference themselves. At the very least, their perception has changed.

Social forces can affect marriages as acutely as the life cycle. For example, two major changes that disrupted marriages in this century, for hundreds and thousands of couples, were emigration and war. The immigrant families who were uprooted from the social supports and the web of relationships which helped maintain their marriage in the old country, often foundered in America. Some adjusted, some broke.

Wars simply divided couples. The men who fought had vastly different experiences than the women who remained at home. In the aftermath of World War II, there was a rash of divorces, as people formalized the long disruption.

It seems to me that on the scale of change, the change in sex roles has carried no less weight. The movement of women into the work force has come slowly, over many years, but during the 1960s and '70s, it accelerated so greatly that it upset the sense of normalcy, the breadwinner and homemaker tradition on which marriage had been based. Marriages lost their old homeland supports.

At the same time, the political force of the women's movement touched and changed women's lives, as greatly as if they had enlisted in the Army. The movement was something they often went into as individuals rather than as couples. It was their change agent. And, the women's rights groups called upon women to look at their lives and their marriages, to question the traditional subservient role of women in the family and to change it.

The women's movement didn't invent marital stress. We have no statistics on how many marriages it "saved" or improved. We can't "number" the traditional marriages which were good or bad relationships.

It is far easier to quantify legal disruption than either emotional strain or increased pleasure. We have only the statistics of divorce. In the ten years from 1965 to 1975, the divorce rate in the United States almost doubled. In 1975 there was nearly one divorce for every two marriages.

To label the women's movement as co-respondent in millions of divorce suits is absurd. In fact, divorce was one of the combined forces which led to this social change. It was a cause, at least as much as an effect. The Catholic Church, after all, had once forbidden divorce in order to protect women from what we now call wife-shucking, the random disposal of wives, especially older women and mothers with children. But as divorce became a more common choice many women who had believed in the security of marriage found themselves bereft in mid-life and mid-mothering. For them divorce was not a choice brought on by independence but a fait accompli which forced independence.

If being a housewife were a secure post with guaranteed tenure, there would always be applicants, women who thought it was a fair deal. There is a strong pull toward security in each of us. But by the late '60s it was difficult to believe in that security.

As the divorce statistics went up, more and more women had to face the reality of second-place status in the world. They became a vocal part of the political drive for equality. But even women who were married began to seek the security in paid jobs which they once sought in marriage.

Divorce had a rippling effect through communities and families. When one neighbor (or sister) watched another pushed into poverty or low-paid employment by divorce, that neighbor (or sister) felt anxious about her future too. That anxiety drove some toward Total Womanhood; it drove more toward economic independence. Divorce had become part of the realistic assessment of the future.

At the same time, the growing economic independence of women did make it easier for them to contemplate living alone, even raising their children alone. Divorce, like any other change, depends on whether or not a choice exists in the world or in the mind of an individual. It depends on the price tag pinned to that choice.

As Robert Weiss noted in *Marital Separation*, the women who were able to support themselves were less likely to go back to the marriage once they had separated. There were more women who were economically self-supporting. They became a role model of sorts for women who might otherwise not have dared to leave the most destructive of marriages. As the number of divorces increased, the visibility and social acceptability of that choice grew. Eventually a woman like Francine was very much affected.

FRANCINE: SEEING A CHOICE, MAKING A CHOICE

Francine was a woman who grew up with strict blinders on her vision of choice. But as an adult, she saw new social options and she made some of them. The major one was to divorce.

"Where I grew up, nobody got divorced. If your husband was a drunk, if he beat you up every Friday night, you told the neighbors that you got a black eye falling into the doorknob and that was it. You kept your mouth shut and you kept your husband," said Francine in her firm even voice, as she puffed on a cigarette.

Francine was divorced, the mother of four children, twelve to twenty-three, who drove a school bus during the winter and a camp bus in the summer so that she could attend college during the day. She and her children lived in a two-family house owned by her sister and brother-in-law. She was slim and short, no more than five feet two inches tall, and wore an Irish sweater over a turtle-neck—her driving outfit. She was an attractive dark-haired forty-one-year-old woman, from a huge Italian family—a family that was horrified when she, the eldest of the girls, announced that she was going to get divorced.

"There is this thing in my family about grit. Endurance. The endurance of pain. The endurance of suffering. This is the thing in my family. The value system. When I went to my mother and told her that I was leaving Tony, she couldn't believe it. She looked at me like I was crazy or something. She said to me, 'Francine, your Aunt Dee, her husband beat her for thirty years, regular, and they stayed together. Your grandmother stayed with my father when he was out every night with a different woman.

My own brother is married to a woman who is only sober on holidays. But they are all married. They kept their marriages together, Francine.'

"Finally, I looked up at my mother and said, 'Ma, are they happy? No. Are they leading decent lives? Are they going to die without ever once knowing any peace or contentment? Ma, look at me closely. I am about to break a tradition, God only knows how many hundreds of years old, a family tradition. I am going to break the longest line of martyrdom in Italian history.'"

Francine finished this story and leaned back in her kitchen on her metal kitchen chair and smiled, like someone who recited from memory a long soliloquy from a play. A woman with a sense of drama and excitement about her, she leaned forward again to repeat the last several lines from this scene:

"My mother didn't say anything for a long time. My mother is a good woman, she really is. It isn't easy for them, you know, all this change. Finally she looked up at me with tears coming out of her eyes and said, 'Francine, the Church . . . it's against the Church.' I said to her, real soft, I said, 'Ma, I'm telling you, Ma, as soon as they have married people, men and women in the Church giving out communion, hearing confession, as soon as that happens, then, *then*, I'll listen to what they have to say about marriage.' My mother looked at me, speechless. She told my sister later that she was sure I was going to hell in a handbasket."

It had taken Francine nearly thirty-eight years of her life to come to the point at which she felt she had to make her decisions. It had taken twenty years before she could choose to unmarry.

You see, Francine wasn't always a woman who felt that she had options in life. She was married at seventeen, halfway through her high school, and was a mother seven months later.

"I got married because I was pregnant. Half of my high school class had, you know, premature babies. Why is it that the first baby is always premature? I didn't want to get married. I wasn't in love with Tony. It was one of those things, I was so stupid. He told me he'd put it in a little way, that I would still be a virgin," she said, laughing now at her own naïveté. "What did

I know? Talk about your virgin mothers . . . But I never had any choice. Abortion? I never even heard of it, except for some woman in the neighborhood who would end up in the hospital because she tried to 'get rid of it' with a coat hanger or a scouring powder douche. That was the way people lived. They got pregnant and they got married and they got pregnant again."

This was simply the Way Things Were.

"I didn't plan to have one of my kids. I lived by the rhythm method. Sally was conceived before we were married. John was an accident. Diane came the night of the Feast of San Rocco. Then the little one, Chrissie, she's twelve, was also a mistake. After Chrissie, though, I started having what the women in my neighborhood used to call women's troubles. I talked about it with one of them and she told me that she had had a hysterectomy, and I could probably get one too. I mean it. That's what the Catholic women I knew did to get birth control. You know how many women I knew who had hysterectomies in their twenties and thirties? Jesus, half of them, two thirds of the women in my old neighborhood are walking around without any wombs, because *that*, the Church says, is okay. So, I had a hysterectomy."

Once Francine knew she would have no more children, she felt much greater control over her life, and began moving in new directions.

When her youngest was six years old, Francine started getting involved in community activities in their working-class suburb. It was the late '60s, and her husband, a trucker, was on the road much of the time. She became increasingly active, first in getting a playground in their neighborhood, then in organizing a group of women to fight the expansion of a road which would have made a thoroughfare out of the relatively quiet street they lived on.

"The thing was, with me and Tony, that we never saw each other. He was gone on the road a lot. I was busy. He was busy. We made sure that we weren't together much. When we were together we would yell and holler at each other. It got so that the kids couldn't wait for him to go back on the road. What did I need this guy for? I used to ask myself that. I would answer, he's the breadwinner. I need him for the money. Well, you know, that's a horrible thing to say to yourself. It's like they say, you are a whore then. If there's no love, you're a whore.

"Divorce never occurred to me, though. It was just not allowed. You got married, you stayed married. What I did, though, once Chrissie went to school, is that I got a job with a community action group."

Her first paid job gave her some self-confidence and was a conduit through which she met other community workers, women and men who were more educated, yet respected her opinions. "One weekend we went to this state conference and there was a women's workshop there; now this was 1971. We're sitting around and talking about some of the problems, in that humorous way, you know how women talk about their husbands sometimes, like they're kids they have to tolerate. Well, some of the other women, the radical types, they started in saying things like, 'Why are you married then?' And we'd come back with answers like, 'Because we're married. You get married, you stay married. He may be a rat, but he's my rat . . .'"

Francine got friendly with some of the other women, the "radical types" who would go to her home and talk with the family. "Tony didn't like my new friends. And while he was for the war in Vietnam, they were against it. He thought they were stuck-up. He didn't like it when I decided to finish high school. I was looking around and seeing if I could make it on my own. I was beginning to think I could do something different with my life."

As Francine began to work outside of the home, she became more upset that her husband wasn't helping inside the home.

"I was working and he was working. But even when he was home, he didn't lift a finger. He didn't lift a sock off the floor. Now before I went to work, I would get mad about something like that, but just inside. It would never show. Just inside. It was like I didn't think I had the right to get mad about that. I agreed it was my job to pick up the socks. Well, my girlfriend and I have talked about this a lot. Once you are working too, you figure you shouldn't have to take that. It got to be so that it was easier when he wasn't home. At least then, if I was doing everything by myself, I wasn't at the same time mad because he was sitting in a chair like an emperor."

In that, Francine was typical of the middleground woman who was Doing It All. But when a woman goes out to work, she almost invariably changes her attitude toward housework as "her work." In fact, one of the things that drives many women to outside work is this hatred of housework. Again and again divorced women told me, as Francine did later, "The best part about being divorced is that I don't have to take care of my husband, cook his meals, do his laundry, pick up his clothes . . . and be mad about it."

Two things happened which affected Francine very much. First, one of the women in Francine's office got divorced and that shocked her. Then Francine and her husband had an argument that she has never forgotten. "We were arguing about Vietnam. My boy, thank God, was too young, but we were arguing about the war and he was saying that he would be proud if John fought in Vietnam and I told him he was crazy and he was going on and on about how there was nothing wrong with our country, America, love it or leave it. I thought, my God, I'm married to this. You know how things start out as a political argument, and they're really personal arguments? You know what I mean? This one got pretty bad. The whole time we're arguing, I'm sitting there thinking, you know, I could get out of this, I don't have to be married. Look at Sylvie. She did it. My palms and hands were sweating, not because we're having a fight, I was used to that, but because I realized that I wanted to get a divorce. And as I'm sitting there, suddenly, he's also telling me that he doesn't like my working and that he's going to put a stop to it. Going to put a stop to it!

"I'm also saying to myself, Francine, you don't have to take this from him. Now, in my mother's generation, they would have said to themselves, you have to take this. If the man said to sit and stay, you sat and stayed. The man was in charge. What he said, you did. I used to act like that, now, that isn't the way it is anymore. Men aren't in charge of women. I know that. I thought of all the times I had sat in my mother's kitchen and heard my father tell her what to do and what not to do and demand this and that. And I thought, thank dear God, Mother Mary, and Joseph, I don't have to take that anymore."

It was two years and dozens of arguments later that Francine finally separated from her husband. It was two years from the moment when she truly felt that she had a choice to the moment when she made that new choice.

Although she never joined a women's group per se, Francine felt herself a part of this story of change. "Look, I never would have done this in another day. I needed a job, you know, and the idea that I wasn't the only woman who was raising her children alone. Nowadays, women give each other help, instead of dumping on each other. Nowadays, it's okay to be alone. I'm happier on my own. The kids are happier. I'm not saying that it wouldn't be nice to be in a good marriage. But it is much better on your own than fighting. This way, now I'm driving in the morning and the afternoon and I've started college. I never would have gone to college if I were still married to Tony. I don't feel ashamed, like I would have in my mother's day. I feel proud that I'm doing all these things and taking care of things. The thing I worry about most is money. Absolutely. If I had twenty thousand a year I wouldn't worry about anything. But aside from that, I think I really like being on my own."

The change in society had uncaged Francine's own sense of possibilities and options. The fact that she could find a job that paid ten thousand dollars a year—enough, with child support, to sustain her family—was crucial. So was the support for changing women's roles that had come from the general consciousness-raising of the women's movement. The existence of a larger group of divorced women meant that she was not a pariah and her children would not have as difficult a time as they might have had in the past. The problems of divorce were still enormous, but no longer overwhelmed her.

But Francine didn't just get divorced to leave an impossible situation. Like most divorced people, she had hope for a different future. "I wanted a better life. I didn't want to spend my whole life fighting. I didn't want to spend it with this man."

Francine's divorce was a story of her own growing-up process. In this time of rapid acceleration of divorce statistics, divorce is often accompanied by the sound of one person growing.

GROWING UP, GROWING AWAY

At the peak of the crisis in men's and women's roles, I knew some people who made a great leap out of their marriages. Some felt a flash of anger so intense that they had to get away. Others in the early '70s especially urged each other—daresies go first—to leave the "pig." They offered each other visions of a brave new world of opportunity and equality, of liberation, just outside the marital door.

But even those stories cast simplistically in terms of "The Women's Lib Wife Versus the Male Chauvinist Pig Husband" are tales of one person changing. The polarization between change innovator and change resister, which occurs in society as a whole, can also occur within homes. As some wives begin pressuring for change, some husbands dig in their heels and push against it.

Within that scenario, however, what is really happening? In part, women who are growing up need more room than can be found in their old roles. If the marriage is inflexible, they sense a harsh ceiling on their aspirations and on the future. Some are compelled to make room for themselves even if it means bursting out of their marriages.

BETTY: A LATE GROWTH SPURT

Betty understood that. It happened to her and to her husband. I met Betty in her Virginia apartment one Sunday afternoon. She was forty-and-doesn't-look-it, with a few crinkle lines around her eyes and some freckles that are renewed every summer along with her tennis serve. It was four years since her divorce, five and a half years since she began to get involved in the women's movement, four and a half years since she got her first full-time job.

Seated on her nubby, off-white modern sofa in a room decorated with turn-of-the-century posters and oak furniture, she talked, as her short hair fell in front of her eyes, brushing it back rhythmically, taking on and off her tortoise-shell glasses.

"Jack blames the divorce on my c-r group. He says I became

discontented, and then I got uppity and roared around being the career woman and forgot about him. That's his story, or it was his story. Maybe it's different now. My story? Well, I suppose the story I had was that he wanted me to be his little woman, sewing buttons on his shirts. Three years ago I would have told you he was just too chauvinistic, that he just couldn't see me, didn't give a hoot about my needs. Now, it's harder to be that simple about it. The whole 'he couldn't see me as a whole person' number. I guess I see it somewhat differently now. It seems to me more of a part of growing up. I had been assigned the child role, which is okay when you're a child. But I became a grownup."

Betty said her story was one of changing needs and an unchanging relationship. Abraham Maslow once listed human needs this way: "The things that people need as basic human beings are few in number. They need a feeling of protection and safety, to be taken care of when they are young so that they feel safe. Second, they need a feeling of belongingness, some kind of family, clan, or group of something that they feel they are in and belong to by right. Third, they have to have a feeling that people have affection for them, that they are worth being loved. And fourth, they must experience respect and esteem. And that's about it."

At one point in life, someone may need most a sense of belongingness. At one time a relationship may fill one category of needs, while leaving another empty. A relationship that fosters a sense of security may eventually threaten a sense of respect or self-esteem. As Betty slowly learned, that may force people into a hard choice.

"I had a very traditional childhood, cookies and milk after school, that kind of thing. The only thing I remember my parents argued about was sending me to college. I knew that my mother was the one who made my father pay for me to go, too, not just my brothers. I remember being so surprised at that. I never heard her fight with my father, and for her to do that for me, for something I wanted, I was very grateful for that. I suppose, inside all of that grow-up-and-get-married stuff, she also wanted me to have more than she had. But she didn't know how or what. Neither did I for a long, long time. I was graduated from college, I'd done well and I was scared. I didn't have any idea what I wanted to do. I had that sense that I had to have a terrific job, if I was going to have a job, or get married and take any old job. I met Jack and we were married three months later and I took a crummy job as a secretary in a tire company, of all things, and convinced myself that it didn't matter because my real life, my real self-image, was in being married.

"Jack was looking for a home, he was eight years older than I. He was thirty then and he'd been living on his own for twelve years and he wanted someone to come home to, he wanted a wife, you know. I wanted a reason to not have to try."

Betty paused and lit a cigarette and looked up a bit sheepishly. "I remember for a long time, in my group, we all went through the number, 'If it hadn't been for you I would have been . . .' I did it too. I am ashamed of that. It wasn't honest. It was easy. If it hadn't been for Jack, it would have been Tom, Dick, or Harry. That's the truth. I was determined to get married and retire. I retired. First to this secretarial thing and then a couple of years later to home and first Robby, then Mickey, then Lucy."

She chose safety and belongingness. At that time the traditional role also gave her a sense of worth. "I think of it as decorating. I kept accumulating things. It was a joke between us. The coffee table was filled with things. The tops of the buffets, the dining room table, all kinds of little knickknacks. I remember this odd feeling I had as I got involved in my group—I started clearing off the tops of things and throwing things away. I threw away ashtrays and little wooden boxes and a collection of porcelain eggs. Anything that was too expensive to discard, I wrapped up and put away in a trunk and when I finally moved I sold all those things or gave them to my brother's wife. It was like all the clutter you accumulate in life not to see the grain of wood in the table top."

Gradually "belongingness" began to feel like a trap.

In her marriage, Betty organized the house around her husband's comings and goings and comforts. The kids were not allowed to be watching television when Jack came home. They were all scrubbed and waiting for him. His return from work, "sacred work," was greeted at the end of the day "like something out of Dick, Jane, and Spot. I was Spot.

"Then, in 1972 one of the women in the car pool for Lucy got involved with the women's movement. I had always liked her, she had stuff and we'd been friends, sort of, the way that women are when they call up about the kids, you end up on the phone with each other for a while. It's funny, that's how a lot of women get to know each other. Anyway, she started going to a group.

"Somehow or other, I knew the minute I went to that group that I was using it to help me move. I never thought of moving out of my marriage, but I did think of moving out of being a housewife. I shared some of the things with Jack but, I'll be honest, not much. He began to have the sense that what we did in the group was compare notes about husbands, that I was violating the marriage contract by talking with strangers about our marriage. You know, Jack is a good man and all he ever wanted was to come home to his little wife and his little kids and, in a way, I was terribly unfair to him. I stopped being his little wife. But in another way, how do you get the right to think of a mate as 'the wife.' I mean, I have the guilt, because I was the one who changed the rules. But the rules were unbelievable."

Betty was aware that she changed unilaterally. The women's movement was her single sex change agent. There were other couples in her group who managed to alter their roles within their marriages. But Betty seemed to think that they had some glue which was missing from her own marriage. "Either they had a kind of commitment to each other or love for each other that saw them through this time, or they were flexible people. Perhaps their marriages weren't as rooted in functions. The you-do-this and I-do-that number. Maybe they were better at answering the questions together."

The nature of consciousness-raising is to question everything. Question the contract, question the status quo. And make changes.

Among the rules Betty started to rewrite were those about her children. She no longer insisted that they stand in place as a welcoming committee when "he came home from the hunt with the deer slain." She no longer behaved as if he had "the real" job and she should be grateful for being supported.

But the other rules were more subtle. Betty didn't ask her husband's opinion all the time as a manipulative way of getting approval for what she wanted to do or buy. She began acting more and more on her own. In their sex life, she began to say no sometimes and other times to initiate sex. But rarely did she and her husband talk about these changes.

"We were both avoiding confrontations. The idea was that as long as nothing was actually said, out in the open, we could go along."

The one thing that she did have to talk about was taking a part-time job. "I was desperate for some positive feedback. I really looked at the job as a way of saving my marriage. I also wanted to work. But I thought if I don't do something I'm really going to blow everything out of the water. I'm going to go crazy."

At this point, Betty was lucky enough for a good job to fall into her lap. She was offered a position working three days a week with a federal agency that dealt with the arts.

"I was incredibly excited and also terrified. I had no idea whether or not I could run anything, although I had run some volunteer fund-raising programs for the arts and had organized some exhibits for volunteer groups. But this job was perfect. It involved dealing with museums and art and I was dying to have it."

Sometimes Betty wanted to be the Vision of Independence; other times she wished she could still be comfortably coupled. But her self-esteem began to hinge on following a new set of possibilities, on risk. In a sense, as she initiated change, Jack was forced to respond. He also had to make choices which he had not initiated and which he didn't like. At this point the pattern of response became crucial to the relationship and Betty's husband chose to resist.

Instead of accommodating, they polarized—the change innovator and the change resister.

"This is a crazy story now. I had an interview for that job on a Wednesday. I had a babysitter, the one I used two days after school and I had told Jack I'd need the car for the day. I'd talked about the job to him. He didn't like the idea, but he said as long as the kids were all right, he wouldn't oppose it.

"Anyway, the morning of my interview, Jack, who was supposed to have arranged a ride, just drove off in the car. I can't tell you how stunned I was. It was ten o'clock and I was due there at eleven. I called Jack and screamed at him and told him to come out and get me, how could he have forgotten? And suddenly—you talk about clicks—I realized that he had sabotaged me. Consciously or not. I put the phone down and said, this is it. I have two choices. I go and take that job and let what happens happen, or I don't take the job and I stay inside this house for the rest of my life.

"I was on the line. I was shaking. I called a cab and borrowed money from my next-door neighbor—oh yes, he had also forgotten to leave me money—and went. How I ever got the job I won't know. I was shaking like a leaf.

"When I came home, after dinner, I could hardly speak to Jack, but I told him I had the job. He looked at me very levelly, and in a deadly calm voice he said, 'If you take that job, I will leave you.' Nobody believes that, but he did. It's too classic, isn't it? But he did. 'If you take that job, I'll leave.'

"Well, I did take the job and he didn't leave but he kept looking at me as if I were a new creature. Actually, I was two creatures. I was really feeling so good at the office, but so bad in my relationship with Jack. It was such a contrast. It's as if there were two people—this interesting vital person at work and this unhappy, scared, skittish person walking around depressed and cautious at home."

Her husband began to seem like the person pulling her down. She felt simultaneously his disapproval, the limitations of the relationship, and a growing number of options for her own separate life. Under these conditions, it gradually became easier (though not easy) for her to divorce her husband than to remain with him.

"We were still living in that house like two zombies that walk around each other. I started to become obsessed about how I would support the children by myself. What was my right to independence if I couldn't be economically independent? While I was thinking that, you understand, Jack was thinking, if she can earn her own living, what does she need me for? I was thinking if he only wants me to be a washer and dryer, he doesn't love me, and he was thinking, if she doesn't want to take care of me and be taken care of by me, she doesn't love me. We had come down to the roots of our marriage.

"Now that kind of rawness, that real vulnerability, the sense that you've gotten down to it at last can be the end or the beginning. It depends on a lot of things. As far as I was concerned it made me realize that after we stripped away the roles and saw each other as we really are, the fact is we don't want each other.

"In the end the women's movement made both of us confront reality. It isn't always a pretty thing to do. When we met as two human beings, there was nothing to keep us there."

While Betty wanted something different, her husband didn't. In fact, eventually he made only the changes of substitution.

Four years after their divorce, the differences in their lives were revealing. Betty lived in a Virginia suburb of Washington with two of her three children—the third was in college—and was unmarried. She had some relationships with men, but not "the one"; she was "hopeful that maybe . . ."

Jack remarried three months after their divorce was final. Because of child support payments and college tuition, this time Jack couldn't afford a full-time housewife-wife. His wife, who was twenty-six when they married, worked, but very carefully. She was home and cooking supper for him and keeping the house. They were saving what money they could, because Janet wanted to have children and they figured that in a few years they would be able to afford to have her quit her job.

"You know sometimes I look at the way he's set up the same thing all over again, and I think, Jesus Christ, that poor son of a bitch could be going through this whole thing again in ten to fifteen years!" said Betty.

Betty was given a new sense of possibility, new standards to judge her life by and new hope. Eventually her husband pushed her to choose "between him and me" as she put it. She chose herself.

"The truth is, I went where it felt best, where I felt best."

If the women's movement changed her, it made her feel stronger and she went with her strength.

In the past it was very common for men to feel they had outgrown the wives they had married in college. As these men went on to graduate school and into professional or business life, their wives stayed in place. Eventually, the Washington senator became uncomfortable with his hometown sweetheart. The surgeon had nothing to say to the wife who had put hubby through medical school and then became involved in homemaking.

But now there is a switch. Now it is often the wives like Betty who outgrow their husbands. Sometimes this happens as the woman rises in her professional career. Sometimes it happens as she grows freer and more self-confident, as she feels more exposed to the world than in the past.

Betty wanted room to grow as an individual, but there are others, women and men, who want their marriages to grow. The women's movement has encouraged many to want more, not only for themselves but from their relationships. Some, like a woman named Lisa, become increasingly discontented with the traditional emotional relationship.

LISA AND SOL: THE RAISED EXPECTATIONS EXIT

"Look, if you think marriage is a relationship between a husband supporter and wife housekeeper, that he does his bit and she does her bit, and it is essentially like a deal, a working deal, then sometimes it changes because one person isn't sticking to his or her end of the deal. But it can also change because one person wants more than a deal out of it."

This remark came from a very intense, divorced woman named Lisa, tall and rail-thin with curly red hair.

I had made appointments to see Lisa on one day and her ex-husband on the other. Both of them agreed that they had not even seen eye-to-eye on the reasons for divorce, and would talk about it.

Lisa described herself to me as a young romantic who had set-

tled into being a wife. Her apartment looked like it was created
by someone who was half the "young romantic" and half the
fifty-five-year-old executive of an international service agency.
The peace posters and Mexican art managed somehow to fit in
with the colonial furniture she had acquired along the way. And
the kitchen in which we shared coffee was both efficient and full
of vegetables and fruits hanging in wire baskets. She had been
living in this apartment in Chicago for nearly a year since she
had broken up her home and her twenty-seven-year-old marriage.

She had left, she said, because she had seen the possibility of
another kind of relationship. "Over the years," said this woman
who is fifty-five, and has a tremendous nervous vitality, "I had
come to terms with the fact that, well, this was the way men
were, this was the way relationships were. It was very difficult
for Sol to express his feelings. It was very difficult for him if I expressed mine in front of him."

She recalled years of self-monitoring. But the worst time was
when she was forty-five. "That was the year my father died. The
kids were teenagers then and I was still at home and I would be
chauffeuring them to art class or to school, wherever. What I remember most clearly during that time was that the kids would get
out of the car to go to class and I would go home and cry. I
mourned for my father in my station wagon. I cried for him going
back and forth. I couldn't cry about it in front of Sol, he really
expected me to get over it quickly. In fact, when his father died
I never saw him cry. In fact, in our whole marriage I never, ever,
once saw him cry. I suppose I must have been lonely for that kind
of thing for twenty-five years. But I didn't know there was anything else.

"I have to say that for better and for worse, the women's
movement showed me that while this might be normal behavior,
culturally normal behavior, it was psychologically sick. I shared
the kind of intimacy with the women I met in the movement that
I was so greedy for. I didn't expect that. When I got into the
group I thought I was already liberated. I was working by then
and we never had any trouble about that. Sol liked me to work
. . . he never approved of the bridge-playing set. But I was

stunned, by feelings. All these feelings came up. I had buried so many of them, sexual feelings, the need for comfort and warmth and sharing.

"I tried to bring that home. I suppose I started being aggressive for caring. Sol got very frightened—it *must* have been scary. You go from a marriage in which you spend a lot of evenings watching television and talking over the kids. Then, the kids are in college and your wife is suddenly at you for feelings. After all those years, I wanted more. I wanted to be important to him emotionally, to have a kind of intimacy that wasn't the sort of side-by-side in the warm glow of the television set. I started talking to him about the conditioning of men, more than the conditioning of women.

"He withdrew more and more. I compared my marriage, not to others, but to what I thought was possible between a man and a woman. Around that time I had an affair. It was an affair out of this terrible loneliness, both for me and for the other man. It was our affair to get out of our marriages. Well, it was very intense and brief and crazy in some ways. But it reinforced my feeling that it was possible to have a truly intimate relationship. It made me feel what was missing in my marriage."

Gradually Lisa began to believe that breaking up her long, long marriage was a less painful alternative than living with that sense of loneliness and emptiness. Very often, when people begin to want "more," the status quo feels like "less." And this was true for her.

There was a time when Lisa lost hope in her ability to change her relationship. She came to a turning point when she had to choose between the status quo and change.

"It's been a relief, in many ways," said Lisa. "At the very least, I have stopped 'wanting' something I couldn't get. It's almost a relief to give up trying to change someone else, walking around 'wishing.'"

Sol's story was a different one. He talked about it the next Sunday afternoon in his bachelor apartment which was the opposite of Lisa's. His home was still sparsely furnished. When he offered coffee, he had to search around for two clean cups and for the instant coffee jar, which he found in the nearly empty refrigerator. It was obvious that Sol was still unable or unwilling to make a real home for himself outside of marriage. He ate meals in the downstairs restaurant or the coffee shop near his office. But when he finally collected the mugs, the instant coffee and dry cream, he gave his side:

"All I can tell you is that before she was in this women's lib, our marriage was very good. We enjoyed doing the same things, we shared the children, we liked each other, she liked me. Then she got in there with a bunch of other women all complaining about their husbands and she didn't like me. She complained that I wasn't open enough, I didn't talk to her enough, I didn't cry or take walks in the rain. Why should I take walks in the rain at fifty-eight years old? She bought me a pair of jeans and was hurt that I wouldn't wear them. I feel like an ass in blue jeans.

"I don't know if she ever loved me, but I do know that she stopped loving me. She wanted me to be something I wasn't. Something I'm not. She got me to go to the therapist with her, and this guy started asking me about sex and how I felt about my life and I didn't feel bad about it. Nobody believed me that I liked our life. I liked going out with our friends, although Lisa started getting a whole new group of friends, sitting on the floor and getting stoned with some people half our age. You know what I think? She just wanted to have an affair. The women in her group encouraged her to be free, go out and get laid. So eventually she went out and got laid. I was sitting at home worrying about whether she was all right and she was out getting laid by some half-assed, forty-year-old professor of something or other.

"I didn't want this divorce. I want my wife back. But she doesn't exist, does she? I want her back the way she was and it's impossible. She's changed so much, it can't ever be."

A gap had opened between Lisa and Sol as wide as the difference in their two "divorce stories." Lisa's tale was one of emotional growth and loss. For her, there was a moment when divorce was easier than living within the status quo. Sol, who didn't want change, who simply couldn't change, considered himself to be the victim of it.

But it isn't always innovators, like Lisa, who initiate divorce.

It can also be the staunchest defender of the status quo. There are some men and women who reject any alteration in their role. In that sense, their resistance to change leads to a crisis. Their attempt to hold on to "sameness" motivates disruption.

In resisting one change, men like Talbott become the agents of another. Talbott, whose identity was grafted onto the male role, eventually decided that if he could not be the dominant spouse, "the man of the house," he would not be a spouse at all.

TALBOTT: THE CHANGE RESISTER'S DIVORCE

Talbott had been a member by birth of the southern aristocracy. Tall, blond, with chiseled features of generations of Anglo-Saxon in-breeding, he had grown up in Atlanta. The others in his clan had lived with servants and horses and hunting dogs. But Talbott hadn't had those things. He'd had the name without the money. He was, in fact, poor southern aristocracy. When he was small his father had died and his family had been reduced to what was familiarly known as genteel poverty. It seemed brutal to Talbott. He grew up hungry for the money and the status that came with his name, his "birthright" that had been taken away from him.

Talbott went to the best schools on scholarships, and attended, in the 1950s, the sort of tea dances where the men wore white gloves. He went through Chapel Hill and then business school with a single-mindedness that was softened only by exquisite manners, a capacity to make amusing conversation with his superiors, charming rapport with their wives, and ability to play intellectual games with his peers.

Except for the fact that she was intriguing, and rather exotically attractive, Nancy was an odd girl for him to marry. After years of dating "belles"—moneyed, secure, southern women of Chapel Hill and Louisiana—he married the daughter of a second-generation Lebanese family with little money and much education. She was intelligent and far more attractive, in a dark, black-haired, lithe way, than she knew. A woman who considered it a stroke of luck to be married to someone like Talbott.

Nancy was determined that she would do everything she could to make him happy. His demands on her were great; her demands on herself were even greater.

Over the years, he urged her to become a gourmet cook, a top horseback rider, and to run the house with the graciousness that fit his status. At the same time he criticized her failings ruthlessly. One year he bought her contact lenses for her birthday, although she had never been concerned about her glasses. On her thirtieth birthday, he bought her a series of facials.

Nancy believed that if she worked harder she could please her husband. She invited the "right" people to dinner, joined the "right" clubs, she moved to the "right" neighborhood in Atlanta.

During all of this, Talbott was working in his investment firm, focused almost totally on making it. The system he worked under was a pyramid one. There were the partners above him whom he had to please personally as well as professionally. There were secretaries below him. With them he had a reputation for being abrupt, thoughtless, making demands. Also, there was his small group of male peers, who were his competition.

When he finally became a partner, he was thirty-five years old and Nancy was thirty-two. They had two small children and a mortgage on their new house in Atlanta. And Nancy was unhappy.

"The least Nancy could have done through all this was to take care of the kids and the house and not complain," Talbott said. "I had all this pressure on me and then there was Nancy wanting more, putting more pressure on."

Talbott felt that her role was to be supportive, to take responsibilities for the home off of him cheerfully, to be his secretary at home with the children, to leave him free for his grueling schedule.

At the same time, Talbott used to like to complain about "what an easy deal" Nancy had. He began to resent her "freedom." His resentment increased with her unhappiness. Unhappiness that he wasn't home every night. That he didn't spend time with the children, that she felt stuck.

Talbott began to feel hemmed in by the demands of his

profession—"Look, I never had any choice in all this. If you want to be a partner, you have to go through this."

He began to make it more and more difficult for Nancy to have any choice, any freedom of her own. He refused to have a housekeeper or a home closer to the heart of the city. He made it hard for her to find babysitters so she could do part-time work—"I figured that she should pay for it, if she wanted someone to take her job then she should have been able to pay for it." He insisted upon dinner parties, and he made biting, disparaging remarks about her competency when the dinner didn't go well. Nancy remembers one night when she used a tablecloth with a stain and put a candlestick over the stain. In front of the company, he made a sarcastic joke about her "housekeeping."

The thought began to solidify in his mind that he had simply married the wrong woman. He should have married a member of southern society, content to oversee the state of the tablecloths.

The last straw was when Nancy began to give up the impossible task of pleasing him. She still wanted the marriage to work out, but through therapy, through misery, she began to realize that it wasn't just her problem. There was the day when she threw away the tranquilizers.

Though Nancy never became a card-carrying member of a women's group, their ideas took shape in her mind. She began to see herself and her husband as victims. And when she needed support for change, there were her old college friends to convince her that she was right and Talbott was a "throwback."

On her own, Nancy went back to school, where she had always felt right, confident, and secure about herself. She found a day care center to take care of the children in return for her putting in some time. Then after Jennie was in school and Talbott, Jr., was in a half-day nursery program, she took a part-time job.

During all this, she was still very careful. In fact, Nancy did everything in the house, as well as her job. There were a few things, however, that she refused to do now. "I didn't get up and make him dinner when he got home after midnight meetings. I didn't make excuses for him to the children. If they asked me why Daddy wasn't home, I told them to ask him."

And they had a low running battle over who was in charge of seeing that his shirts got to and from the laundry. Nancy took one of those odd stands of principle on the matter of the shirts.

"It got so that Talbott would go out and buy himself new shirts—cotton ones, he didn't believe in drip dry—rather than pick up the ones at the laundry. I told him I would pick them up, but he would have to take them." It was funny and it was deadly serious.

Nancy still felt enormously tied to her husband, but she no longer felt proud of that tie.

The night that I first met them was one of the last they were together. As we talked, their histories and relationship came into shape slowly. Then in front of me there was a startlingly vicious exchange, and the evening degenerated into a scene from Edward Albee's play *Who's Afraid of Virginia Woolf?* Now forty years old, the product of a lock-step life that had brought him to a successful partnership, Talbott was into his fourth scotch and talking wildly, out of control.

He began to discuss the women's movement. "I don't know why women would go to those meetings where pretty soon some other woman has her hand up her skirt. I'm not saying they're all a bunch of dykes, but the movement is ruled by them. Now I can understand, maybe some women who've been involved with a bunch of premature ejaculators would turn to other women for sex. But they aren't normal. Normal women aren't like that."

He continued, laughing, into an analysis of why Nancy was the "wrong woman," for him, as she sat, passively, like someone who'd been struck.

"A woman like Nancy shouldn't marry a businessman like me who needs a wife at home to take care of the kids and the house and the things he's too busy to deal with. He needs a wife who'll understand that he's busy and that his work comes first. Around here, I can make a million-dollar deal and come home and find out that Nancy is mad at me because I didn't pick up the shirts.

"Nancy doesn't have the vaguest understanding of my career. If I'm not available to take care of customers, pretty soon we don't have this house, the car, vacations, anything. I can't be sharing housework like some asshole and say, 'No, I'm terribly sorry, I can't talk to the head of IBM, I'm doing the vacuuming.' She wants the money I make, but not the responsibility for the home. She wants to get out of her job. Well, fuck that, there are times when I would like to get out of my responsibility too, but I can't and neither can she."

Talbott had locked himself in so tightly that he bitterly resented any measure of freedom around him, and any further demands on his own life. He felt that choice had been wiped out of his life. The only changes he could tolerate in his marriage were those in favor of the most rigid traditional roles, the ones that offered him service and status.

Finally, he was the one who walked out. "I blame it on Nancy. I warned her that if she couldn't get off my back, I wouldn't stay with her."

This most traditional man embarked on a radical amputation of his family. He wiped his life clean of them and rarely even sees the children. In some of the best restaurants in the South, he can be heard blaming his divorce on Women's Lib.

THE DISRUPTIVE CHANGE RESISTERS

Talbott resisted change right out of his marriage. His relationship, indeed his capacity to love his wife, had been based on a dominant-and-submissive relationship. As his wife began to come gradually out of her role, he felt his own power erode and with it his "love."

The hardest part of these stories of divorce is the effect of change on the rather mysterious bonding we call love. There is clearly an emotional tie which helps one couple withstand all kinds of buffeting in the world. There are also more fragile bonds and, on the other hand, more powerful winds of change.

"People fell in love with one person and found themselves ten years later with another," says a Boston marital counselor. "Some didn't want to relearn that person. They found it easier to start all over again."

There were others who fell in love as one person and found themselves ten years later becoming another person.

But it isn't always women who play the role of change innovators, and men who resist (even to the point of divorce). There is also something you might call a Men's Lib Divorce. At least Zack thinks so.

MEN'S LIB DIVORCE

Zack is a large expansive man who would fill the "ethnic quota" on any writer's panel in New York. At thirty-eight, he still fought weight—"No one ever called me slim on the streets, you know"—and could eat and drink any of his friends under the table of the neighborhood restaurant. He was a man who was raised under the eleventh commandment—"Thou shalt be guilty"—and just now is beginning to drop the mantle of guilt and responsibility that he took on when he was a child, the boy-child, the eldest in his Polish family.

"Where I came from, work wasn't 'work experience' that would look good on your application to Harvard University. The four-fifty a week you got from schlepping the goddamn newspapers around and collecting the fees—I was a teenage collector, it sounds like something from the autobiography of a mafia chief—that money meant the difference between spaghetti and meat."

Zack wanted to get out of his environment and the only route open to him was education—"due to the fact that I couldn't get a basketball scholarship. That was the only way you got out of my neighborhood, through brains or athletics, and I am the only kid in the block who could miss the basket forty-two consecutive times."

He became a writer, a storyteller, reworker of the tales of childhood, using the dialect of his neighborhood. The stories made him a modest success by his mid-twenties. They also helped him find a wife. "Priscilla. The Golden Wasp." "I couldn't believe that someone with blond hair would look at me with my puss. She was gorgeous and cool and refined. I always felt nervous around her that I would slurp my soup or burp at the wrong time, but, Jesus, I fell in love with her. My self-destructive streak, I guess.

"She wanted a steady income and I was enough of a traditional schmuck to think that I was a bastard unless I provided her with it. It was the country club and the tennis lessons and all this crap. The house with the lawn—me, with a lawn? I've got allergies—and then after it was the expensive schools and the stuff for the kids."

He gave up writing his stories and took a job in California writing for ad agencies and then television scripts. "The ultimate thing was that I actually once bought a three-piece, pinstripe suit to please her. I was on my way to becoming a damn executive. I would have had plastic surgery on my stomach to please her, to be a Man."

When Zack hit thirty-six, he suddenly felt, "I'm on the wrong track. I look around me and I see relationships, I mean marriages where the husband and wife are pulling together and where the guy is able to do what he wants with his life, because maybe his wife gets a job for a while and helps, because maybe his wife doesn't want him to be Robert Redford."

Zack became more aware of his own needs, as he finally went through a long therapy. "I went to a shrink. Now, where I came from you only went to a shrink if you were sitting in a corner counting butterflies. But my friend Paul, who was a guy I went drinking with, told me one day that he had been through therapy and he was now only mildly nuts. I figured if Paul could do this, and get something out of it, what the hell, I could. I wasn't Mr. Together."

This therapist, as Zack described him, convinced him that "I had been put in a male role and they'd thrown away the key. He said such earth-shattering things as: 'Where was it written that you had to be the sole support of your wife and children? Where was it written that she was in charge of the children and you couldn't have a relationship with them the way you wanted it? Where was it written that you had to support her in the style to which she wanted to become accustomed? Where was it written that I didn't get to live my own life?'"

So Zack wanted to change. His wife didn't. "Have you any idea what it's like to tell a woman who's looking forward to a life of developing her overhand smash, that you don't want to work your ass off to pay for the country club? For a guy like me to tell his wife to get off her ass and help out? To move out of the fancy neighborhood, to take a chance on his talent, to let me do what I want to do? Shit, it was very tough. Talk about guilt. I was drowning in it, but I was determined. I wasn't going to let my life go down the toilet."

Many things had happened to Zack. He realized that he didn't feel loved for who he was, but for what he could provide. He had also begun to lose respect for Priscilla. He compared her to the other women he knew who had energy and ambition of their own. Now that the children were both in school, he no longer felt that she was justified in her life choices. "The truth was that I began to feel that she was a leech."

For two more years, Zack tried to change their relationship. He spent more time at home, more with the children. Because he had always loved cooking, he now took charge of it. But Priscilla couldn't move. She half-heartedly took a course or two, but she was increasingly resentful and resistant.

He took a less-pressured job teaching and started writing stories again, oiling the rusty creativity of his youth. Then, unilaterally, he made a series of decisions. Their income was halved, and he found that they could live on it if they moved to a less lavish home, or sent the children to public school. "I always felt uncomfortable with the private-school thing. The kids never got a sense of the real world."

But Priscilla's resentment was such that they finally were feuding and arguing, most of the time about "his responsibilities."

"She had always given me sex as a reward for being a good boy. It was a pat on my head for behaving well. When I stopped behaving well, I was cut off in bed too."

A gap grew between Zack and Priscilla. He changed in ways that made him more comfortable with himself and less comfortable with Priscilla. It was as if he and she loved different "Zacks."

"I had to choose between being the guy she loved, or the guy I loved. Now, I mean, I have to be able to live with me. That's more important than being able to live with Priscilla—and that sentence only cost me $5,700 in therapy." Zack laughed.

Later he put it this way: "If someone only loves you in the

role you're playing, and that role isn't the real you, then, how the
hell can you con yourself into thinking they really love you?
They just want someone to play the damn role."

Months after they split, Priscilla remarried. Her second husband is an executive in the television business and they live with
her daughter in a plush suburb.

Zack now lives with his son in a small apartment in San Francisco. He wrote one television script "for the rent money" and
spends the rest of the time working on a novel that is nearly
finished, about growing up Polish but Protestant in Cleveland.

"Priscilla thinks I'm a nut, to this day. I am a nut, that I grant
you, but this divorce is the sanest thing I ever did. I have felt
more comfortable in the last year than in the twelve years before
that."

Very few of the people I interviewed felt that their divorce
had been a tragic error.

Lisa, the oldest of the women in this chapter, who had emotionally outgrown her husband, felt that she might never find
what she wanted in a man in her own age group. Yet she was not
regretful.

The others acknowledged that divorce was the most disruptive
experience of their lives, but when asked if it was worth it,
responded that it was. Some felt that they could not have
changed within their marriages the way they have outside of
them. As one woman put it: "The fact is I'd rather be the person
I am today, even alone, than the person I was three years ago,
with my husband. It's a tough thing to say, but there you are."

So while many people in the middleground fear change because it might bring with it the loss of divorce, many of the people who had been divorced said that they had already suffered
an intense sense of loss within their marriages before they ended.
For them, divorce, however disruptive, was often experienced as
the change of reintegration.

But the most difficult, the most painful decision comes when
the alternatives seem most evenly balanced, when it is obvious
that the decision to remain in the status quo and the decision to
disrupt that status quo are both perilous.

In the intersection between competing losses, the most tragic divorces seem to be those in which the relationship is disrupted, despite a very strong love. For these people, the pain involved in staying within the marriage is almost evenly balanced with the pain of separating from it, and divorce is the saddest and most crisis-loaded change.

THE ANDREWSES: A MARRIAGE THAT FELL BETWEEN THE CRACKS

For the Andrewses, separation has not been a "creative" experience but a wrenching loss. They were among the people whose marriages were casualties of timing, the people who may have just missed going through change together. After meeting both of them, I was convinced that they never fell out of love. They fell out of synch.

Today their separation finds Theresa, thirty-eight, living on the East Coast, and John, forty, in his home in a western city that annually makes the Ten Most Livable Cities list.

From the beginning they were almost symbiotically matched. John was the son of a businessman and a librarian, who named him after the poet she admired so much. He was a boy who grew up alone in his mother's affection and attention until his sister was born ten years later. John was the one who was admired and "expected" to achieve. It was no surprise when he was the only one in his town to be accepted to Yale.

Theresa was the eldest child of a working-class family in New Haven, born to a young mother; she grew up taking care of the children who came along after her. No one catered to Theresa. She went to college on a fluke and a scholarship.

She and John met each other at a concert at her college in Connecticut. John, tall with reddish hair, and Theresa, short and dark with expressive hands and brown eyes, began a volatile romance. "When I met John," said Theresa twenty years later, "I didn't want to be serious with him, because he wasn't a Catholic. We had different ideas about lots of things. He was very passionate and really it was the first time I had been involved with anyone that emotional who really romanced me. He even sent me poetry. We always argued and fought. It was a challenge for me to be with someone like that. I didn't like to be bored, and we were never bored."

Theresa talked about the marriage haltingly, with a great deal of feeling now, six months after she left it. We met in her New Haven apartment, a far cry from the elegant home she'd left behind. Her home now is brightly colored but furnished from Salvation Army stock.

"My husband was an only child until he was ten. He was accustomed to receiving a lot of attention. His mother devoted her whole life to him and they expected a lot from him. All eyes were focused on him . . . I was used to giving and not expecting much. It was a perfect match," she said, with just a hint of an ironic smile.

Theresa and John were married while he was in law school. Almost immediately she became pregnant.

By the time he was through law school they had two children and she was pregnant again. That was when they moved back to John's hometown. "We never really talked about it. It was John's decision," says Theresa. "That's the way it was then really. You had to go where your husband's bread and butter was."

It took Theresa six grueling years taking care of three and then four children before she could even tolerate living in this town, so far from home, in a house that was isolated from the city, and from any other young mother and children. She and John drifted apart as his life became increasingly involved in law practice, hers with the children.

"I was alone so much," she said. "I was alone all the time. I remember one sweltering hot day, I had one baby in a little car bed and another one in the bedroom and the third was in my arms and the fourth was in my stomach and it was a hundred degrees and I started to cry hysterically. My life was out of control. I remember thinking that I had been trapped in another body."

John was literally never home. He worked from eight in the morning to nine or ten in the evening. He worked weekends. "He'd go to work, he'd come home for supper, go back at night, work on Saturdays—and on Sundays, we'd go visit his relatives. That was life.

"It was very sad. I kept thinking: now is the test to see the value of my liberal arts education, if I can survive this without going crazy. I was reading things about people being in solitary confinement or being in Korea and I compared myself to that. This was a test to see if I had enough inner resources."

Throughout all of this, she and John had an intense attachment to each other which both have described as "mystical." But Theresa seemed to live in a perpetual state of wanting more from her husband, while he seemed increasingly compelled to remove himself from his romanticism and to be rational and "strong" and a successful lawyer. The more successful he became the more remote he became.

"Whenever we had a discussion I would comment, and he'd say, 'What's your source?' I'd say, I think it was the *Ladies' Home Journal* and he would play the lawyer with me, putting me down, making me be logical."

The one thing Theresa did was to read. In the early 1960s she even read *The Feminine Mystique*. But the book disturbed her so thoroughly that she could only read a little bit at a time, putting it down, feeling angry and frustrated.

Somewhere in the mid-'60s after their fourth child was born, Theresa "took control" of her "stranger's body." "In this state it was a crime to talk about birth control. The doctor wasn't allowed to mention it. You had to initiate it. I didn't know that. I was too naïve. Besides, I was still a practicing Catholic. The pill had just come out then and I called the priest and asked him if it was all right. He said, 'Well, you can take it to get your period regular.' That's all I needed. I took it. I said, 'My God, this is what it's like for other people who don't have to worry. It's such freedom. I don't care if I ever get regular.'"

She and her husband had always had a strong sexual relationship, even during the worst times, and now they could have sex without terror. She describes this as a pivotal change in her life, a taste of freedom and choice.

But it also prompted her to start questioning everything in her religious past. "I had been devout, but it started crumbling. It took me two years to come to a decision. But then I said, 'That's it.' I left the Church. When I go through changes, I seem to do it abruptly. But a lot of thinking had gone into it."

In the '6os her husband became involved in politics and Theresa herself started meeting new people. She was pulled into organizations, went speaking before community groups, and slowly began gaining self-confidence. "This was John Birch country and I had to put up with a lot of attacks because we were liberal. But doing it was great for me."

She made a circle of friends from her political work. They weren't intimates, but women she liked. By the early '70s, when she was in her thirties, she began to hear more about the women's movement and gravitated to it naturally.

"I didn't join a consciousness-raising group. I started one. We got together at my house and talked. We weren't going to call it something awful like Women's Lib. We called it a book group."

Theresa couldn't explain exactly why she started this book group except that "I wanted something to explain my life. I had that feeling there was a thread and if I could only pull it, I could unravel the problems."

She wanted to unravel the problems, not her marriage. She wanted more of John, not less, and more in her life, not less.

"I remember one of the first things we did. We went around in a circle and said, 'If you just had yourself to consider alone, what is it that you would do to make yourself happy?'"

This was as subversive a question as any of them had ever asked themselves. "These were mostly women who were married and had children. I remember one woman started to cry. She said, 'I can't think of anything that would make me happy—I'm going to have to think about this.'" They were teaching each other that they had rights.

Gradually, they read and talked through the process of consciousness-raising. "I grew more in that one year than I had in four years of college." The anger came up, the combined anger at herself, at her husband, at society. She thought about all the old things that she had repressed and was furious. Furious she had followed her husband to "his" town, furious that he never helped raise their children, furious that he wasn't home, furious that she was only at home. She was angry at the big things and at the little things.

But for Theresa, as for many women, the anger grew into a deeper realization of the bad bargain both men and women had made. The women's movement was her change agent and she became the agent of change for others. In her town, she became a spokeswoman for feminism and helped other women start groups. This was a good time for Theresa. Even her husband seemed to understand and their relationship was growing stronger. "I really felt things were getting better. I was very happy at that time. I had great hope for the future. I had just begun making some demands. I had started saying, 'The children are all little. Let's enjoy life. Take some time off, we'll go camping. Anything.'"

But at that point, just as she started making her own needs known, John made another ambitious leap. He decided to run for statewide office. "I was terrified. I was just getting to do what I wanted. I saw him so little that if I saw him any less, I thought we wouldn't be married. And I was uneasy because of what I knew of political wives. I didn't want to be Mrs. John Keats Andrews.

"John thought I was trying to stand in his way. I said I didn't want to work for something that was going to destroy our marriage. I felt a lot of pressure to be the right kind of wife and it was horrible. I felt that I was being pushed back into something I was trying to get out of."

When her husband lost, many people in the state said that the publicity about her involvement in the women's movement hadn't helped.

John was disappointed and resentful. And Theresa felt that she was hemmed in on all sides. "I didn't see how I could lead my own life at home. I went looking for work. People wouldn't hire me because they'd say, 'Your husband's a lawyer, you don't need a job.' One place wanted John's permission. They said women work better if their husbands are in agreement.

"I became very tense. I broke out in a rash and I was severely depressed. In our relationship, well, I had learned how to be a widow while he was running for office."

The fact was that Theresa had begun separating. "I cried all fall thinking about him. He was so much a part of me that I had to detach myself from him. I started getting prepared to go. I wallpapered my bathroom. I did all the Christmas shopping. We talked about it, but I was practically in a coma.

"I told John that he needed to get close to the children. I told him, 'Your boys are going to leave before you know them.' I told him, 'You have to really talk to people, really listen.'"

Finally Theresa flew back to New Haven, telling her family and friends that she was going to school.

"I don't think there's any such thing as a women's lib divorce," she said. "There's only a personal divorce. But this was the time for women to go off. I had come to admire women who somehow made a life for themselves. I always wanted to know how they did it. You feel it's going to happen to you, sooner or later. I wanted to know if I could survive. But this was, I think, an act of desperation. I didn't feel I had any other choice."

She still felt that she had left half of herself behind, the half that was committed to her children and husband. She felt that this separation was also "for" him, that she had made it to force him to change enough to connect with their children, and face his problems. Leaving the children behind was an enormous wrench for her, which she interpreted as "something I had to do for John and for them. So that they would get to know each other, have some affection for each other." For the first several months, she found it almost impossible to talk with him on the phone. She was so painfully aware of her feeling for him. When she started to talk about it, the day we met, the emotion came back; she shook herself and remembered, "I missed him more when we were together than I do now."

JOHN'S DELAYED ACTION

John Keats Andrews did finally begin to change. It was only after Theresa had left that John understood what she had been saying and in a rush made a series of innovations in his own life. Only after they were separated did he make the adjustments she had wanted in their marriage.

Again and again I have seen this delayed reaction-action. I have known many ex-wives who have bitterly watched their ex-husbands—the same men who thoughtlessly moved them back and forth across the country, who never lifted a diaper pin for their first families—become models of nonsexist marriages the second time around.

One man in a suburb of Chicago told me: "It's a sad fact that, for us, things are possible in new relationships that simply couldn't have worked out in the old ones. There was so much more mistrust. So many old wounds and angers. Now I feel so much more me. It's as if with my second wife there's no old baggage."

For some men, the shock of being on their own is so shattering that they change more in one year than in twenty. Other men discover that they can't find or afford the traditional marriage. Still others change too slowly, too little, too late.

John only found out later where his personal life—his own emotions and his family—should fit in his life. It was as if, at forty, he finally shook off the dictates of his childhood, which led from grade school to the political career.

Six months after separation John was working a five-day, forty-hour work week in a new law office located in the renovated school building where he once attended grammar school. Six months later, John was a working father, who learned to take care of the office and the children and the home. Six months later, he was going through the most intense period of change, searching through therapy, through books, through a men's consciousness-raising group, to understand his own life and what went wrong with his marriage.

When he talked about his marriage, in his taut and monosyllabic way, we were sitting in the one restaurant in his town that serves quiche and wine for lunch. Throughout the three hours we were there, around the oak table, people stopped by to say hello and to find out who the stranger was. John was obviously a figure in his town, of curiosity as well as stature. With his hands folded, he struggled to be "open" and to try and convey his own sense of life and marriage, as the feelings pushed up through the stiff words.

"I think I was to a very large extent formed out of the cultural pattern that most of us have been brought up in that there are certain husband attributes and certain wife attributes, and that there's a role involved. The model is what caused a lot of the basic problems in our marriage."

He described the early years of his marriage from his point of view.

John married Theresa less than a year after his mother died. That first year of law school had been a shock to him, but one he rarely talked about or acknowledged. In the process of caring for his mother those last months, he missed so many classes that for the first time he ended up near the bottom of the class. During the next two years John struggled to pull up his grades, and to be competitive with his classmates at Yale.

Then, with two children and a third on the way, he went home to private practice. "What I wanted to do was to get into trial practice in a medium-sized community and the more I thought about it, the more I said, it doesn't make any sense to go to some other medium-sized community when all my contacts are at home." But, in fact, it seemed that this man, who never liked exploring new places, even day trips around Connecticut, wanted to go home. He was never as secure as he felt he had to appear. In some way he had a plan, a life plan to fill.

At home, he dedicated himself to that life plan and to his very real fears of not being able to support a growing family. "I became immersed in the practice of law and trying to make ends meet. I became a very compulsive lawyer."

John had a very grim philosophy of life which made him feel that work was everything. "My basic feeling was that life is maybe not nasty, brutish, and short, but certainly it isn't a pleasant experience to breed an organism to go through."

His own "organism" was put to work. "From the period of, say, 1964 to 1974, I was just involved in lawyering and politicking and community affairs to a degree that really shocks me now.

"I'm not a person to do just what needs to be done to get by," said John earnestly, as he leaned across the oak table. "I'd become compulsive and it has to be the best. My ego was on the line and a whole lot of other things. I was involved in many, many things that were not actually necessary."

In this he agreed totally—belatedly—with Theresa. But when he talked about finances, it was clear that there was just a gap between his and her feelings about the importance of money. "I felt that things like financial matters were worked at out of necessity. There was a shortness of income and longness of expense. I was always juggling to pay certain things and then I had insurance policies. I felt a responsibility to the children. I would say that Theresa protested my working this hard, but I also felt she wanted the things that my money provided."

For both of them, the significant change began when she started that "book" group. "Theresa also makes a total commitment to what she does. She became a kind of provocateur of the group and brought other people into it. I was well aware of what was going on in the sessions. Most of it was not troublesome to me. But I think there is some antagonism created when you know somebody's talking about you and your circumstances. One thing that bothered me most . . . when they began discussing how little voice they had in financial affairs, when that subject was raised, I know I reacted rather violently.

"I realize now that in terms of the male psychology, this is at the very core of what the traditional male role has been. We have a fear that unless we're right on top of the financial picture, we may not be able to pay our bills. And the traditional male role has been that the man earns the livelihood and therefore should have control of it." John had thought very little about all this, before their separation. He had gone on, leading his own life, believing that she would stay in line. "She is an artistic person. I'm a verbal analytical person. We've had that problem all during our relationship. At the time we separated I was very dissatisfied with a lot of things that were going on with me professionally. I had just lost something I'd wanted—public office—and then I lost Theresa."

At that point, John crashed. He went through a crisis, reevaluating his life and values both personally and professionally. The combination of losing his work goal and his wife precipitated a kind of breakdown of his whole personality. And an attempt to restructure it.

"I have been trying everything, everything, to learn how to relate to people, to learn how to express myself, to come to terms with an emotional life. I have also, since Theresa left, taken over complete responsibility for the children. I do everything. I am the emotional support for them, I cook their meals, wash their clothes, send them off to school. We have become very, very close."

He began studying himself—in psychotherapy and in a men's group—with the same intensity he brought to his legal career. "I have learned that control is a very big issue with me. I have had to have control. I had to believe that I controlled Theresa. When she left, I saw that I didn't control her, couldn't control my life the way I had foreseen. I'm trying to deal with all that.

"I've discovered that the stealing from one's self, the amount of energy and amount of time that's involved in compulsiveness is a large part of what impedes a relationship. Unless you're there with the children and with your spouse through the casualness of some daily activities, you can't walk in—as I think so many of us have been prone to do—and say, 'All right, family, now I'm here, now's the time to have fun with Daddy.'"

John said all this with a sweating anxiety. It was apparent to me that he made an enormous effort to talk about his feelings and his distress. "In the last several months, I've learned that the building of relationships depends on being there . . . being there." The last thing he said was: "If I'd come to the realization maybe even two years earlier . . . one year earlier, I think it's very probable that things wouldn't have gotten to this point.

"The hardest part is that I still love Theresa. You know, how do you deal with that?" asked John. "The most painful thing is that never, through any of this, have I deviated from that. Starting about two months ago, I had visions of Theresa and me walking across a field with a tremendous sunrise coming up. It was the two of us and there was the sunrise. I thought of this as symbolic of a fantastic new relationship and I guess one of the really devastating things is that it hasn't developed. Theresa doesn't believe in us anymore. I can't delude myself any longer that it's going to work out."

When I last talked with them, they were still living a thousand miles apart, still separated, and planning to share child custody. Two children were moving to live with Theresa and two were staying with John. Apart, they missed each other enormously, and together they fell back into the same patterns which caused their divorce. They were unwilling or unable to divorce or reunite. Of all the couples I talked with, their ambivalence was the strongest. Their "losses" were the most equally balanced, and their crisis was the most difficult to resolve.

THE RISKY INTERSECTION

The accident rate at the intersections of personal and social change is higher than on the familiar street of the status quo. A change in roles does mean a renegotiation of the marital contract. At the most common level, the emergence of women into the work force means that "breadwinner-homemaker" marriages are now often "two working parent" marriages. As one person changes psychologically, in a new growth spurt, the marriage changes. They come to a point when the "I" can collide with the "we".

Not every change ends in a disruption. Not every disruption is caused by this change. But there is and always will be a risk associated with any change, whether it's of an individual or of society. The price of growth may always be some kind of loss. The new choices we have to make may always precipitate the most difficult decisions.

Among the divorced people I talked with, I found a profound understanding of how hard it was for two people to maintain a permanent relationship over years and decades, over a lifetime, during which each is inevitably subject to separate pulls and life changes. And yet, I found permanent marriage—and not serial marriages or "open marriages"—to be the ideal. People talk about lifetime marriages with a kind of longing and wonder. And hunger.

I heard again from Betty, the divorced woman from Virginia,

months after I had written her story. We had lunch. She was, she
told me, over hamburgers in downtown Washington, thinking
about a second marriage with a man she'd met shortly after our
first talk. At least they were going to try living together.

"I'm scared. That's the truth. I see so few 'good' marriages
working out over any time. There are the very rigid kinds of
marriages where they just hang on to each other and lock out
anyone else and avoid any kind of change like the plague. Those
seem to me to be the kind of people who are committed to commitment. They stay together, because they *stay together*," she
said, raising her eyebrows and her glass. "Then you see the people who are open and flexible and half the time they end up
being open to other people and their marriage is so flexible that
it ends up in pieces. But I really want a marriage in which the
two of us are together because we make it better for each of us
separately. I want a marriage in which I can keep on growing
without worrying that I'm moving away from my husband. I
want my own life and our life. I want to believe that it's possible," she said fervently, and then leaned back and asked, "What
do you think? Is it possible?"

Chapter 7   The Housewife's New Blues

"Sometimes I envy my mother. When she got married, everybody was a housewife. She never had a sense that she had to justify it. Now it's awfully, awfully hard for women my age to be at home. I feel sometimes that I have to justify it to everyone. I even have to justify it to myself."

"What do you do?" a Washington political aide asked a friend of mine at a Georgetown party of professional couples—and I wait. "I am a housewife," she answers, looking at him levelly, to see whether he will turn away from her as if she's just suggested that she's a transsexual.

"You see, I am married to a housewife," says a New York editor, across the table at a French restaurant. He says it with a certain pained emphasis, as if that will explain everything, even his affair at the office.

"What are your hopes for the future?" a Time magazine editor asks mass murderer Caril Fugate, after she is released from a Nebraska state prison in 1976. "I'd just like to settle down, get married, have a couple of kids, dust the house, clean the toilet, be just an ordinary, little, dumpy housewife. That's all I want to be," she answers.

Until the 1970s, it was most often the employed mother who felt the harsh judgment of society. She was the one criticized and put down by men and women, and especially by the mothers at home.

Now, however, things have changed. As more women work outside the home, it is the housewives who have begun to feel that they have been left out. As working mothers receive the praise and stroking of society, the women at home have begun to feel keenly a loss of status, and with it, a loss of self-esteem. Housewives, especially the young middle class and educated housewives, are on the defensive. "I'm an anachronism," wrote a housewife in the New York *Times* in December 1977. That same month, a woman named Sally Sullivan, a housewife from Chestnut Hill, Massachusetts, wrote a strong defense of her role in the Boston *Globe*.

They were singing the New Housewife Blues.

Superwoman—the successful, married working mother of two—the Woman Who Could Do It All—is the new improved image of superior American womanhood. However mythical that image proves to be—a transitional role in the middleground—it has a strong effect on the ego of the housewife. As the working mother image rises, the image of the housewife seesaws lower. It seems to many that the woman at home is not only "just a housewife." She is now also the Old Woman—old-fashioned, stuck.

FEAR OF LOSS IN THE STATUS QUO

People traveling through the Shuttle Zone are most afraid that a rapid change in sex roles will precipitate the loss of their most intimate personal relationship. They see around them marital accidents and they want to move ahead cautiously.

But very few want to retreat to the time when men and women were assigned their roles for life. Few want to shut the doors on choice. Yet many housewives wonder whether their choice is being phased out.

Once homemakers literally "made" everything in the home. They had a virtually assured lifetime post as a housewife. Marriage was social security. Women lived shorter lives and spent more years in child-raising. They were vital, if separate, partners in marriage. But as people began to live longer, have fewer children, and more of the homemaking functions were taken over by the economy, there was clearly a loss of function and a loss of meaning in the old homemaker role.

The women's movement expressed that pervasive loss. The movement didn't create the housewife's blues, but by encouraging women who move into the world, it has enlarged the general sense of loss for those who stay in the status quo.

In many ways personal growth for women has become associated with moving beyond the world of home and children. While there is surely much personal stretching associated with raising children, feminists are pushing the horizons of people who have known that. They encourage them to want more.

Women have been pushed in two directions by this pressure. Millions have joined the ranks of employed mothers. Others have fought back proclaiming Housewife Pride, or insisting that the only real security lies within the home.

The housewives and their husbands in the middleground are the ones who feel the conflict most keenly. They respond to both the values embodied in tradition and the hopes located in change. They experience and fear the losses from remaining within the traditional sex roles, but they also are vastly altering the meaning of the role, opening up new alternatives and new conflicts.

THE NEW BLUES

It is, in many ways, very hard to choose a traditional role now —and this is true not only for housewives. It is true for secretaries, nurses, indeed, any woman in the "woman's place."

Ironically, the women in families who can afford to have the woman be a full-time homemaker are often the ones most sensitive to the new messages of society. Even when they want to be at home and feel committed to the values of the homemaker job, many are angry at the image. Moreover, like those I talked with, many look around at their peers—women they have grown up with or identified with—and feel diminished. They feel like people left behind in the old neighborhood, while the upwardly mobile around them move out to the suburbs. In fact, their lives have not changed, but their attitudes toward those lives have changed.

CASSIE: THE OLD WOMAN

One of the housewives who very much experienced this loss of self-esteem and status in her own life is a woman I met named Cassie.

While we talked in her kitchen one morning, Cassie reached down under the Formica-topped counter for a sponge, cut open the edge of the economy-sized package and took out a pale yellow one. Then she wrapped a plastic tie around the rest and put them in place. With the sponge, she wiped the counter clean of stray Cheerios and crumbs that lingered from breakfast.

It wasn't until she had put the breakfast dishes in the dishwasher and put the baby into the plastic mesh playpen with her *Pat the Bunny Book* that she sat down for her own quiet cup of coffee time.

Cassie, dressed in blue jeans and a long-sleeved T-shirt with a bandanna over her straight brown hair, was one of 32.8 million women in this country who are classified as housewives. She was, according to the dictionary, "the woman in charge of a household, esp. a wife who does all or most of the cleaning and cooking in her own household and who holds no other job."

When I read the dictionary definition to her, she reacted simply: "Good God, is that what I am? Do they have to put it quite that bluntly? It makes it sound like I'm Harriet Housekeeper, like my largest ambition in life is to keep the cobwebs away from the cabinets. I guess I've gotten to hate the word 'housewife.' It sounds as if I married the house instead of Brad.

"On the other hand," she said pointedly, "I am not a Mad Housewife, Trapped Housewife, Oppressed Housewife, or Household Slave."

That out of her system, she laughed, "At least not always."

It was obvious to me that Cassie had come to a time when she felt great ambivalence about the word that described her current life choice.

"Sometimes I envy my mother. When she got married, everybody was a housewife. She never had a sense that she had to justify it. Now it's awfully, awfully hard for women my age to be at home. I feel sometimes that I have to justify it to everyone. I even have to justify it to myself."

This was one of those "sometimes." It was May when we met and in about three weeks it would be Cassie's tenth college reunion at one of the Seven Sister colleges. But Cassie wasn't going.

"I just don't want to face all those other women. They're all doctors and lawyers. Isn't that awful? It hit me when they sent out the questionnaires about what we're all doing today. I wanted to write down, 'Nothing.'"

Of course, Cassie wasn't doing nothing. She was doing a job she felt was important and meaningful to her. Having grown up an only child, she wanted to raise the kind of family she had fantasized about. As an upper-middle-class-income family, she realized how lucky she was to be able to afford the "luxury" of staying at home with her children. And yet:

"The other women in my class are always writing in class notes about their latest promotion and degree and who got tenure where and who's going to work for the Secretary of State. You never, ever see someone write, 'In the last five years, I have taught three children to tie their shoelaces and remembered to close the baby gate at the top of the stairs 433 consecutive times.'"

Cassie put the mug of coffee down on the round table and absently picked at a piece of stray banana that had escaped her sponge. She pushed her hair back behind the bandanna and smiled a freckled, youthful grin.

Cassie was "in-between." She talked about herself as a member of the last generation that would "drift" into the role of housewife. She became a housewife as part of the package of expectations she had grown up with as a female. Yet at thirty-two, she was a young woman with choices, who acknowledged that she chose to remain at home.

She made a decision—out of the web of alternatives she saw during her formative years, and out of the alternatives she had available to her now.

Cassie was born in 1947, the year when it seemed that everyone was having babies. Her parents bought a house in a development in Pennsylvania with other young couples and their children. In those days all the women were housewives and there was a spirit of camaraderie in the development that is lacking in Cassie's own life. "They had a sense that everyone was in it together. Everyone led pretty much the same kind of life. Especially the women," said Cassie, looking back at that vision nostalgically.

As Cassie's father's business did better, they moved to a bigger house in a wealthy suburb of Philadelphia and eventually sent their only child to a private school that regularly sent its graduates to the Seven Sister colleges.

From college, she drifted to Boston and a job in her "field." "Actually, I had been a fine arts major, so I got a job working for a fine arts professor. But I was really a secretary. He was a very nice man, very thoughtful. He used to worry that I would get bored and leave, like all the other Ivy League women and he did everything to make me comfortable there. I got days off, I got vacations—all that was great. But when I was working, I was essentially typing his revised textbooks. It was really grim."

The reality about her options in the work world of the late 1960s, surprised Cassie. "At a school like mine, you spent four years being told how smart you are, how cream-of-the-crop you are. We knew that for every ten applicants only one was accepted. All this kind of stuff. Then you graduate and you become a secretary. Excuse me, a faculty assistant."

In another woman, or another time, this disillusionment might have prompted a new career direction. But Cassie had already begun to make the series of incremental choices which she described as "drifting."

If she had found work more rewarding, perhaps she would have been more motivated to invest some of her hopes in that area of her life. On the other hand, if she had not been so sure that the future lay in marriage and the family, she might have been more ambitious about work.

In any case, Cassie met and married Brad, a tall, skinny man with brown curly hair and tortoise-shell glasses forever falling down his nose. Brad is the kind of man who wears Brooks

Brothers suits, drives a vintage Volkswagen, and runs five miles a day. He considers every purchase as an investment and chooses the styles that never change.

When they were married, Cassie's job didn't seem as crucial to her life. It was easier to accept the on-the-job boredom because it was now seen as temporary. Her job was a way to support them "for a while" until Brad got his degree and they began their "real life."

"We both assumed that I would have children and stay home with them. I had a fantasy of having six of them, if you can imagine. This was my expectation from the time I was a kid. My parents had that same thought. I mean that I would stay home— not that I'd have six kids. Even though I had gone to high-pressure schools and all that, it was also seen as preparatory school, and the end was that I would be a mother."

Cassie and Brad had their first child as soon as he had landed a job for a Cambridge research firm. During that year and the next, Cassie was busy, even overwhelmed, learning about the routines of child-raising and homemaking, marking schedules and struggling to learn the variety of tasks and timetables that would help her get on top of the job. It was a year of excitement and great change.

"I was learning so many things. I think the change from having a job to being at home is amazing. You have to learn to do nineteen different things at once with a baby under your arm. I think that was a pretty proud year for me. I became very competent. The problem is that after you learn how to do it, you've learned how to do it, and you've got twenty more years of just doing it."

For Cassie that sense of routine came slowly. Two years after her first son was born, they had a second and then last year, after they had moved into a suburban house twenty minutes from Brad's Harvard Square office, she had their baby daughter.

"For the past year, I have been feeling that raising three children is a very tough, totally consuming job and that I am mostly unappreciated for doing this job—by society, by anybody. I hate to sound like a spoiled brat. I don't need to be told that I'm wonderful every day. But the fact is that you get almost no credit for raising your own children. If I were out working in a day care center and someone else were hired to come in and take care of my own children, then everyone would be saying, 'Isn't she marvelous, the way she organizes her home, the job that she does.' I think that's crazy. But I know that it does have an effect on me.

"I think housewives are getting battered on every side. Every time I see *Ms.* magazine, it's either dumping on housewives or patronizing them or feeling sorry for them. Then there are the other Total Woman idiots running around telling housewives to greet their husbands in boots and negligees. That makes us sound like dum-dums. It all does something to me. I should be immune by now. But I think, good grief, is that what the world thinks of me? Are my kids eventually going to think I'm that stupid? It's partially the ring-around-the-collar stuff. I want to live long enough to see the woman in the ad turn to her husband and ask him why he doesn't wash his neck."

Cassie's husband, Brad, was supportive of her decision in some crucial ways. "I once saw *Diary of a Mad Housewife,* and I got so angry at that mousy little woman. I wouldn't stay married to a creep like that guy for anything. Brad is, on the whole, very admiring, even awed at what I do. But he's conflicted about it, too. For a long time he really thought I had it easy. I don't have a boss, I don't absolutely *have* to do certain things at certain hours. Then last fall he was home with a bad back for about two weeks. The baby was four months old; Jamie, the four-year-old, hadn't started nursery school. Brad got a good dose of seeing what I actually do all day. At the end of about the third day, he said to me, 'My God, how do you do it?' It made him appreciate what I do. Since then, we worked out a time when he takes care of the kids—Saturday afternoons—and I just take off and do whatever I want. It's been great. But I also think it occurred to him at that time that there was something weird about me that I would do that all day long. He told me it would drive him crazy . . . Sometimes I wonder what he really thinks."

Cassie also found herself wondering about the attitude of some of the younger women and the working women as well as the working mothers in her husband's office. "I'm jealous. I'm jealous of them. I am jealous of them being peers with my husband, working with him. It's not a sexual thing. But they share things with him that I don't. There's one woman in his office who's divorced with a six-year-old boy and he thinks, wow, is she terrific, the way she's handled her life. He takes her opinion to be more valuable than mine. He asks her opinion about things that she knows about—work things—that he would never ask me about.

"The other thing that bugs me is their attitude toward me. The other women in the office think of me as Brad's little housewife. We had a dinner party once and not one of those women picked up a dish from the table. They all talked to the men at the table, only the other 'wives' talked to me. The women in Brad's office were perfectly comfortable letting me serve them while they didn't even talk to me.

"That's part of it. Nobody really thinks you could conceivably be interesting if you're just a housewife and after a while it gets to you," said Cassie. "I begin to wonder if I'm interesting, or if I could do anything in the real world."

She got up then, and took the baby out of the playpen and said sheepishly, "I sound like I'm really complaining. I hate that. It's not that I want to go to work. I really don't. I feel very strongly that I'm the best person to raise my own children. I can't imagine that anyone else would do as good a job with them, because they wouldn't care as much as I do."

Holding her baby, Cassie poured apple juice into a bottle, casually, instinctively repeating certain words, like "bottle," smiling at the baby who repeated back a string of ba-ba-ba sounds.

"You know, I feel that I'm doing the right thing being here. And there are so many really wonderful moments. I wouldn't want to miss them. I get such a kick out of it, when Jamie comes home from school with his papers and all the rest of it, and he's full of what happened during the day. That's just really a good time, and I think, I'm so lucky. Then about a half hour later when he and his brother are fighting and the baby's cranky, I'd like to take to the highway and drive the car straight to California. But I have chosen this, I really have, and I feel that I'm very important in this house."

The choice that she made was one that she was sticking to. But her ideal was still somewhat different. "What would I do if I could have anything? Sometimes I think I'd like to be the curator of the Fogg Museum. But other times I think, wouldn't it be wonderful if my parents were around and two mornings a week I could leave the baby with my mother. Then I'd be really content.

"In about three years, two more years when the baby starts nursery school, I would love to start doing something in the mornings, or two or three mornings anyway, a job or school, something to keep my sanity. I do think about what I'll do when the kids grow up. I don't dwell on it. She's only fourteen months old. But you know, I'll be forty-nine when she goes to college. That doesn't sound so old to me.

"But, on the other hand," Cassie said, picking up the questionnaire from her tenth reunion class, "I'm ten years out of college already, and what have I done with my life? Learned how to make Play-Doh?"

I had talked with Cassie at a particularly vulnerable moment. It was her tenth reunion that prompted her to take stock of her life the way she had. As we talked she was aware that the entire reunion was geared to praise Women of Achievement and that neither she nor her schoolmates nor society gave more than lip service to the notion that a housewife was an achiever.

Cassie's generation was hardly the first to feel the onerous label of "just a housewife." Another "Seven Sisters" graduate, Betty Friedan, had reacted against precisely the same set of feelings. But Cassie's peers, friends, classmates, neighbors had begun to make other choices. Her former roommate, for example, held a $28,000-a-year job in Washington. Two of her Boston friends had full-time work and used the local day care center for their children. Cassie knew these children and couldn't label them "neglected." A third woman friend who had shared coffee and playgroup with her three years ago had gone back to school, to rechannel herself into work.

Cassie felt then a "relative" loss of status, relative to those with whom she compared herself, in terms of background and competence.

"I think it's fine that women who have to work or want to work can do that now without other people throwing sticks and stones at them," said Cassie. But she felt that the changes which have made it easier for them have made it much more difficult for her, for those who choose to be a housewife. Among her friends and peers, to be a housewife meant having to deal with a loss of self-esteem not only compared with men, but with other women. This was a feeling shared by many of the college-educated housewives I talked to—they shared a fear that as times changed, they were left out or left behind.

Many housewives share Cassie's sense of the loss of status. It is as true among working-class women as among the middle and upper classes. Many internalize this message. They feel the loss of public esteem as a loss of *self*-esteem.

CHANGING INTO THE TRADITIONAL ROLE

Cassie had at least grown up expecting to be a housewife. Her sense of loss came from "staying in place" while many around her changed their lives. But very often in the 1970s, young couples carry into their marriage egalitarian ideals. They establish a "young married" lifestyle in which both work and share housekeeping. Eighty percent of the married women between twenty-five and thirty-four years old, without children, work outside their homes. Those who "become" housewives have to deal with an enormous change in their lives. They often feel that intensely, as a step "backward" into dependency, precisely when the momentum of the times encourages women to go "forward" into independence. They are, in many ways, far less prepared and less able to accept or cope with some of the side effects of that change.

Again and again, these couples express a sense of shock at the discovery of how hard it is to maintain a relationship of equals in a situation of economic inequality, and how insidiously their lives change along separate patterns.

STEVE AND JOHANNA: THE TRADITION FEELS LIKE CHANGE

Steve and Johanna were a couple who changed "back" to the traditional roles of breadwinner and homemaker. This change came as a disruption, packaged with loss for both of them that they found surprising.

For three years before Zoe Elizabeth was born, Johanna, a twenty-seven-year-old honey-blond, model-thin woman with eyebrows that arch over her bright green eyes, and Steve—thirty, a sober-stylish man who wears a handlebar mustache under his brown curly hair—used to drive to and from work together. Three times a week they would go jogging, Johanna sprinting two miles and Steve steadily logging four miles.

They worked in the same department store, Johanna as a window display artist, Steve as a merchandise manager. At home, Johanna took charge of the cooking, making dishes with the flair of her Greek parents. Steve made breakfast, because she didn't eat anything before 10 A.M. They shared the housework; the laundry was Steve's job, making beds and vacuuming was hers.

They had their differences, of course. Steve had been born into a family that was security-minded. His mother had urged his father to stay with the city payroll in Miami because of the pension plan, and he had. His mother was the kind of woman who believed that wasting money was sinful.

Johanna, on the other hand, was someone who believed that an occasional extravagance was "necessary for the spirit." Even when she was an art major on scholarship, she'd managed to buy some special piece of material or a drawing which Steve might have considered frivolous. While occasionally, when they were first married, Steve disapproved of her purchases, he didn't say too much, because it was her money.

On the whole, they lived a rather integrated and easy life. Then, three years ago, they became planned parents. They had waited for and wanted Zoe. But what they hadn't entirely planned was the change that would come, when they separated into the woman at home and the man at the office.

When I met Johanna, Zoe was an almond-eyed blond-haired child of two with a passion for taking apart the yarn whenever her mother sat down to do some weaving. She was a plump child who only sat still for *Sesame Street*. And her mother could still describe and chronicle the changes Zoe brought in their life.

"When you called me, I couldn't imagine why you would

want to talk to me when I was just a housewife," she said as we settled down in the room decorated like a comfortable stage setting out of plants, wicker furniture, and bright homemade pillows.

"Aren't I what hasn't changed? Same old thing? Then I thought, that's what's happened to me since Zoe was born. I don't think anybody will believe I have anything interesting to say. Isn't that awful? Why should I feel that way? I'm the same person I always was. Maybe it's being at home with an infant talking baby talk."

Johanna hadn't known that becoming a housewife would be such a major turning point. She had looked forward to having a baby and looked forward to being at home. "I've always thought of myself as someone who would love to have a lot of time to make things with her hands. I thought of being at home as having a great deal of free time. I really wasn't thrilled with my work. I wasn't miserable, but after three years of dressing mannequins in the window, it didn't leave very much to be desired. If I never see another Christmas display it will be too soon.

"Of course my fantasy of being able to create wonderful things while my baby toddled around me went out the window pretty fast. But I got over that. I feel that I really get a lot out of taking care of Zoe. She's been so much fun. Sometimes I'm ready to strangle her, but I don't resent being home with her all that often.

"The things that shocked me though were the things that come with it, like my relationship with Steven. We'd lived together for a year before we were married and we lived together married for three years before Zoe. I really didn't think that having a baby would change what went on between us to the degree that it has."

Gradually, because she was the one at home, she took over more and more of the chores, and they lost a great deal of their shared time.

"Some of it is just natural. We can't jog together anymore without getting a babysitter. You know what I mean? You don't get a babysitter to go jogging, you take turns. Or one of you doesn't go that day.

"But the biggest shock to me was that gradually I've become like a maid, an unpaid maid. I had supported myself from the time I was eighteen. I'd never even taken any money from my parents to go to college. They didn't have any. But I'll never forget the day when I suddenly didn't have any money and I had to ask Steven for money. Maybe it shouldn't have bothered me, but I felt somehow, like, humiliated."

Johanna and Steven were now living on less money than when they were both working, although Steven had gotten a raise to $21,000. The paycheck is his paycheck and slowly his attitude toward spending money has come to be the one that prevails.

"I don't feel that I can spend money the way I choose, because it isn't really mine. I feel that I have had to adopt his standards of what's expensive and what isn't. I don't agree with it. Steven gives me an allowance—just saying this to you makes me squirm—and I have to budget within that amount of money. Steven puts whatever money is left over in a bank account so that we can buy a house. Well, if I were in charge of the bank account, I wouldn't do that. I'm not as worried about the future as he is. I'd like to do some things now. But," she said, repeating it slowly and incredulously, "it isn't my money."

Johanna felt that a joint decision—the decision to have children—had significantly different effects on her and her husband. Johanna, like others I talked with, missed her "own" money, and the equality and decision-making role in marriage.

"It's not that Steven is a male chauvinist pig or anything. He does a lot more at home and with Zoe than my father ever did. It's just that it's less than I expected. All of a sudden, I'm the one who's here, so I'm the one who can throw in a wash and do all the cleaning and the shopping. Before, if the laundry didn't get done, or the house was a mess, well, that's the way it was because we were both busy or something. Now, it's my fault."

Johanna basically was uncertain whether this change in her life, the change toward being a mother at home, could be made without a loss of self-esteem that had come from a paycheck, and loss in their relationship which had been based partially at least on their ideal of a partnership marriage.

"I really want to be here for Zoe at least until she goes to school. Everybody's always saying, 'It's not the quantity of time, it's the quality of time.' Well, I just don't buy that. I think you have to be here at home, with your kids, to really have the kind of kids you want. I want Zoe to feel loved and secure and I think I can do it best. Besides, I want to be here with her. But it seems to me that you have to pay an awful price just to raise your own children now. I want to take care of Zoe, but I don't want to take care of Steven as if he were a second child, and I hate being taken care of financially by him.

"I think my generation of women doesn't accept all the stuff that comes with being a housewife very well. We want to take care of our kids, but most of my friends resent the fact that it's a package deal. You take the kids and the house and the pick-up-after-the-husband, and not having any money, and being less than he in the relationship—and I'm not saying this like a women's lib thing, it's just true. You either take the whole thing, or you go to work and leave your kids in a day care center."

Johanna wasn't alone in her ambivalence. Her husband was also uncertain and uncomfortable with the change "back" into the traditional life, as I found when I went to see him.

The contrast between Johanna's "workplace" and Steve's was vivid. After leaving the warm sun colors of their living room, with the sounds of *Sesame Street* and Zoe's screeches of delight— "A," "B," "C," "D,"—Steve's office was as cool as the sleek gray chrome and glass. He worked eight floors up, above the display windows which Johanna had told me, with a measure of disgust, to "check out." (Two weeks before Mother's Day, the front windows were an unimaginative collection of square boxes with red ribbons boasting "For Mom", and mannequins in expensive bathrobes.)

Steve leaned back in his black leather and steel chair and turned a pencil with the company's name on it around and around in his fingertips. Slowly he began to talk, and answer my questions:

"I don't think of Johanna as being a housewife in the sense of the word 'HOUSEWIFE,' with capital letters. I mean, not a dumb housewife, if you know what I mean. I think of her as a very talented, creative person. The work that she did here was incredible. They have never been able to find anyone who could touch it. Have you seen the work of that clod who's doing the windows now?"

Does he still think of her as talented?

"Oh, absolutely. She could come back here or anywhere. She's good enough to do Bloomingdale's."

Talented at home?

"Oh, I see what you mean. Well, she has done a great job with the house. All of the curtains and cushions and everything, she made. And there's her weaving. Is there anything creative about housewifing? Not much. She's a fabulous cook. There's that. But basically she's busy taking care of Zoe. I mean, that's what she does. I'd like to have more kids. I guess I think it would keep Johanna busier. One kid leaves her with a lot of time on her hands and she is bored sometimes. I can't blame her for that. Staying home with a two-year-old for someone as sociable as Johanna is lonely and when I get home she is a lot more eager to have someone to talk to than I am. I've noticed that change since she was home."

Steven sat thoughtfully turning the pencil around and around and then started talking about how different it was now to be the husband of a housewife.

"It's hard for me to know, to step into my father's shoes, or my mother's, but it seems to me that it was easier for a man and woman who just assumed that this was it. She was a housewife, he was the worker, there wasn't any other way. If my dad resented it, well, he sure as hell didn't say anything about it. That would have been really unmanly and stuff like that. Maybe it was easier, but on the other hand, it must have been pretty grim. I don't know. My mother was a very insecure woman. She just wanted my father to hang on to that job. It was like her whole life depended on someone else and all she could do was to force that person to be dependable. She never had anything for herself. They really restrained each other in some ways I don't fully understand. But they weren't happy people. They didn't have any capacity for joy that I ever saw.

"I think that was why I married Johanna, she had a great capacity for joy. She lit up. She really saw things, when I would have been buried in books.

"Now sometimes I'm afraid she'll lose some of that.

"But that isn't what we're talking about, is it? Maybe it is. I don't know. I mean, sometimes I think, you take a woman like Johanna with such spirit and creativity and you put her in a box with a baby or two, and twenty years later you let her out and what have you got? That's an exaggeration. But I feel guilty sometimes, I really do, that it's her who's at home. After the years of doing everything together, now she's at home and I'm here. Not that being at home is bad. I think it must be damn nice not to have to go to an office every day," he said. Steve buzzed for his secretary and asked her to bring tea for us. He absent-mindedly took the cups, forgetting a "thank you," and kept talking as if the secretary weren't in the room. "I think it's important for the baby. I know she loves the baby. But what happens to us? Is that selfish? What happens to her?

"I guess maybe I think the only way I can think about it is that it won't last forever. In a few years she can start getting out again."

After his secretary left, we talked about money—obviously a sore spot in their marriage—and Steven's empathy and ambivalence all but disappeared. Some resentment, some guilt, and some fear solidified into his resistance.

"Okay, now, I know all this stuff. I read those articles about how much a housewife is worth and all that. But let's look at this thing in black and white. Okay, now when we were both working and we didn't have Zoe, we had very few expenses really. We could save some money and spend it. So, if Johanna was extravagant, I bit my tongue about it. I didn't want to get like my parents who always fought about money.

"Now, I'm the one earning the money. There's less money and more expenses. We have to budget. It seems to me, since I'm the only one earning the money, I should be budgeting it.

"Johanna wanted to stay home with Zoe. Not that I disagreed, I didn't, I think a mother should stay home at least till the kids are in school. But if that's the way it is, then at least if I'm earning the money, I should be making the decisions about it.

"I'm afraid that if we start negotiating about everything, then we'd be fighting all the time and we wouldn't be saving anything.

"Besides, I understand about money more than Johanna does. I deal with money here. That's my job and I don't understand why Johanna doesn't just let me deal with it."

Steven admitted that he missed having the second income. In their early years together they had gotten used to working together and having a joint income. He had been somewhat unsettled to discover that as Zoe came along, he was the one with the total responsibility for earning a living: "I feel more tense about it than I did. In those early years I learned to think in terms of our money, and what we could plan with both salaries, and it's difficult to adjust to less."

Was he angry about it? "No-o," he answered a bit slowly. "How can I be angry about it? I want the best for Zoe, and Johanna is the best." Steven talked fondly, even sheepishly, holding the desk picture of his wife and baby. Neither of them wanted their relationship to drift into separate places and yet they both saw a potential for that. They had many of the expectations built up over their early years together, expectations of sharing; and as well, the reality of their "temporarily" separate specialties. Because they were not married on equal terms, because intellectually they didn't accept this difference in roles as inevitable, it was harder to accept it all. A new conflict emerged between their goals as parents and their goals as partners. Johanna and Steve wanted the kind of partnership marriage they had known to begin with, but they also wanted a chance to bring up their children with a full-time mother at home.

AN OLD ROLE, A NEW MEANING

Even while people like Cassie or Steve and Johanna identified housewifing as the traditional role, they were examples of the changes that are being made in (not beyond) that role, in order to conserve its meaning.

There have always been two parts to the "work" of the housewife. One part is housekeeping and the other is mothering. Once, the housewife's most time-consuming and economically valuable role was in homemaking. Now, most housewives, certainly those I talked with, consider housekeeping the least meaningful task in their job description. Housewives are sure they care less about cleaning, dusting, mopping, and shining than their mothers did. They despise the ads that show housewives glowing with pride over the spotless glasses. Simultaneously they feel disparaged at the implication that a woman is at home to *serve* her husband. In this time of Equal Rights, the dependent "little wife" is not their role model.

Increasingly the meaning in their lives as housewives is invested in the other part of the job: mothering. If there is one task which is indisputably worthwhile to the woman at home, it is child care. One of the most popular sentiments is described on the button sold at the National Women's Conference in the fall of 1977: "Every Mother Is a Working Mother."

This change has occurred slowly. But now it is complete, and it dictates the new life pattern of even the "traditional" woman in the middleground. Cassie's mother and Johanna's mother had been housewives since their marriage. But Cassie and Johanna had become housewives only when they had children. Very few young wives without children stay home. Very few young women expect to be housewives after their children are grown.

The modified traditional life pattern for homemakers represents an enormous change in the tradition, although this change has come about gradually, and hasn't always been recognized as such. The investment in "mothering" helps to conserve meaning within the tradition—by changing it. Yet again, the solution which is arrived at in the Shuttle Zone often contains latent conflicts which may be seeds of further change.

NEW MEANING AND NEW CONFLICTS

The women at home whom I talked with expressed pleasure in and concern about their children. They believed that they had a meaningful job, one that required a wide range of skills and sensitivity. Moreover, they believed that their children needed them. The notion that there was something denigrating about devoting their lives to their children angered them. Again and again, I was asked questions like "What is so much better about working in an office than taking care of your own children?" They balked at the idea of their own children in day care centers or after-school programs or in the care of a paid sitter. And they were largely convinced that the children who grew up in a home with their own mother would be better off.

But, at the same time, the emphasis on mothering increased some areas of discontent. The woman who is now a homemaker only in order to be a mother often suffers some increased anger (which Johanna experienced) at the side effects of that role: housekeeping, economic dependence, service to her husband. They feel that the only way to be a full-time mother is to accept the rest of the package and that is not always attractive.

Moreover, in this changing tradition, as child-raising becomes the only reason to be at home, the housewife's life has a built-in time frame and limitation, which again predicts change.

In the "new traditional" role, a housewife is faced with a gradual diminution of usefulness at home as her children grow older and need her less. The in-between years can be the rockiest ones, as they were for an angry housewife named Belinda.

BELINDA: THE IN-BETWEEN YEARS

Belinda was a thirty-six-year-old housewife with a twelve-year-old master's degree, a son who was eight and a daughter who was ten. She was at the awkward age, when her "nest" was empty for six to eight hours a day. She found herself with a building resentment about the nonmothering aspects of her life and concern for the future. When we met it was 9:30 A.M., Belinda's children were at school, and the neighborhood in the hills surrounding her Washington State home was peopled only with young children and housewives.

Belinda was dressed in her tennis clothes for the eleven-o'clock game she had scheduled at the local sports club. She was brown-haired, stocky, and intense, the kind of woman who played field hockey at prep school in the East. In the mid-'60s, she married an architect and they moved West with the hope that Allen would be able to build houses in the mountains and the rugged terrain of the Northwest Coast. Instead, his firm specialized in renovating doctors' offices.

When I came into her house, Belinda was waiting for the washing machine repairman who had promised only that he would be there "before noon." As we talked, Belinda revealed that now, in this "awkward" age of part-time mothering, she felt herself in a holding pattern, filling more of her hours in service to her family and less in active "mothering."

"Isn't that typical," said Belinda of the late repairman, "I mean it. Everyone assumes that housewives aren't really doing anything. They are just home anyway and they can spend all their time waiting. It's one of the things that irritates me about going to the doctor's. You always have to wait for *his* schedule. Everyone assumes that if you are at home, you won't mind doing this, that or the other things."

Two years ago when both children were finally off to school, Belinda was overjoyed. "I thought of all that time. Six hours a day! I forgot about sickness, vacations, summers. But still, I really was ready to have some time to myself."

But gradually she felt that she still didn't have a space of reliable time that she could call her own. "I'm up at quarter of seven. I make breakfast for the kids and they're off at eight. Then Allen comes down. He hates to eat breakfast with the kids—it is a bit of a pig show—so he eats next. And he is very picky about what he wants for breakfast. Did you ever see anyone who wouldn't eat an egg if it has a hint of uncooked white? You have to get the egg off the fire at the moment the yellow is still soft, but the white is done. It makes me feel like a nuclear engineer, planning it just perfectly. Then he leaves me a list of things to get done. Shirts at the laundry, people I have to call, all that sort of thing.

"Then there are the days when I have to be at school for something or other. But basically I have to pick up the house, beds, dishes, do at least a minimum of vacuuming, a lot of picking up. My kids strew things behind them. They tend to litter the house. The only thing that gets me out of the house is my tennis. I'd go mad otherwise. And some of the P.T.A. stuff, which isn't very rewarding, but I have met some other women through it. Then I also have the shopping to do and I have to plan dinner. Stuff like that. I'm always chauffeuring the kids here and there. I have at least one or two car pools a week. Oh, and I'm the one in charge of both cars. He drives to the office. I have to get both cars fixed or inspected. If one of them is broken I am the one who drives him to the office.

"I also pick up after my husband. I do the laundry every other day, and I put away all the clothes. I do dishes all day long. Isn't this fascinating? What else do you want to hear? I clean the refrigerator sometimes on a really *big* day."

Belinda's children were at an age when they dashed in from school and then out again to play with friends nearby. "Some days I feel like I could be replaced by a revolving door," she said, nervously lighting another cigarette.

The most important part of her job was "just being there."

"Somebody has to be there when the kids come home from school. The idea of my children with a latchkey around their necks would just wipe me out. And I'm the only one who can do it. Who else? Certainly not Allen.

"I don't really resent the things I do for the kids. Sometimes I grouse about it, but it's also fun sometimes. But I find myself getting terribly angry when Allen is sitting in his chair, or reading a book and I am running around, picking up after dinner, yelling at the kids to get into bed, brush their teeth. He just sits there, as if they weren't his children at all. I also feel that I don't get any weekends. He says that weekends are his 'free time.' But *I* don't get any free time.

"I think that feminism has just made me feel more servile. I resent doing household things much more than I did when we were first married. I was brought up to serve the men in my home, and I did that when we were first married, just automatically. Now I feel, well, if I have to do that, why doesn't he?

"For instance, I've said to myself, I'm serving the coffee in the morning and he's never questioned that. I've set up this thing where I am the 'mother of the coffee' somehow. I see it as my job, part of my responsibility. But now there are times when I feel like telling my husband to get his own coffee! I see him as another child to take care of."

During the time that we talked, the repairman was late, and Belinda had to cancel her tennis game. She took meat out of the freezer section, answered the phone, made notes on the calendar she used to keep track of her children's schedules, rearranged car pooling, added items to the shopping list, sorted the laundry from the washing machine and ran vinegar through the electric coffeemaker, "as long as we're just sitting here."

She talked about the time before she felt this restless discontent. When the children were small, before they went off to school, even the housework didn't bother her as much. It was something that she did with them, making a game out of rolling up the socks, and chatting while she cooked dinner. When her little boy went to school, she experienced both a sense of release and emptiness, since her time of being most needed was over, and there was nothing really to fill the gap. More of her time was involved with housework, less with the children. She was less vital to them now and yet, "If I were to go to work, I'd have to replace me with me. The thing about kids at this age is that you're not dealing with diapering and keeping them away from the Bab-O under the sink or stuff like that. You're teaching them values. When they come crying into the house because the kid next door whacked them, you're teaching them how to deal with their lives and all that. In a way, someone like me is more vital now than when they were little. But then there are all those days when it's two-thirty and they both call up from friends' houses that they aren't coming home, and I have from two-thirty to five or five-thirty left with nothing to do except stuff I hate doing, like cleaning the house or something."

As for part-time work, Belinda said that she didn't have enough control of her schedule to be a responsible employee. "Last winter, Beth had bronchitis for three weeks. Then Bobby had it. There went six weeks down the drain. I don't know what other women do, but I can't really count on much except being at everyone else's beck and call."

It's obvious that Belinda felt more uncomfortable in her role as her children grew older. More of her time was spent in less meaningful tasks, and yet she didn't think that she had the time to make a change. She felt trapped. While I observed her alone and interacting later with her children, it was obvious that she was torn between wanting to be more vital and more in control in her children's lives and wanting total independence, a new life for herself. The pushes and pulls created a stressful relationship with the children, who were her "work."

THE JOB OF CHILD-RAISING

The housewives I interviewed, like Belinda, seemed to have more anxiety about the issues of child-raising than the mothers who worked outside the home. It was not that they cared more about their children, but that they spent more time and energy discussing and worrying about the problems of development, the psyches in their charge. They simply discussed their "work" more, and were more likely to have read and believed the various child-care experts, especially those who supported the notion that children need mothers at home. I wondered whether other women are more likely to stay at home because they have that interest and anxiety. Or does it come from being at home?

It seemed to me too that full-time mothers are more reluctant to share the decision-making power over their children's lives with fathers. Although many expressed the desire to have fathers participate more fully in family life, they are the overseers of the father-child relationships more often than not. Many say simply that their husbands don't have the expertise.

Some women at home seem reluctant to lose the one traditional power they have, power over their children's lives—a power that ranges from the supportive and nurturing to the benign and loving, to the overbearing and intrusive.

If child-raising is a primary job, then surely the woman at home has a motivation to resist having that job phased out unless she has her own future plans in order.

THE HOUSEWIFE'S HUSBAND

The problems faced in the shift of meaning from housekeeping and wifing to mothering aren't only internal ones. The overwhelming majority of housewives are economically dependent on their husbands and on their husband's work.

As they begin to consider the wifing part of the job less important, their husbands are also affected. Today men and women are more likely to make the decision together that she will stay home "for the sake of the children." Implicitly, the husband is now the sole wage-earner "for the sake of the children."

This means a shift in male expectations and there are many men who have begun to feel that they are not getting the same deal that their fathers got, even though they are playing the same roles.

Belinda's husband Allen was one of the husbands of a housewife who had become increasingly discontent with his own bargain.

When I went to his architectural office to talk with him, he was not looking forward to it. He was aware of the strains in their marriage. The first thing he said to me was: "If you are interested in talking about how oppressed the American housewife is, I'd just as soon go back to work."

Allen's eyebrows, a straight line across his forehead, broke apart to make room for a frown. After a while, when he was sure that he wouldn't be assigned the role of the Guilty Husband, he began to relax, looking an almost boyish thirty-eight years in a three-piece yellow-tan corduroy suit.

Finally, as if he'd been given a permission slip, Allen lit up a cigarette and started talking. "You are sitting before an endangered species. The white Anglo-Saxon male head of household with two point zero children, a mortgage and a job that allows him to take a dentist's office and turn it into a chiropodist's office. I have the pleasure this month of planning a perfect environment for the geriatric feet of a chiropodist named Alvin Shearer."

Corns weren't part of Allen's plan when he left the East for the Northwest. "I had loved this part of the country ever since I was a kid. When I was in high school, I had driven out here with two friends, and I had just been awed by the coastline. I came out really with a vision of building houses into cliffs—a Frank Lloyd Wright cultist. Instead, I am trying to find satisfaction in podiatry."

Allen's voice had softened for a minute: "In retrospect maybe it would have been better for Belinda if we'd stayed in the East, near her family. I don't know. I really don't. I know that she's miserable. I feel that I've gotten it in the neck for doing what I'm supposed to do. I was raised to believe that the worst thing a man could do would be to not support his family."

When the children were babies, he worked nights and often weekends to establish himself in the firm he had originally joined in Portland. If he had become a partner, he reasoned, then he could have supported his family and built the houses he dreamed about. But it didn't work out. In the architectural hard times that followed, Allen and two of the other younger men were let go. They formed their own firm and struggled to make a living the first several years, before one of the partners got linked into a rental agency with a medical clientele. For the past several years, Allen had been doing the "bread and butter" work of this group.

As he went on it was clear that his attitude toward his wife's work was reflected off his own discontent. "When we decided to have Beth, we talked about all this and we decided that we both believed children should have a mother at home. My feeling is that if you don't want them, don't have them. But if you want kids, you have to make a decision that you'll take care of them. We pretty much assumed the other things. That if she stayed home, well, she'd take care of the house and all that. I can't run the washing machine from my office.

"About three years ago, when the baby was four or five years old, she started wanting me to do what she called 'my share' of the housework and child care. Well, I don't mind looking after the kids sometimes. And if she were sick or really pooped, or something, I'd be glad to take over. But my share? My share? Does she do her share of the podiatrist's office?

"When the kids were little, you know, and they were under foot all the time, I could understand how she might not be able to keep the house perfectly neat or something like that. I didn't complain. The funny thing is that now that they're out of the house, the house is even messier.

"She is now substantially free six hours a day. The fact of the matter is that housewives like Belinda have a very, very easy time of it. Going to pick up the kids at school, taking care of the house is a lot more palatable than negotiating the color scheme with these idiots.

"Belinda wants all the rights of being a housewife, staying at home, not earning any money. And she wants all the rights of being equal, independent, whatever you call it. Well, I don't buy that."

It's not that Allen thought his wife should work, at least not full-time. He too appreciated the fact that she wanted to be home for the children. In his own childhood, there was often no one home. His mother had been out volunteering in one organization or another. One of his own clearest memories is coming into the house after school when no one was there. He used to envy his friends who came home to platters of egg salad sandwiches and smiling mothers. But he had absorbed the idea that she might be "better off" with a part-time job, like the one his partner's wife had found in the university library.

"She goes to work and is home in time for the kids. It doesn't interfere with her taking care of them or of the house. Compared to Belinda, she's a white tornado. I basically don't think I'm the kind of guy who would be angry if she got a part-time job.

"With the kids gone most of the day, there just isn't the same reason for her to be stuck in the house."

Both Belinda and Allen played ring-around-a-rosy with their options and their ambivalence, exploring their choices and their lack of choices. Belinda wasn't the only one who had a changed attitude and unchanged set of circumstances.

By the end of our interview, Allen spelled it out pretty clearly: "From my point of view, what I see has happened by all this stuff about women's equality is that I've gotten the shaft. I mean it. A decade or two ago, a man like me, who was filling his side of the bargain, would have gotten some service in return. He would have had a wife who took care of him, who bolstered his ego, who was proud of him, who appreciated the fact that he worked to support her at a job that didn't thrill him.

"Now, what happens. Not only am I supporting my wife and kids, but I am supposed to be guilty for keeping her at home and unfulfilled. Not only am I supporting her, but I personally am not supposed to ask for a thing in return."

The one thing that Allen and Belinda had in common was resentment. Their conflicts were not universal, not even "typical." They were a product of their own family histories and their psyches and their interaction as a couple. They were hardly what you could call happily married. But their problems were also specific to the way that this couple met these times of change.

Those who perceive their role as "mothering" are less tolerant and more conflicted about the aspects of housewifing that don't fit under that heading. This forces husbands to make difficult adjustments. If egalitarian couples move into a "traditional" role structure when they become parents, the husbands often fall back into (or assert) a traditional mindset, seeking the rewards and services which their fathers had received. Many of them accept the notion that their wives are there "for the children," but they have difficulty adjusting to this revised vision of the house-wife-husband structure. As Allen said, almost guiltily, "What am I getting out of it?"

THE IMPERMANENCE AND THE OLD GUARD

The new consensus that "housewifing" is a temporary position, limited to child-raising, has yet another effect. It threatens those women who once went into the role as a permanent assignment. Very often during the last few years, older women have bitterly complained that the "deal" was changed on them. As one woman told me, "I put in my twenty years. I feel that I shouldn't have to apologize for relaxing now. Why, even the Army gives you a pension after twenty years! But all I ever hear is, 'What are you going to do with the rest of your life?' I don't want to do any more than I'm doing." She saw the "new choices" as new pressure and new threats.

That vision is shared by some younger women who would also prefer to be at home. The existence of new patterns and new choices forces many younger housewives to regularly re-evaluate their commitment to be at home, and to plan for a different future. For some housewives this is a relief. But for others, like Sally, it is an unsettling conflict and pressure.

SALLY: CAN I STAY HOME?

Work held no allure and no glamour for Sally. This twenty-seven-year-old Boston mother worked from her sixteenth birthday, when she got working papers, to her twenty-first birthday when Sean was born. Six years later, Sally was fighting off the time when she might "have to" go back to work.

Sally had grown up within six blocks of where she and Bob lived and she'd finished high school with a clerical course behind her. The summer she was eighteen, she went to work full-time in the insurance company where she'd worked summers before. There she did typing, filing, and filled out forms. It was well-supervised drudgery.

"I liked the other girls. I liked earning the money and deciding what I wanted to do with it, you know, after giving some to my family, of course," she remembered as we talked on the second story of her three-decker house. Her three oldest children, Sean, six, Allyse, four, and Bob, Jr., three, were playing outside and she had put the eighteen-month-old baby in for her nap.

At home, as she described it, Sally felt more useful and more in control of her life, freer in fact than she ever felt at the insurance company. "Oh, they used to clock us. They used to watch us, and monitor our work. It was like being in high school, only you had certain quotas that you had to do, so many forms, that sort of thing. You only had so much time to go to the bathroom and if this supervisor caught you, it was like a teacher at school. It was pretty bad, you know. I suppose if we get really stuck, I can go back there. I had a good record. But what a dump."

The insurance company had been one of those large chrome and plastic offices with rows and rows of desks that had to be cleared off every night before anyone left. Her home was definitely not that sort of place. There was the long railroad corridor down to the back bathroom that was an obstacle course of kiddie toys. The living room was a mixture of the furniture she took from her family house when her mother died, and some of the items they bought as newlyweds. In the kitchen there were new cabinets and linoleum floor that she and her husband put down together over last summer's vacation. There was a new Early American style dinette set in the kitchen which they bought on time two years ago and just paid off. She shared a washer and dryer with in-laws who owned the house and lived on the first floor. In the reluctant soil in the backyard, there was now a garden which she nurtured each summer.

"It's not my dream house," said Sally with a smile that suggested that she was not dissatisfied. "Well, you know, I was depressed after Sean was born, and we moved in here, to the old neighborhood. I had in mind a house like in a suburb or something that would be all new. But you know, there are some advantages. Like if I want to go out, Bob's mother can babysit the kids. Basically I do like being in charge of this house. And the kids. I mean, I am the boss here and I don't have to answer to anyone what I do all day. I don't have to ask to go to the bathroom. I can cook whatever I want. I can do the wash when I want to. If I don't clean up on a day, there's nobody to get on me about it."

Sally knew that her life was different from that of her mother's in one very big way. "I was one of seven children. My mother worked herself to death. I mean that. She died at fifty-four years of age. But we're not having any seven children."

Sally started thinking much more about the future than she used to. Last year her husband made $14,000 as a house painter. Because they were living in a three-decker wooden house, owned by his parents, their rent was very low. But they still wanted to move out.

"It's the schools. Bob and I both went to school here and it wasn't terrible. At least, when we were growing up they were very strict about teaching reading and writing. Now, with all the kids being bused, they aren't learning anything. I don't care if they go to school with black kids. But I do care if they spend more time worrying about fights and all that than they do learning.

"So we both kind of want to move out. But I don't see how we can afford it. If I went to work now, then it would be possible. I could make $120, $130 a week. I could leave the children with my mother-in-law, and pay her something and go back. But honestly, my husband really hates the idea of the kids spending all that time with his mother. She's all tied up with the Church. She's always praying dear Mother of God this and dear Mother of God that. It drives him crazy. He thinks she'll have the kids on their knees all day.

"Also, the truth is that I get a kick out of being here. I just enjoy them—not every minute, sometimes I could strangle them, you know how kids get on you—but I like it. I don't like cleaning up, but I don't mind it, either. It gets done. I think most of my friends are slapdash cleaners, but it isn't actually dirty, either.

"The big thing is that I want to raise my own. I want to help them get a start, like with reading. My six-year-old is just going into first grade and he can read a bit already. I have my four-year-old picking out the words on signs. We've got the alphabet letters on the refrigerator and she does real good with them. She's the smart one. Her and the baby."

What Sally said she would like to do, "if we can manage it," was postpone going back to work until the baby was in school. Then, she said she would feel that she had gotten them off to a good start.

"If I went ahead now, I'd miss this time with the kids and it's the only time they are going to be little like this. I'd hate to miss this. It would be nice if in a few years maybe Bob would be making enough money for me to stay with them for longer, but that is hard now on one salary. Around here I'd say about half of the mothers, even with little ones at home, are working. I see them, and it's running here and there. I just would like it to be that I could stay with them until they are grown up. It's like you see the high school kids hanging around, and they get into trouble around here all the time. I don't think that would happen if they had someone at home."

On the other hand, Sally felt very guilty at times when her husband was moonlighting. "He's tired and then he's cranky around the kids. I feel like I could be helping him with the earnings. But I can't be split up like that. The kids need me here.

"You know when I felt worst? The other day, last week, the

oldest were visiting with my sister's kids and the baby was taking a nap. I lay down over on the couch and was reading my magazine, and I fell asleep. It must have been about four because my husband came in and there I was asleep. I heard the door shut and I jumped up like it was a burglar. Like he'd caught me. There was this second when Bob looked at me, like what is she doing taking a nap. Now I didn't say anything to him. And he didn't say anything. He's not that kind of guy. But I felt guilty. I feel guilty if I do something strictly for myself, because I think sometimes just being here is a luxury."

For Sally, being a housewife wasn't a "must" or a "should," it was a luxury they might not be able to afford much longer.

CHOOSING TO BE AT HOME

At least part of the reason Sally wanted this "luxury," wanted to be at home, was because work seemed unattractive to her. In fact, her own work experience had been unpleasant and she saw very little likelihood that she might find a job that she would like anywhere nearly as well as being at home.

But there are women who make this choice out of a broader range of options available to them. While they may be also ambivalent about their decisions, some of these housewives are now able to look at mothering as a middle career. They see that, yes, the housewife is now a mother and that the mother's job lasts only as long as the children need her. But that seems to be an advantage. Their time at home looks like a part of a flexible life plan.

Many of the housewives who maintain a sense of equilibrium while living in a transitional time, have one thing in common: a feeling that they have some measure of control over their lives. They are often women, not surprisingly, who feel some economic security. (But that sense of security doesn't hinge solely on income.) They are also women who feel they made a decision about motherhood and about the number of children they would have. Moreover, these women feel competent as mothers, and have husbands who are supportive and sharing in the raising of their children, and of their decision to be at home with children.

They are not immune to the changes in their role or in the status of housewifing. They accept the fact that mothering is a sequence in their lives. They seem to have the capacity and the interest, the internal resources to plan and prepare for the future, to see their time at home as valuable but finite.

As one Michigan housewife put it: "The women's movement made me realize in a new way that I was making a choice to be here. I lost the excuse that I had just drifted in. I had to really look at what I was doing and decide when and how long to keep doing it. I have to re-evaluate it pretty regularly, and I have to feel that I'm planning for my future, not just my kids', and that I can, if I have to, take care of myself."

DIANE'S "STAGES OF LIFE"

For Diane, being at home was a stage of life.

Diane was thirty-nine years old and the mother of three children, ten, eight, and five, who live outside of Los Angeles. Five feet three inches tall, with black curly hair and a forthright manner that was at once aggressive and humorous, intrusive and friendly, she was clearly a woman with a vast number of interests, from running a volunteer gift shop to handling the public relations for a nonprofit organization. Diane was the kind of woman who carried around a historical record of the accidents and illnesses of all the children in the neighborhood and in her extended family. If her own children were late from school, she could panic. If there was a fire engine coming down the street, she would assume it was headed for her house. A woman quick to anger and quick to forget, Diane was also a woman convinced that "if I didn't have a sense of humor, they'd have carted me away a long time ago."

Diane had grown up in Miami, one of two children. When she was a teenager, her father died, and she remembered vividly how hard it was for her mother to survive. In many ways, Diane, as the eldest child, took over the sense of responsibility for the family, after her father died. She worked from the time she was a teenager, worked her way through college, and into a high-pressure job with one of Los Angeles' leading advertising firms.

By the time she was twenty-four years old, back in the early
'60s, she was earning $20,000 and accumulating shares in the
company.

She met her husband when he was just beginning business
school and married him in 1962, with no frilly illusions about
marriage. "You know, my favorite joke when I was growing up
was that the fairy princess married the fair prince and, if they
were lucky, they both died after the wedding, as they rode off
into the sunset. Because that was the only happily-ever-after
there was. When I was walking down the aisle I was laughing
my head off. Larry started to laugh too. This was the silliest thing
we'd done since we'd met. But . . . it was what was expected,"
she said, throwing her hands up.

They were married for five years before they had their first
child. During those five years, her husband finished business
school and set up his own business, while Diane continued the
"hysterical" pace of her advertising job. Until 1967 she was the
one who earned much more money than her husband, and it was
her savings that went into setting up the business and putting a
down payment on their home.

"I'm not the sort of person who makes half a commitment. You
get married, this is your husband, you're in this together and
that's it," explained Diane with a firmness she brought to almost
everything. She was not a person who easily deferred to others'
opinions.

When Diane and Larry had their first son, five years after their
marriage, it was a joint decision that she would stay home. "I
quit a week before Jackie was born. I had worked six years then.
Enough. I wanted to stay home with him. I knew I was going to
be breast feeding. I felt that I couldn't give the effort to my job
and have the baby without putting much more pressure on myself than I was willing to. That's me. I couldn't do anything halfway. I think if I'd kept working, I just would have been a nervous wreck."

This transition was still a shock to her. "It was something! I
was suddenly cut off from the day-to-day excitement and hyste-
ria that went on in my office. The screaming! The yelling! The

people fainting!" She laughed and did a two-minute rap on the advertising agency hysterics.

Then in a whisper, she remembered: "My God, it was so quiet here. Really quiet. First of all, Jackie was the most inactive baby. He woke up to nurse and then he went back to sleep. He was never awake. I was much too restless to stand for that. I started making friends with people I didn't even like because they were there. I went to other mothers' houses to sit and chat for the first time in my life. I was very, very itchy.

"I became a person obsessed with dinner parties. I mean, you got to get your kicks somewhere. I had to have people saying, 'Ooooh, that's fabulous.' They weren't going to say, 'Ooooh, it's fabulous the way you scrub your floor,' so I made dinner parties."

Soon Diane realized that her anxiety wasn't going to be restored by parties. Or by long afternoons sitting at pools with other mothers. It just wasn't her style. Nor was she interested at this time in going back to work.

Over the next half dozen years, she found outlets for her vast energy in several ways. Her son, the quiet baby, grew into an energetic elder brother of two sisters who came at two-year intervals. In some ways, she re-created the kind of hectic, energetic dynamic in her home that existed in the ad agency. Her children were all forceful and active, even demanding.

"Sometimes I think it's wonderful that I've brought out all these children. Repressed they aren't. Then, other times I think: what's the matter with a little repression?" Diane said as her middle child cartwheeled through the living room on a third go-round.

Diane also became one of the women most vitally involved in community and school work. She was continually called on to run meetings and fairs, to plan projects as complicated as after-school day care, to chair and moderate encounters between the parents and principal of the local elementary school. When anything happened in the community, it was Diane who could be counted on to monitor the situation from the telephone with the eternal busy signal.

During these years, Diane always considered herself to be primarily a housewife. "A housewife is a woman who is married, and whose primary interest is in running the home and who has children. That's what I am."

She was also a feminist, and had been almost from the first moment she heard the word. "I recognized that that was what I was. I didn't become one. I *was* one. First of all, I had always known women living different lifestyles. I was never shocked by women who were aggressive. I was very aggressive."

Moreover, Diane never felt a conflict about being a feminist-housewife. "I just never took the messages about housewifing personally. You know, 'all those poor unwashed housewives.' I saw the bra-burning and all as just another advertising campaign. They had to do something very dramatic to get attention. I certainly never saw myself as a victim. My mother, I would say, was a victim. She was a very beautiful woman, raised to be a beautiful woman, to find a husband and get married and live happily ever after. She was crushed by the expectations to be a docile housewife. To some extent I went the opposite way. I'm very aggressive. I never wanted to be caught the way my mother was caught, widowed without a way to make a living. At the time I quit my job, I was making twice what Larry was making. So I knew and I know I can support myself if I have to."

In many ways, Diane felt that the changes in society made it easier for women like her to be a housewife.

"Well, first of all, I've never, ever felt that I was the kind of oppressed housewife they were talking about. I was never as stuck as many, maybe most, women are. I was always able to go out and be out. We always had babysitters, even when we couldn't afford it.

"But one big difference I think is that my friends are more concerned with understanding each other. I have spoken to my mother about this. She was afraid to tell people a lot of things. They didn't confide in each other the way we do. She would say, 'How can I tell Mrs. Jones that I'm lonely and miserable and blue when she looks so happy?' Everyone had these beautiful façades." But the dropping of the façades helped Diane deal more directly with the good and bad parts of being a housewife, to feel some understanding and support. And to feel "permission to talk about them."

"Well, there are the physical aspects of the job, the drudgery that I hate. I hate the repetitive jobs like going for food, driving the kids places, doing housework, cleaning, doing the beds. I hate that.

"But when you know that *everybody* hates that part, well, you can deal with it. There's a difference. I mean, if dinner isn't on the table right on schedule, I don't worry about it. So it goes. If I want to lie in bed and read a book, it doesn't bother me to call a babysitter over so that I can do that. I don't feel guilty. I would say now that I have to have time to do those things. The women's movement has put into focus that women have needs that are just as important and aren't fulfilled by mechanical drudgery."

Diane said that both she and her husband worked hard. He wasn't guilty about his long hours, nor was she resentful. In fact, he loved his work, even when he came home exhausted.

"Who's got the better deal? Oh, I think Larry does. He would say he does. He's taken care of the children while I was away. When I came home, he said, 'I don't know how you do it.' Larry appreciates it. If he didn't I'd kill him," she said, laughing. The best part about being a housewife, she said, is the wife part. "Being married to a man I really like. That's what's best about it. Period. A husband who likes all the things he has now and appreciates it. He has encouraged me to have a job, but believe me, not a full-time job that would take me away from the things he thinks are important."

Diane planned for and avoided the emptiness that might otherwise have come when her youngest child started school. After a few months of "relief," she began part-time work, which she could do at home and at her own pace. When I met her, she was doing public relations for a small, new nonprofit business run by two women she knew. It didn't take away from her main job, but it was part of the step-by-step pattern which many women choose to keep the balance in their lives, to prepare themselves, to keep pace with their own sense of the present and future.

"Well, you have to do something," she said simply. "I mean,

this isn't going to last forever . . . Thank God . . . No, I don't really mean that . . . well, maybe I do . . ."

But for a while she enjoyed and felt right about being at home —for the children and her husband.

"It's not that I think I'm so much more terrific than a babysitter. I mean, my sitters would give the kids all kinds of comforting when they got hurt. I'm much more likely to say, 'Well, goddammit, go get a Band-Aid, can't you see I'm on the phone?' I'm not some ideal mother, you know.

"But, well, I have obligations and commitments that I made that I can't disavow. I have three children, all brought into the world because we wanted them. I don't have time to do everything I want to do. If I want them to have the things that I consider to be important.

"As far as Larry is concerned, I've never had to say, 'No, I can't meet you downtown for dinner. I can't meet that customer. I can't go here and there.' I think he would deal with that all right, but I don't think he'd like it. The biggest problem we have is that we don't have enough time alone with each other. We go away just to stay up all night talking and fooling around."

Diane mused quietly for a moment, as the hubbub in her house wound down and the three children watched television.

"You know, I see a lot of silly women who hear from the movement that up to now everything has been full of shit and go out and find yourself. So they walk out on their husbands and homes and they can't find themselves because they aren't there. They never became anybody. But that isn't what *I* hear the women's movement saying. I hear, well, this has been okay but it's not the only thing, it's not enough. Women have been discriminated against and all that. I hear that we should encourage our sons to cry and our daughters to be dentists—better yet, she should be an orthodontist—and what on earth is wrong with being a mother at home to teach them all that?

"On the other hand, I am not going to be one of those women sobbing as the last kid goes off to college. By that time, I will be involved in something else. Knowing me, I suspect I'll be racing around doing God knows what. I really think that you have to plan; that's one thing that maybe a lot of other housewives don't think about. I have time, more time already for part-time things. As the kids get older, I will have to plan more and more for my own future. But there are a lot of rewards from seeing children grow up and being with them."

In many ways, Diane was a good example of the pervasiveness of change even within what people still thought of as the "traditional role."

The sense of meaning in the role had been relocated into child-raising. Her sense of personal security no longer rested exclusively on her husband, but rather on her own individual marketability in the work world. It was her confidence and independence which, in fact, made her comfortable taking time at home.

In a sense, it is ironic that the ability of women to comfortably choose to be homemakers depends now more on the success of the change innovators than of the change resisters. So many other women like Diane spoke to me of the necessity of part-time work or flexible time or social security for housewives. They spoke of the need for re-entry jobs. It seems that if women are to have the continuing option of homemaking, they too depend on changes in women's status and in the world and public policy. Right now, the only change in status housewives see is a lowering one. The insecurity of the role and the image reflected back to them from a society right now fosters feelings of loss, even betrayal.

Diane herself suffered very little of that. She had a sense of balance about her job and a perspective and control over her life. Yet, I did not leave her believing that this would be an easier choice to make in the future.

You see, Diane herself was neither training nor expecting her children to follow the life pattern she had known and which had been a perfect middleground solution for her.

In that she was typical. There has been a general change in the attitude of mothers, whether they are change innovators or resisters, in their aspirations for their children, especially their daughters. This, I think, predicts an escalating "Movement of Women" in the next generation because girls are being raised with new expectations.

Diane, for example, saw herself raising independent, achieving daughters who, she said, may very well not take time out for housewifing.

"I think that's true. For one thing, I don't even know if the job of housewifing will be there," she said before I left her home. "Will my daughters be able to stay home? Somehow I expect they won't. In any case, I feel it's my obligation to train them, to encourage them to take care of themselves, have their own professions, be independent. Then whatever else happens, happens. It isn't my job to raise them to be housewives but to be their own people. It's a responsibility I have not just to them, but to the world they will live in."

Chapter 8 Choice

"At the sound of the word 'children,' I freeze. I think our whole generation is postponing that decision as long as possible . . . Yet, somehow I'm not ready to think about living my life without kids."

The speaker was a tall, forty-seven-year-old woman. After her name came a number of initials spelling out ABMAPHD. She stood behind a makeshift podium in the long church hall and told the meeting: "We are lucky to be living in a time of greater choice than ever before. Women have almost unlimited options in their lifestyles. They can choose to marry or not. They can choose to have children or not. They can choose to be house-wives or working mothers or part-time working mothers, they can drop out of the work force and re-enter. We have more choices than any previous generation of women in history."

Many heads in the audience nodded affirmatively. Choice. Yes, that was what the change had been about. That was what had been won in the last decade. They all seemed to agree.

And yet. In that audience I knew one thirty-eight-year-old woman who was looking for a re-entry level job. There was an-other, recently divorced, who was suddenly the sole support of her three children. Further back near the large coffee urn was a third woman in the throes of an economic decision. Would her husband take a second job to pay for the dentist bills and to put away money for college, or would she take a job, and who would be home when the children came back from school? Still further back in the audience was a forty-five-year-old woman who had just had an unsettling conversation with her twenty-six-year-old daughter, recently engaged: "Jamie and I have decided that if we both want to work and we want to have time to do things for ourselves, we probably won't have any children."

New choices, yes . . . but.

By the late 1970s, "choice" had become the knee-jerk answer to the Woman Question, the question Freud posed, "What does a woman want?" But choice is after all a peculiar word. It defines both options and decisions, free choices and hard choices. Choice is both something we have and something we have to make.

The speaker at the YWCA meeting was observing society from a high altitude. She was taking a social overview. "Down there" she observed a variety of lifestyles for men and women, and reasoned backward that these must exist—like courses listed in a catalogue—for every one of us.

It's true that men and women have more options in terms of their relationships, their work and family patterns, than in the days when they were virtually predestined to follow a pattern based on their sex. But there are severe and obvious limits to choice. Biology, economics, geography, health, life accidents, prior commitments, personal abilities, and social policy are the most obvious ones. But there are also psychological limits. Can anyone, for example, choose their needs? Maslow suggested a hierarchy of needs, from the need to be fed to the need for love, achievement, growth. Can we choose these? As individuals with our own private histories and psyches, we clearly do not have completely free choice.

If then despite all these limitations, "choice" has become a watchword of the Shuttle Zone, I think it is for very special reasons.

In the late 1960s and early '70s, it seemed that the New Woman and the Traditional Woman threw stones and names at each other. Gradually now people have begun to talk with each other more openly and less defensively. They have begun to acknowledge ambivalence. The argument has become a discussion, the threat has become an alternative.

By adopting the motto of "choice," the people in the middle try to keep the dialogue open between the different members of society and between their own ambivalent responses to change. By suggesting that there is a norm-free, should-free, judgment-free range of possibilities, they free themselves from having to deny the past while moving tentatively into a different future. They don't have to reject the lives of their parents or neighbors, they don't have to disrupt their social bonds.

Under the same banner, people are also studying the choices being made, especially by those who are living on the cutting edge of change. These are the role models of the future who can assuage or increase our own fear.

The people living in the avant-garde of this change are important guides. They may be the couple next door, the man who works at the next office, the sister, the brother, even the couple featured in *People* magazine. But they are the people who make change seem closer and more real. The sister who survived a divorce, the co-worker who accepts new responsibilities at home, one child who suffers from coming home to an empty house, another child who copes and grows with new responsibilities. People anticipate the consequences of any change before they embark on it. They look ahead to see how it has affected the lives of others.

Today, the young, the avant-garde, those who are living what we popularly call New Lifestyles are our messengers, sending back signals of what's ahead. In that sense they can indicate the new conflicts emerging and point the direction of further change.

Perhaps the most common, the most supported "new" lifestyle is that of the young partnership marriage, begun according to what were originally considered "feminist" ideals. Now this model has been so generally accepted that it is looked upon not as a "political" marriage but as a typical one for the young educated couple. These marriages, often involving the offspring of traditional families, also exhibit the pleasures and conflicts of new transitions—as they did for a young husband named David.

DAVID: NEW DEAL HUSBAND

David was a freshman at Columbia in 1970, when sociologist Mirra Komarovsky studied male college seniors and found them "unrealistic in describing the future." According to Komarovsky, they believed that "girls will not, unless they are really stupid, get satisfaction out of just keeping house for the rest of their lives." Yet, they felt some conflicts. They said things like, "It is only fair to let a woman do her own thing, if she wants a career. Personally, though, I would want my wife at home."

Komarovsky noted: "All too frequently, wishing to enjoy the best of both worlds, they did not foresee that the zestful, competent independent women they hoped to marry might not easily fit into the semitraditional roles they preferred for their future wives."

David would very easily have been one of the young men who answered the questionnaires that way. Now, seven years later, the lanky twenty-six-year-old was married to one of those "zestful, competent independent women" and was learning firsthand about the values and problems of the new deal marriage.

David, blue-eyed with curly brown hair that he pulled along the ends when he talked, seemed both quick and ambitious. He had a wit that could be vicious or delightful, depending on the target, but one that had, he insisted, mellowed over the last few years into humor. A generation ago, David would have clerked somewhere for a judge when he finished law school. But when I met David, as he faced the bar exams, he was not so sure. David's wife, Carolyn, was also a law student and they were considering their lives together in a very different way from the way their parents did.

Their West Side apartment in New York was wall-to-wall law books, on bookshelves made of bricks and boards. The furniture was 1940s Salvation Army, their walls were filled with Carolyn's photographs. On a cold winter night, they were eating "our specialty," Kentucky Fried Chicken bought in a franchise store owned by a Cuban down the block. After a bottle and a half of wine, David started his game of "True Confessions" this way:

"I was a teenage prince. I took it for granted that the world revolved around me. I've talked about it with my sister, my poor sister, and her answer is, 'Look, kid, the pressure was on you, not me.' Well, I got the pressure and the attention and I am still a glutton for attention. I'm going to be trying a case before the Supreme Court some day and I'll throw a moon for the attention. I'm a pig for it.

"I am also a snob. I mean an intellectual snob. Carolyn says that when we first went out she had this weird feeling that if she couldn't spell Kierkegaard, I'd leave her on the corner of Amsterdam Avenue.

"Anyway, we started dating two and a half years ago. I wanted her to move in with me right away. And she said to me, 'No. You just want someone to make dinner for you while you're studying.' Zonk. I confess to you that the thought had crossed my mind. Not like an idea, but like a visual flashcard. Me, sitting there, reading a law book while she gets dinner ready. But I couldn't admit that. If I admitted that, I'd be the one who'd be left on the corner of Amsterdam Avenue."

David picked at the sole of his boots and said: "Even back then I knew it was wrong, I mean *wrong*, to expect my law school classmate to make my dinner. But I'm telling you, if she'd said yes to making the vittles and sewing the cuffs on my corduroys, I wouldn't have been the guy who would have said, 'No, no, you mustn't.' I'd have sat back and said, 'When you're through with that, would you mind getting my slippers?' But I think I would have ended up hating myself and there's nobody more hateful than me when I'm hating myself.

"I knew that I wanted to marry Carolyn. But she was really giving me a hard time about it," said David as Carolyn came back in and settled down in a chair. Carolyn pushed her glasses up onto her brown hair and said, "The only thing I ever said to you was that you didn't want to marry me, you were crazy, you wanted to marry someone like your mother who would bring you chicken soup on a tray when you were sick."

David changed a lot, so did Carolyn. But they knew, after a year of marriage, that there were some tough decisions ahead of them. "You know, Carolyn gets the raw deal," said David, swinging his leg over the sling chair. "If I do the dishes, I'm a hero. If she does them, it's her job. If I go into practice with Carolyn or we find some firm in East Oshkosh that would take both of us, I'm the hero. Everybody says, hey, wow, the liberated man, hotshot. If she does it, nobody says that to her. Now supposing we decide to have a baby. Our baby. Now, again, if I stayed home one day a week, I'd get a pound of candy from the local NOW chapter. She'd get zero. It's really weird."

On the other hand, he was still the one with stronger professional pressures. "Okay. Now, I've been programmed to become Louis Brandeis. Maybe Douglas, but nothing lower than that. Now, let's say my father was the one programmed to be Brandeis. If he had wanted to be a law clerk for a judge, he'd have been a law clerk. If he wanted to go to San Francisco for a year to study something and go to Washington to be in an agency, he wouldn't have had to figure out whether his wife would find a job, whether she'd like San Francisco. He said, she did. He got a job, she moved. He didn't have to worry about having children, and would he have enough time to be with them. He wouldn't have asked the Supreme Court for a paternity leave."

Was David saying then that his marriage limited his possibilities for achievement?

"Right. If it weren't for Carolyn, I'd be a Supreme Court Justice," he said and then leaned back laughing and hitting the side of his head with his palm. The sentence hung in the air until he rewrote it. "The thing is, it isn't as easy an answer as that. Carolyn was the first person who made me question the plan. She said to me, 'Okay, so you spend the next thirty years plotting to be a Supreme Court Justice, or whatever. There are four possibilities. One, you don't make it because you're lousy. Two, you get so close, so close that you hang around waiting for a seat to open until you die. Three, you make it and you hate it, the robes give you hives, whatever . . . Four, you make it, and you love it.' She made me think, do I really want to work solely for some distant goal I may not even want? I just don't know. I don't know if I'll be more sorry that I spent years trying to become a judge, or more sorry that I was held back from it, that I held myself back from it. I mean, when you lose your programming, for a while, you're like a computer, the lights are flashing, the wheels are turning, but you don't have any information coming out."

Like most of the men who were his peers, David didn't really "feel" that he had the option to retire and be unemployed. "I guess I do. I mean, abstractly, I could sit back and let Carolyn support me, but I'd feel like a kept man. I couldn't do that. I could take a legal aide job and let her bring in the money. I think I could, maybe. But I couldn't ask her for carfare and I couldn't end up keeping house. My mind would go soft like a grape. That's why I understand that she couldn't do it.

"The fact is that you don't get someone like Carolyn and get someone who is going to be really concerned about whether there are fuzzies on the rug. I think you can choose between a slave or a Carolyn. You don't get them in the same package. I'm not going to fall in love with someone who picks lint off the sofa. I need someone who excites me, who thinks with me, and pushes. So what are you gonna do?"

Later I talked with Carolyn, a slight woman who wore her khaki slacks and T-shirt with a certain style. Her brown hair was pulled back into a casual bun that showed a long neck and dangling Mexican earrings. Speaking carefully she told me: "I still feel guilty in funny ways, as if I am the one preventing him from being more aggressive, tracking off to the big firms. I feel that he's doing a lot of his rethinking for me and that's an additional pressure on me. But I try to deal with it. I do honestly feel that he was so highly pressured at home, that he is happier and more relaxed being this way. But it's also true that I don't want to be a partner in a big firm like Sullivan and Cromwell. I want to lead a somewhat balanced life. If that's possible. Sometimes I do think I have been very attracted to David's energy and part of that is his ambition. I've seen so many women who really, deep down, want their husbands to be big strong successes. And how conditioned are we still to think of success as public success? The thing that David and I have is the ability to talk about it with each other. David especially. We have a lot of thinking to do. About how to manage our lives, our careers, our relationship, to keep it all together. Sometimes I think our only problem is that we have so many choices, and that we're greedy. We want it all."

Both Carolyn and David were raised in what they would label traditional households. Their mothers both were at home during their childhood and they were very aware of their parents' relationship and the limits of their lives. Carolyn's mother had become a school supervisor in Illinois, but a woman who was still in total charge of the home. David's mother was "a professional shopper." To some degree, they, like many of us, defined "choice" as the ability to live differently than their parents. Very often the college generation and the generation in its twenties, the children of the feminine mystique generation, choose at least not to make the same mistakes. To many young women this means being anything but a housewife. To young men it may mean being anything but a corporation executive.

Yet among young married couples like David and Carolyn, there is a fear that they won't be able to have "it all"—marriage, work, and children. It is the word "children" which terrifies them most.

This is the option they want to "have" and the choice they find most difficult to make.

On the whole, I found that they preferred to keep this choice by postponing it. In that David and Carolyn were typical. The one subject they rarely discussed was children.

"At the sound of the word, I freeze," said Carolyn. "I think our whole generation is postponing that decision as long as possible. I keep reading articles about amniocentesis, you know, for older women," she said. "I still have the article in *Ms.* about having babies after forty. I don't want to think about that for years and years.

"I just don't know if I could do it all. We seem to be so busy now and what would happen if we had a baby? Just the thought of it overwhelms me.

"Yet, somehow I'm not ready to think about living my life without kids. It's just that there's a lot of time to worry about it."

There is a strong likelihood that David and Carolyn will have children, or a child, and become part of that emerging majority, the two-working-parents family. Many, perhaps most of these working-parents families in America follow the transitional pattern of the middleground—a pattern in which the mother "adds" work, subtracts some housekeeping, and "juggles." The father is still seen as the primary wage-earner and adds a more significant parenting role, but not a significant housekeeping role.

This "compromise," which seems satisfactory for so many transitional couples, would, however, be regressive for Carolyn and David and many others of their background, and their expectations for the future.

The role model for them are couples like themselves—with a thoroughly egalitarian vision. As they think about having children, they will look to couples like Chris and Aaron as an advance preview of the new life choice they will follow.

CHRIS AND AARON: AND BABY MAKES THREE

Chris and Aaron were only about five years older than David and Carolyn, but it was a big five years. To be more accurate, it was a big one year. The year since Jessie was born.

Chris and Aaron were city planners who worked at desks no more than a hundred yards away at a firm that lived on government contracts. They met in their office right after Aaron's first marriage had broken up and he had moved to San Francisco from Washington.

In the "old days," before Jessie was born, they used to walk to work together from their house and then stop after work for a leisurely drink, and occasionally dinner at a nearby Chinese restaurant. If one had to work late, it didn't really matter, the other would put in a few extra hours as well.

But after Jessie was born they began to go to work separately. One took an early bus, while the other waited for the babysitter. One had to leave the office by 5 P.M. on the dot so that the sitter could be home at five-thirty. There were occasionally frantic phone calls back and forth to see who would leave first. More significantly, the six thousand dollars they paid a babysitter meant the end of their vacations and entertainment—they were on a much tighter budget. Both were very aware that they had chosen a different way of life and child-raising than their parents. Though Chris came from a Maryland Episcopalian background and Aaron from a Methodist family in the Southwest, their backgrounds were similar in one way. They both had professional mothers who had given up their careers upon marriage. They were both aware of the costs that their mothers and, they believe, their fathers had paid for that.

"My mother adjusted," said Chris, a lithe, athletic blonde who let her hair curl into its own halo around her head that seemed to go with her oversized glasses and pale green eyes. "I don't remember her telling me specifically that she was unhappy or anything like that, but I felt somehow that my father led the more important life. And that she was much more interested in his career. She had made his career hers too."

In fashioning their lives, they have both been very aware of their parents' decisions. Indeed, Chris referred back to her mother as a regular counterpoint. "I've never talked with my mother directly, I mean, asked her if she feels her life was wasted. I don't want to hear her say yes, I guess. Because I'm the one she wasted it on."

Aaron was wiry, and muscular, dressed in western boots and jeans, with his after-work work shirt. His brown hair was sleek and straight, shaped carefully. When he held Jessie, as we talked in their Victorian-furnished, turn-of-the-century townhouse, it was with assurance and familiarity.

Aaron had gone through college and graduate school, and been married at twenty-five to a graduate student at Berkeley. That was 1966. A year after their marriage, he had been sent to Vietnam by the Army and he had been deeply affected by the devastation of the country.

"It was a surreal experience. When you are in Vietnam, there is only Vietnam. Anyone who isn't there, doesn't understand.

"My life with Judy [his first wife] just divided. She was in Berkeley as part of the antiwar movement while I was in the war. She was at rallies while I was walking around Saigon stoned all the time. It was the only way you could survive. We had one weird week together in Tokyo and then she went back to Berkeley and wrote me a Dear John letter. I don't blame her. There was nothing to hold us together."

Chris's expectations, which she'd brought to her first live-in relationship, had been similar to Aaron's. "He was older and I was the one who put in 80 percent of the effort. I never felt quite secure and I would run around trying to please him. I only bought the kind of clothes he liked. I never wore a pantsuit until 1972, can you believe that? Plus, of course, I was working and paying half the rent and most of the food money and it was awful. I swore when I got out of that, I would never again change myself to please someone, be so anxious about it . . . I get the crawlies just thinking about it."

When Aaron and Chris met, four years ago, she was twenty-eight and he was thirty-one. They were married a year and a half later and slowly made a series of decisions that would determine the way they lived.

"Well," said Chris, "I knew that I wanted to keep working. I think it was a combination of things. I felt that my mother was strangled. Let me put it this way: I always felt that I didn't want to be so dependent on my children as she is on me. I mean, she is bored. She makes work to fill up her days. Even now, she will spend all day looking for the right blouse or the perfect pot. I remember when I would come home from school, my mother would spend all afternoon preparing dinner. She would wash the vegetables in the afternoon, she'd have the butter melted and ready. She would always have a nice dessert. She spent so much time doing so little, to be perfectly frank about it.

"That vision scared me, genuinely scares me to this day. I always have this feeling one false step and I will be my mother," says Chris. "Well, then, too, I could see the economic situation that if I dropped out of our firm, well, there aren't that many jobs in city planning. I might not be able to get back in. I could see myself stranded."

Aaron added, "When we decided to buy this house, it was a decision that meant she wasn't going to stay home with the baby. I mean, there's no way we could live here on one income. We wanted to stay in the city. We're just not suburban types. So we bought this house which is damned expensive and now, well, we couldn't keep it if she weren't working."

"I just couldn't imagine myself living out in the suburbs or someplace. It would be like I was another person," agreed Chris. When they had Jessie, Chris stayed home for three months, then found a babysitter. "I replaced myself. It's the most expensive kind of day care. It's certainly not a solution for the average working woman, because she just wouldn't be making enough to pay for it. Even *we* aren't making enough."

They both learned about some of the tradeoffs of the life they have chosen, to be the avant-garde in a semitraditional society, one which still has little public policy support for the two-working-parents family with preschool children. "First of all, child care. It's strictly a do-it-yourself operation. Either you stay home with your child or you replace yourself, or you find a situation for the baby. There isn't any support for this, not really, except from the other working mothers who give you some hints about how to interview, where to advertise, the pros and cons of their situations.

"Then, to be honest about it, there's work. There's no real allowance, in our office, for the way we are arranging things. We're generally regarded as doing something vaguely suspicious," says Chris.

Aaron agreed, "I think that's true. The head of the firm is a fifty-five-year-old man, whose own wife stayed at home. I am convinced that he thinks Chris should. He isn't about to fire her or anything, but he disapproves. And I get a lot of disapproval myself, from the older men in the office. If I leave to go home to take care of Jessie, well, to be honest about it, I'm pegged by them. They don't think I'm a 'go-getter.' Some of the guys my age live the way we do—although they don't work with their wives so it's a little different—but they think I'm gutsy . . . or foolhardy to be open about it. I have a feeling sometimes that if it weren't for the wife of one of the senior partners—he's been very supportive of us!—we'd have gotten a lot more grief than we have. These people are really good to us. They've become almost surrogate parents and that's because she's one of the women who've gone back to school, and work, she's done the whole women's number."

"And," added Chris, "because they feel that their own kids were really screwed up. When they were babies, John was traveling all over the world and Sybil was going bananas, and I think he's guilty about that."

Chris and Aaron genuinely shared child care with each other and with the babysitter who came in eight hours a day. One of the things Chris had learned was to share mothering.

"One of the things that always amazes me," she said, "is how possessive some of my friends who are at home are about their kids. I have a theory that a lot of them really don't want to share their kids. That's their part of the tradeoff. They want to be Big Mama. Now I don't know which comes first. Maybe, if you are at home all the time, that is your reward. I also know a lot of working mothers who have trouble letting go and that makes life much harder on them.

"I don't think I feel competitive either with Joyce [the sitter] or with Aaron. The other morning, just as Joyce came in, Jessie fell and she wanted Joyce to pick her up. I had a twinge, I have to say that, but really, honestly, no more than that. I know I'm her mother, and I feel lucky that she is that close and loving with Joyce. As for Aaron, Jessie goes to either of us, really, and that's because we both take care of her."

Yet Chris was aware that she made a tradeoff.

"You do miss something not being home. But you miss something if you're not working. After Jessie was born, I enjoyed the daily contact and watching her change so fast. But I felt my mind going.

"It's just that when I'm not home I think I'm missing something. I call home twice a day and I run to get home because I really want to see her and I feel that I've missed something. Then if I am home all day, I spend more time pushing her off. After a while, I've had it. I figure if I were home all the time, I wouldn't be anywhere nearly as good with her. I know I wouldn't."

Chris had a sense, shared by many of the young working mothers I interviewed and she put it succinctly: "Our generation has traded boredom for anxiety.

"The truth is both Aaron and I have more hassles than our parents did. I'm sure of that. My father had the work hassles, my mother had the home hassles, and we have both of them. We have no time. I mean, that's it. *No* time. We run from home to the office to home. We throw dinner on the table. Aaron doesn't even make a salad anymore. It's a one-course operation. On the weekends, we have errands to do, shopping, going to the cleaners, all the things that we used to do at lunch or after work. We almost have given up socializing. I think we've had two dinner parties since Jessie was born. I mean, we have all we can do to work and spend time with Jessie. And that's really all we want to do."

When I asked how they would change their life, they both answered, "More money." Aaron elaborated with good humor: "All we need to be perfectly happy is about ten thousand dollars a year more."

Yet, they also shared anxiety about the bringing up of Jessie. To some degree it was the anxiety that entered every new parent's life. But it was accentuated. They were the first generation in either family to live outside of traditional roles.

"I don't know, who knows? Will all of our kids be screwed up at twenty?" asked Chris. "Obviously I don't think so, but it's a concern. I feel like we don't know, really. Nobody's studied the effect of the whole generation that is now growing up. People just seem to think, well, if you have a warm, stable environment it doesn't matter who is the primary child-care person. Obviously I think it will be fine. And, I don't think it was so terrific for all of us with our mothers at home. Aaron is lucky he survived his mother. My mother, well, I love her, but I pray I won't aggravate my daughter as much as she aggravates me. She needs me too much.

"On the other hand, we went to a party the other day and we brought Jessie along and there was this woman who came over and said, 'Oh what a beautiful baby, doesn't she have sad eyes.' Well, God, I was so worried. I went around thinking, does she have sad eyes? Oh, God, is she really sad? The past four nights I had the most terrible nightmares. Jessie's just walking and she's so proud of herself. This has been the best time we've ever had with her, and I suppose my dreams were because things have been so good. Anyway, I just kept having nightmares, one after another. That she was in a fire. That she was kidnapped. I can't stand to watch TV shows with a baby in them now.

"I do have a terrible fear that something will happen to Jessie

while I'm at work. But I know it¯isn't rational. Two weeks ago
the kid next door who is eight was hit by a car riding his bicycle,
while his mother was right there at home. Oh, it's not rational, I
know," said Chris, throwing up her hands.

Aaron for his part was overwhelmed with being a parent.
"I cannot believe now that there are fathers who come home
and spend a half hour with their babies. I think of the way
men have given up their children to women. It's amazing. My
own father did that. I shouldn't fault him for it. I think that must
have been the only way he knew. And when we got older, he did
spend some time with us. But I just feel now, how could you
miss being the parent of a baby! I'm just insane about her."

One other thing that Aaron and Chris shared was a sense of
partnership. Watching them care for Jessie and make dinner, I noticed that neither of them apologized to the other, and neither
overcompensated.

And neither of them was guilty. "What has Chris lost by having
me as a husband? Well, she might have married a guy who made
a lot more money. But she probably would have been miserable," he said, laughing. "No, to be honest, I think that she likes
being married to someone who shares work as well as home. I
mean, ours is a bit odd, working practically next to each other,
but . . . I don't think she's lost anything. She wouldn't be able to
stand some guy who stuck her at home with the dishes."

As for Aaron, Chris said, "Oh, he could have found someone
to wait on him maybe and I don't think he would have minded
that . . . What else? Not much . . . Actually, I think he's a lucky
son of a bitch!" she said, and they both laughed.

Chris thought that she traded in boredom for anxiety, for the
hassles, but she didn't think it was actually a harder life. "I don't
know how you calculate 'harder.' Certainly I have worries about
work and worries about the baby and worries about Aaron. I
guess my mother didn't have the pressures of a job. We have
more hassles, we have more ups and downs, and much less time.
I think time is the ultimate pie, if you know what I mean.

"But harder? I really don't think so. You only have so much
space for worrying anyway. And, then, I love my work, and I

love my family. I couldn't choose between them any more than you could choose between children."

Couples like Aaron and Chris do have a sense of being a part of changing times. Though, as Aaron put it, "We would like to live our own way, privately and quietly, without making a big deal out of it." They were not really able to do that.

They were still "the first." The first working-parents couple in their office, the first generation of their respective families to break a pattern of many generations. But they are not alone. Around them in the other brightly painted early-twentieth-century homes in San Francisco, and in similar areas filled with professional couples in many major cities, there is a chain of somewhat elite, educated, "liberated" couples who take sustenance from each other and form a network of support. They are perhaps more insecure, and tenuous about some aspects of their lifestyle decision—because the lifestyle choice hasn't been tested and turned into a tradition. But they are also excited by being part of change, and they derived a certain status from their lifestyle.

CHOOSING A "HARDER" LIFE

There is something energizing as well as fearsome about being part of a sizable avant-garde—not so far ahead that you become sacrificed, the "loss leader," but on a comfortable cutting edge.

Caryl Rivers, an author, and not the sort of person to label herself part of an elite, has written extensively with humor and insight on her "liberated" marriage. She and her husband, Alan Lupo, are both writers and share child and home care in their style, without contracts or even, necessarily, agreements. Their house resounds with cries of "Mom," "Dad," and barks of their hyperactive dog, Jane.

In fact Caryl testified that the secret of role-sharing marriage is just plain flexibility. That, and a drastic lowering of some kinds of expectations—"like passing the health board examination of the house." On the whole, she said, they were lucky to be living a nontraditional life in a transitional period. "I get to thinking, aren't I terrific. Now, I'm good, but I'm not terrific. I am not one of the great writers of the western world. But I think that men compare themselves to Pulitzer Prize winners and we compare ourselves to housewives. It has to do with expectations. I'm doing better than anyone expected. Than *I* expected. I would have been thrilled just to have a job writing obituaries. I suspect that Alan compares himself to the Pulitzer Prize winner."

On the other hand, Caryl said, she compared herself as a parent to full-time mothers while Alan got a lot from "women who go around telling him what a terrific parent he is." The very fact that he had taken care of the children qualified him for that praise. Both Caryl and Alan were called on regularly to be on "Liberated Marriage" panels. "I feel like wearing a badge sometimes that says, 'Yes, I'm Married and I Have Children, and I Write.'

"The college kids I meet are so afraid. It's not that they don't want to have kids or something, it's just that they think they can't. I keep feeling like I should be in a shrine or something."

But Caryl and Alan felt more often as if they have stepped incrementally into a new life.

Alan and Caryl started out together in the early '60s with a semitraditional mode. They began their marriage at a point many have arrived at with difficulty: the middleground.

"The idea was that I would work, but it wouldn't be as important as Alan's work. It was like all animals are equal but some are more equal than others."

But there came a time when Alan wanted out of the daily journalism job he was in, and Caryl found a post as a teacher that allowed her an income with enough flexibility so she could still write. Gradually, Alan moved in and out of jobs, including a period of bookwriting when his income was negligible and Caryl maintained a steady teaching job.

"On balance he's gained the freedom to make some job moves he would never have made.

"At the beginning I think he wanted me to be a superwoman. He would have liked to come home and find that I had made dinner, with two vegetables and a piece of meat, and the house was immaculate and the children well scrubbed and everything perfect, and I have just finished a novel that day. Fortunately I'm too lazy. I just wasn't about to try and do it all.

"The tradeoffs have been in terms of more work for Alan at home. Yesterday, for instance, he was grubbing around looking for some clean underwear. But he's much closer to the kids than he would have been. Economically, if he'd had to bear the burden of the family, I really think he would have been physically ill. He looks upon a lot of this as a health thing.

"The other tradeoffs have been that we've given up our social life, virtually. We don't have time to plan it, let alone do it. I haven't painted in an age; we haven't been to the theater, to a concert. I've become a cultural moron. We're just not what you'd call laid back around here."

They have been lucky. Their professions are relatively free ones, with some independence and a flexible time schedule. They don't punch a time clock. Neither is climbing a corporate ladder that is geared to traditional expectations of roles.

There are other men who are discovering more pointedly the conflicts of new choices. Some of them are discovering conflicts that were once almost exclusively female.

FEAR OF SUCCESS

There was a time, for example, when the fear of success was considered to be a female problem. Matina Horner described the "motivation to avoid success" among college women who feared that being successful would make them ineligible for marriage, even unlovable.

Among many on the further side of change there is now a revised "fear of success" that comes from a new reckoning of what success has meant and requires. Men are figuring their families into the cost-accounting system of their lives in a very different way.

Barrie Grieff gives a course to couples at Harvard Business School, the most traditional high-pressure school, in which he talks directly about this cost accounting.

As he said: "The course is valuable because it gives people options to think about. There is always a conflict between personal needs and a corporation's needs. The individual must create a mechanism that allows him to participate in a little of each. It may mean giving up some goals and aspirations. It may mean talking to one's employer. It may mean quitting and taking another job. People have to think clearly what their options are, what their priorities are, and what their tradeoffs are."

Now it's very often men who are faced with, and make some of, the new hard choices between career aspirations and family life. Not unlike the decision Patrick had to make.

PATRICK: CORPORATE IMMOBILITY

Patrick described himself as "someone who always had to learn the hard way." A large-boned forty-two-year-old man with sandy hair and huge hands, Patrick was the one of all the kids in his family who was dubbed "stubborn."

"What stubborn meant in my family was that if you didn't do what my dad told you to do, you got the shit kicked out of you," he said in a voice that comes out of his large body an unexpected tenor.

He was the most rebellious of the six kids who grew up in Gary, Indiana, where his father worked in the steel mills for forty-five years. The only thing that distinguished Patrick's father from the others in the rundown working-class parish was that his dad was a union man. His father was a leader in Detroit during the toughest days. He remembered the fighting at the River Rouge plant and he was proud of his role.

Yet by the 1930s, when Patrick was born, he was a man caught, in some ways, between his intense and bitter class consciousness and his desire for his sons to make it.

"We were driven. It was tough for my dad. He drove us out of Gary. In a way, he drove us away from him and yet he was never reconciled to the fact that we did make it. Here's this union man, and we all became management men! He was proud of us and he hated it at the same time. I think he just hated the whole class system and yet he didn't want us to spend our lives at the mill. My dad was a very complicated man. He was toughened up by life. There was nothing soft about him. I hated him for a lot of years. Now, boy, I try to understand the kind of mixed-up feelings that he had. I guess I understand better now because I've had some mixed-up times myself."

Pat met his wife, Fran, during his junior year of college in 1960. When he graduated and was offered a job with an executive training program of a major manufacturing firm, Fran quit school to marry Pat and began following him. In the first ten years of their marriage, they had four children in four cities. Every time the company asked Pat to move, he did. It meant more money and more responsibility each time. It meant that Fran was uprooted, the kids were uprooted, "but there was never any question about moving. Fran was unhappy but she kept it to herself. It was just the way things were. We didn't think of it a whole lot. Now, I see, that it was easy for me. I would go off to work and I'd be busy and pretty soon I'd meet the other guys at work, you know. Corporations were like the Army, you kept on moving and the idea was that the families would adjust." The word choice hadn't entered their emotional vocabulary.

Each time, like a pioneer wife, Fran was left behind to close down the old house, and sell it, to pack the packable, to sort out what they would take and what they would leave behind. Then she would come out to the "new territory" and help settle into a slightly more expensive house. She would then try to scurry around and find out which schools, which teachers, which music lessons, which stores to use.

By the time Fran was thirty, she had children eight, six, five, and three years old, and her husband, then thirty-two, was a manager. This time, they knew they would settle in for a time, and Fran put down some roots.

She and the children made friends, real friends, over the next six years; she decided to go back to school, and gradually and eventually finished a degree in music teaching. First she took some students in their own home for piano lessons, and then, after the youngest child was in school, she got a job teaching music.

"Now, the thing is that we'd both been fooling each other. You know what I mean? Not for bad reasons, but there it was. I was real proud of her for doing all this, the school, the music. I'm not a musical man myself, but I thought it was great. It didn't change anything in my own life, if you know what I mean, because basically, from my point of view, she was there when the kids were home from school, I always thought that was real important. I still do. And she was there when I came home from work. She was getting a kick out of what she was doing. The money was a nice extra. We took a trip one year and she was real proud that it was her money. And that was great. I wasn't totally hung up on the ego thing. She put some of her money in a savings account for the kids' college."

The only major trauma they had during those years was right after Fran had gotten her school job. She became pregnant in April. "We were both raised Catholic. Not all that Catholic. My dad used to rant and rave about the Church and my mother used to cross herself. But we had gone to church pretty regular as kids. The only piece of advice my dad had given me—and, mind you, I was one of eight growing up—was not to pay any mind to the Church about how many children we'd have. Even my dad couldn't come right out and say to practice birth control, you know. Well, we pretty much didn't. We used what they call Vatican Roulette until the fourth was born and then it was Fran who went and got the Pill. We never talked about it, not really. She did it and it took me off the hook. Neither of us wanted any more kids, but it was Fran who did it, and I see now that was the way I copped out on her. I just left all those decisions to her."

Patrick took another cigarette out of the pack and lit it. He held it then between his fingers and let it burn, wrestling with his tale of the fifth pregnancy. "Well, my side was, first I was angry that she had gotten pregnant. She'd forgotten to take a couple of pills and then taken three of them. Anyway, I was mad. Then I said, okay, we'll deal with it. It won't be the worst thing in the world. Well, it was Fran who said no. She wanted to have an abortion. An *abortion?* That was, well, I was brought up to believe that was murder. But I didn't want any more kids either. It was all we could do with the four of them. In any case, I tell you this and I feel pretty bad about it still, I just left it up to her.

"This is, now we're talking about 1973. Fran got on a plane and went to New York and had the abortion and was back in two days. Boom. That was it. We almost never talked about it. I

wanted to pretend it never happened and she did too, I guess.
But I see now, it was like everything else. We didn't talk about a
lot of things."

It was a year and a half later, after his oldest had started high
school, and Fran had worked hard to turn her music teacher job
into an innovative music program for the town's grammar school
system. She was going to be appointed the following September
to test this program out herself. In some ways Fran had been
testing herself and planning for the future—now only less than
ten years away—when her children would all be gone. She had
struggled hard to create an equilibrium in her life, to balance
her obligations to her family with her "own selfish" interests (this
was how she thought of it) in her work.

Pat, for his part, had been very comfortable in his own mana-
gerial role. The department had weathered some rocky economic
times, he felt competent in both personnel work and in keeping
tabs on production. He liked the idea that the town where they
lived was small enough so that he could get to work in twenty
minutes and that they could drive to the lake, all of them, put
the boat in the water and spend the weekend days sailing. He
also loved his home and had personally, with one of his brothers,
built on an addition.

Then one day the president of the company called Pat into his
office and, with a big smile, congratulated him. He was going to
be the new vice-president in charge of the Chicago operation.

"Everybody's congratulating me. I had known in some ways
that this was coming. And I have to say, I was really pleased to
be given a promotion. Who wouldn't be? On the other hand, the
idea of leaving wasn't great. I really loved my house and our life
here. But you didn't say no to a promotion. The fact is that if
you said no, you were probably courting disaster. They'd kick
you out. That was what I thought, anyway.

"So I went home to tell Fran. I knew this would be tough.
And it was. She didn't want to move.

"I wasn't unsympathetic to her, but I figured, well, she'll come
around.

"Fran said it wasn't fair. I remember her words: 'It's not fair.
You had your moves. I kept a home and raised the kids and it's

just not fair. This is my chance.' Up until then I hadn't realized a lot of things, like how important the music thing was to her. And that she hadn't wanted to move with me or to take care of all these things in our life. I went into a kind of spiral, you know. My thought was, Jesus Christ, she never wanted to do all these things. She never wanted to take care of the kids, she probably never wanted even to have them. She was probably resentful of me, of them. I thought, Christ, I don't know her at all.

"This broke a big dam in me and in Fran and we talked the next month more than we had for the past ten years. You know, a thing like this can make or break a marriage."

Pat gradually realized that Fran hadn't hated the choices of the past. She had simply moved beyond them. She had made a series of decisions—not all of which she'd shared with him—and the cost to her had been significant. "The abortion had really hit her. Going through it alone." But the pleasures of change, the sense that she was learning and contributing, important beyond her family world, had also been enormous. Now, Pat was threatening to take her away from the self she had been building over the years.

"It never got to the point where she said, 'Pat, I'm not going. The kids aren't going.' But it was eggshells all around."

The entire family was thrown into an uproar. Pat and Fran never let on that there was tension between them, and the kids assumed, miserably, that they would be leaving. But Fran went ahead planning her music curriculum as if she weren't moving. In the spring, Pat's superiors sent him to Chicago on several preliminary trips to meet the people he'd be working with.

On one trip to Chicago he drove down to Gary to visit his father. "I sat with my dad. We talked a bit about this move and about Fran. Now, my dad and I had never really gotten along that well, as I said. I think he was so damned conflicted about us, you know, and then he was worn out, working and the union. But visiting with him that time, I saw the strength in the guy. He'd worked in the steel mill forty-five years, he'd been a union man. Hell, it didn't matter that he hadn't been a big shot in that place. He'd done what he thought was the right thing. The fair thing.

"I drove back to Chicago. I wondered how he had let me get to the point where I would have thrown my family down the toilet for the job. How had I gotten to that point? I thought, I can get a job. Nobody in my family has starved since they left Ireland. That was the thing, you know. I was afraid, if I didn't take the promotion, I'd get the can. That's the thing with us, with men, all of us, we're afraid we're gonna get the can. Well, my dad hadn't been afraid. He'd spent his life bucking that management and here I was, a bowl of Jell-O.

"When I got back to Chicago, I drove straight out to O'Hare and came home. I told Fran that I was going to tell them I wouldn't move and that she should know that they might fire me."

In fact, they didn't fire Pat. But subtly, the attitude toward him at the office did indeed change. He was given a lateral move, no longer on the line moving up, but in charge of a small department that was a self-contained subsidiary.

"I have changed a whole lot from that decision. Work isn't as important to me as it once was. That's the truth. I do a good job, don't get me wrong. I put in my time, there're no problems in my area, but I've changed. Going through this made me realize that it's the whole thing that's important to me, keeping the whole thing, the family and all that together, that matters the most. We don't make as much as we would have if I'd moved to Chicago, but what with the cost of living there, we don't live a whole lot differently than we would have. I think about other things at work than I used to. Fran, for example, has helped me to see how to make the office a better place to work. I've been able to loosen up a bit, make the hours for some of the people more flexible. The other day, one of the women in the office, well, her babysitter didn't show. She's divorced, there's nobody else to take care of the kid, so she called me up and I told her to bring the kid in with her. Well, I wouldn't have done that a few years ago. No way."

It wasn't easy to make this switch from a single vision pointed to "success," corporate success, but Pat weathered it well.

"I thought that if I kicked the ladder, I would feel shitty, like a failure, but I don't. That's the Jesus H. Christ truth. Things have been better. All around, I feel better."

A lot went into Pat's new choice and the way he felt about it. The value on "fairness" which he inherited from his home; his sense of having to make independent decisions, against the system, which came from his childhood experience. The changes in his family that had come from his wife's revision of her role and aspirations had bred a new level of conflicts. In the old days, Fran simply, reflexly moved with her husband. Whither Thou Goest. Now, he simply wasn't as mobile a man.

In a sense Fran had softened the changes for Pat. She had evolved into a semitraditional role. But the crunch came when a choice was presented, a hard choice, that required a new process of decision-making. The problems facing a two-worker marriage are more complicated and this was the first time Patrick consciously had to recognize Fran's work and then family as important factors in his own professional life. That choice turned out to be a significant turning point in their life directions and their marriage.

On the whole, it worked out very well for their family. Neither Pat nor Fran—certainly not the children—thought that this change diminished them. Pat was able to say that he hadn't ultimately made this choice for Fran, but for his own values. In retrospect he saw the gradual life changes that led up to this crisis.

But it was also true that the new opportunities for Fran had closed down at least one of the options for Pat. He was no longer able to make all of the decisions for his family. He couldn't have his vice-presidency and his family too. Other men in similar circumstances might have felt constrained, disappointed, or even embittered at having to make this kind of choice. But one person's new possibilities may be another person's new limitations or losses.

ONE PERSON'S CHOICE MAY BE ANOTHER'S LOSS

The men that I met agreed that their clearest gain from the changes in roles had been an improved relationship with their

children. The message that the middleground men accepted
most easily was that they might have a greater involvement in
their children's lives.

But again, this new choice of equal parenting may bring with
it new social conflicts. In this case, for example, there is a new
side effect of divorce. It is clear that we are at the threshold of a
vast increase in the number of custody disputes and decisions
that will award greater rights to fathers, and, therefore, lesser
rights to mothers. More men, like Peter, will be granted custody.

PETER: FATHERING, A SINGULAR EXPERIENCE

Two years ago when Ona and Peter finally decided to separate, the tall black man left the house feeling dazed but assum-
ing, "This was the only way."

"There I am and I'm moving into this apartment," Peter said,
describing his first days of separation. "Like I'm thirty-four years
old and I am supposed to go back to being a playboy, a bachelor, and I guess that was the fantasy, that men could just pick
right up on their bachelor days and not mind that they are
without their children. But I was in this godawful quiet apartment, with the rented furniture and the TV set and the refrigerator with a limp head of lettuce in it, staring, just staring. I felt
like someone had dropped me on Mars. Where were my children? I had nightmares that my little girl was shrinking. I had a
dream that my son was wandering around looking for me, that
he was looking around and only seeing these white faces and trying to find one black face, mine." Then and there the slim athletic father decided to try to get custody.

He talked about this intensely, in the attached coffee shop of
the tennis club which he operated in a Connecticut suburb.
"When we had Melanie, man, I thought she was the most beautiful thing I ever saw. I thought, this is yours, a child, this is
something no one can ever take away from you. Sometimes, I
would hold that child and think, this is it, this is good right now,
to be sitting here with her.

"Ona and I both always worked. I always believed that if we
were both working, we were both taking care of these kids. It

was my mother who watched them during the day, and lots of times I would come by, especially since I've been working here, I would come by or the kids would play here some in the afternoons. Ona couldn't do that at the insurance company. That's not her fault, it just wasn't in the cards. It would have blown their minds to see two little ones playing around her desk.

"Anyway, when things really hit a low point for us, I didn't want a divorce because of the kids. It was Ona who said all this stuff about how it was worse for them to hear us fighting than for us to separate—now I agree with that—but all I could think of was that I was going to lose these children, my flesh, my children. I never even thought of having them live with me, even though, as I said, I looked after them as much as she did.

"I was in this dumpy little apartment going crazy at night, not sleeping, and during the days I would go by and call my ma all the time—because she was still looking after them. Finally, one of the members here, this woman was saying to me, why don't you get custody of them? I was so crazy at that time I hadn't even thought of it. So I said to her, 'I can't get custody. She's their mother.' But the idea stuck in my head. I kept thinking, now what's going on in this world? Nowadays everybody talking about men taking over child care and here I am, a guy who changed in my life, and I just say, okay, you have the kids. What's going on here?

"There was something extra in our case. Me being black and Ona white. I figured these kids are going to have a tough time with a white mother and them being considered black. I also figured, I'm the one with the freer schedule. I'm the one who can run over to school if Melanie or Saba forget their lunch money. I'm the one who can run over to the school plays and stuff. This doesn't make sense. Deep down, I just wanted them. They are my kids and I don't want to go through life without kids. They mean home, they mean that I got a place in the community, that I'm a real person, not some floating, rootless nobody. I'm willing to go through the hassles for that.

"When I first told Ona that I wanted the kids, she was stunned. She just freaked out. She told me I was just trying to

punish her and all kinds of stuff. I tried to tell her no, it's just
that I want my kids and I'm going to get them.

"And I did. I went to court and got custody and it wasn't easy
like that sounds. I don't know if I could have gotten them if it
weren't for the thing about them being black. Maybe the judge
was just a racist and that helped me out, but they live with me
now and their mother is getting used to it, gradually. I think
somewhere she knows it's better for them and she is reacting to
the public thing, you know, that she must be a whore or something to have lost her children.

"But I've been looking into this thing for a while now since it
happened to me. I keep running into more and more single fathers, like me. The way I figure it, women and men are going to
be fifty-fifty on this thing, if the women's lib and other things
mean that we'll be all working and looking after kids equal-like,
well, now you can't just cut men off like that in divorce. You
can't just say to them fifty-fifty in marriage but in divorce, tough,
man, hit the road and be a visiting daddy. You're going to have a
guy who has a bigger stake in his kids and who feels that he can
do the job. Nothing so mysterious about raising kids, you know.
You love them, you take care of them, Mama, Papa, it's all the
same."

In some ways it seems inevitable, as Peter said, that the men
who participate in child care more, who incorporate fathering as
an integral part of their identity, won't accept the loss of that
role as easily in the event of divorce. The trend toward father
and shared custody may mushroom. There may be more custody
conflict and many more joint custody decisions. And this new
"choice" will breed some of the most intense new conflicts.

On the other hand, we may also see—for better and for worse—
a new reason for "staying together"—for the sake of the parenting.

THE INDEPENDENT WOMAN

Divorce is not a "new choice" in a time when there is one for
every two marriages. Yet I found, despite a pervasive fear of divorce, the single-again woman was in many ways a new role

model. One of the strong forces behind the changes in sex roles had, after all, been women's need for self-sufficiency in case of divorce or death. As one widow told me sadly, "There's one thing I never knew. No woman can feel secure unless she can make it on her own." This is a very prevalent feeling that runs through our transitional society. Since every marriage ends in either death or divorce, a great number of women look at these single survivors. As one said of a divorced friend, "Sometimes I think she's my Ghost of Christmas Future—I'm rooting for her."

The lives of divorced mothers are also often labeled "alternatives" and "new lifestyles" in this change. Some, like Sylvia, even give themselves a new label, the Independent Woman.

SYLVIA: INDEPENDENT WOMAN

If you wanted to find a woman in New York who had made it on her own, someone who had raised children and paid her bills and made her job work, someone who had done all this and grown stronger and more interesting with the years, you couldn't find a better specimen than Sylvia.

Sylvia was forty-four years old, five feet five inches tall, with graying black curly hair, Afro style. She lived in a West Side New York apartment with two noisy teenaged children and a dog who was afraid of grass.

When I came into the apartment, she was standing in her kitchen with one ear on the phone attached to the wall by a long extension cord. In front of her was a beige paper pad with the big brown lettering MEMO. She was taking notes with her right hand and talking, the pencil exchanged during the pauses for a long wooden spoon with which she stirred the frying onions.

Although we had never met, she had invited me to dinner with a kind of casual friendliness, promising only that "I'll throw something together." It's the style that had made her apartment a center for the kids' friends.

Sylvia was energetic and noisy and a coper. She only screamed once a month, she said, when the hassles in her life built up to a shriek; the rest of the time she managed everything from plumbing to her daughter's tears to changing the tires on the bicycles in her hallway. She described herself as "good sturdy peasant stock."

But as we sat down to hamburgers, she insisted that she wasn't always as active or energetic.

"I was a slug. I was one of the women who waited for everything to happen to her. I waited for a husband and then I waited for him to make everything all right."

About eight years ago, when they were divorced, she realized that she had to stop waiting and start doing.

"There I was with these two kids, and no money. My ex-husband went through a charming number where he declared personal bankruptcy and you couldn't squeeze a nickel out of him.

"We'd been living in this brownstone in Brooklyn which I had redecorated with my hands. I had personally exposed every brick in the place, and he claimed that the house was his! I realized then that what I had done had counted for zero."

For the first eighteen months after her divorce, Sylvia lived in a state of panic. The money she finally got out of a long divorce action was enough to pay for only the rent. She learned about "independence" firsthand.

"I made the rounds with my portfolio. I'd been a commercial artist before I had the kids and I had done some stuff since. I still had an agent anyway.

"But I was starving to death. My mother would come over with food, for chrissakes. I couldn't ask her, but I'll tell you, there were times when that pot roast was the only protein the kids had all week."

Finally, her agent made her an offer, to be an agent herself. "I didn't have any idea what it was about. I heard the magical words, 'fourteen thousand dollars a year,' and my eyes lit up like a slot machine. I thought . . . FOOD, SHELTER, CLOTHING . . . YES! I think if he'd asked me to be a stripper I would have said yes.

"I got that job at just the right minute. I had been wallowing in the Poor Me, Poor Me, deserted by my husband for another woman. Poor Me . . . Save Me. I thought if I could just replace him, get another daddy, everything would be dandy. Well, thank God, I didn't."

Her impulse to substitute—the kind of change that often seems appealingly easy—gave way to the changes of growth.

"I don't think I thought about anything but money, for years. I was obsessed with making enough dough to get out and keep this family together."

She "chose" to make it on her own. She "chose" an income over art. She "chose" to put her energy into her professional life rather than her personal life. Free choices? Hardly.

"You do have to decide what to do with your energy. It's like I wasn't interested in wasting it on a lawyer, pursuing the husband, going to court and doing the whole number. I was lucky and I worked hard. I was able to do it on my own. Well, I still know that money is the difference between being independent or not and I'm very aware that what separated my life from that of another woman today is that I now earn a goddamn good income. And, I am proud of that."

Over the past three years in the agency, Sylvia's income went up over forty-five thousand dollars. She was able to have one child in private school—the other at one of New York's select public schools—and she had some degree of confidence that she would be able to pay part of college for them.

She was aware that all of the changes she made in the past eight years had been in the direction of independence.

As we talked late into the night, the dishwasher humming while we drank the French wine which had replaced the Almadén chablis of her poorer days, she talked about the "choice" of remaining single.

"When I say I've chosen to be single, let me tell you that it's taken two years for me to say that. To me it means taking responsibility for my life. It's not like I said, 'Hey, guys, what I really want out of life is an empty bed and I'm gonna get it.' It's more like I made decisions that have, for now, ended me up in this situation and that, on the whole, it's okay, it's no better or worse than a lot of other things.

"When I was first divorced, you know, I just didn't have the time—correction, I just didn't make the time—to have men in my life. The first one I fell in love with was married, and a client to boot—that was two years ago. There were a couple of other possibilities over the past few years, but every time I think of getting married again, I think of it as giving up something. Something I worked really hard to get.

"Oh, there are other things too. It's this damn city. All the single men in New York are either involved with each other, or they date teeny-boppers. I am forty-five years old. I have a daughter who thinks I am ready for social security. I still live in a time when society throws women over forty into the trash barrel and if my partner tells me one more time that I look great for my age, I will spit.

"My friend Jason told me that I was unwilling to make any compromises. Compromises! I spent ten years of marriage as a doormat. Now, I'm afraid that compromise means compromising myself.

"I think I would like to meet a man and fall in love. Sometimes, when I'm in a funk, I get into this weird thing where I say things like, 'Boy, I wish I were miserable enough that I would let some man take me away from all this.' Do you know what I mean? Like if I were miserable then I'd have a better chance of getting married. That's nuts, of course, but sometimes we all get a little nuts."

In fact, the changes in society have made it much more possible for a single woman to feel comfortable with her life.

"First of all, you can earn a living. That's one way the women's movement has made things much, much easier. I can survive, lead a decent life, nobody in my office pays me less because I'm a woman.

"Then, too, I don't feel like a failure because I'm single. I don't think of myself as a failure at all. In fact, I see myself as a success story. Housewife makes good. Self-made woman.

"I feel comfortable being in an aggressive business. I'm given a certain kind of respect. Remember when I was in college, if you didn't have a date on Saturday night you hid in your room, so that no one would see you. Now, it's no big deal if I go out to dinner with one of my women friends. There's a lot more flexibility for women living alone.

"Nobody ever questions my credit, either, that's for sure."

But, in just the last few months, since she turned forty-five,

Sylvia said that she'd been nagged by a question, "What next?"

"I thought so hard about making it, getting independent, getting in control of my life. Now I am. Not altogether, but pretty much. Now I think that what none of us knew, thank God, is that once you're on your own, you got to keep on living your life, doing what you do, day after day after day. There used to be these fantasy escape clauses for women. Somehow or other they'd get out of it when *he* came. Now I don't have that. That's okay, but I have a feeling that I'm ready to make some changes again.

"I think, and this may be my new fantasy, that I'm beginning to get to a place where I can think about having a Man in My Life, rather than thinking about giving up my life for a man. Maybe. On the other hand, it may not happen. I can say that I have chosen to remain single, but I can't choose to fall in love, and have someone call up the right guy and deliver him over here." She poured the end of the bottle of wine into her glass. Philosophically, she added, "You know, men are still like five or ten years behind the women. I wonder if they'll ever catch up."

As she walked me to the door, Sylvia said: "My friend Joanie the other day said to me, 'You know, Sylvia, on the whole, if I had breast cancer, I'd rather be married.' That sort of summed it up. This is great for me now. My kids are still here, I'm healthy, it's terrific right now. But I don't know if I want it forever. I think a lot of women of my generation will have to come through the time where they know that they can make it on their own. But they may not want to live alone their whole lives. I don't really know. I do know this: I can survive; I'm not miserable; I like my life."

In the spring of 1978, when I was finishing this book, I was also spending a good deal of time on college campuses. Here were the people who had the most choices still in front of them. I wanted to talk with them about their own perceptions of the changes in society and the future as they saw it.

For the most part, the students I talked with were children of middle-class parents, most of whom had themselves been college-educated. Many of their mothers had married into traditional roles but now lived in modified middleground patterns. Some had returned to school or to work while these students were in high school or college.

I found very few students who believed that the woman's place is in the home. Psychologist Alexander Astin, who has surveyed four million college freshmen over the last decade, found that in 1967 a majority of them agreed that "the activities of married women are best confined to the home and family. Males agreed by 67 percent and females by nearly 50 percent." By 1976 he reported less than 30 percent of both sexes agreed. In all my 1978 interviews I found only a few men who admitted to such an "old-fashioned idea" and they readily—occasionally belligerently —agreed that they were "out-of-step."

For most of the young people, the middleground was their baseline, the status quo in which they had grown up. But they didn't really operate themselves with a great awareness of choice. They, like Nancy, were more conscious of the limitations and conflicts.

NANCY: CONFLICTS, NOT CHOICES

Nancy came up to me at a reception following a speech I'd made on her campus in the spring of 1978. A senior, with straight brown hair, she was almost six feet tall with freckles and a serious, rather intense manner, broken only by her smile that revealed two rows of braces.

She told me intensely that she was a senior and that she had only three more months before she was out in the "real world." I could see her almost visibly shuddering at the prospect.

Nancy had just been home for the weekend and she had tried to explain to her parents the kind of anxiety she felt as she faced commencement.

"My parents just didn't understand. My mother kept telling me that I should feel lucky graduating from college in a time when women could do anything they wanted to. My father kept saying, 'You have everything in front of you. You can do anything.' They just don't understand."

After the reception I sat with Nancy in the corner of the

Alumnae house and we talked that night and again the next day.

As we did, I couldn't help thinking again of Rollo May's remark: "Without some new possibility, there can be no conflicts, there can only be despair."

Wasn't it possible that one generation's despair bred the next generation's conflicts? Nancy's mother, it turned out as we talked, had been desperate her senior year to get an MRS. Nancy, it turned out, was desperate to get a JOB. She wanted to work in television and if she didn't get a start in her career, she was convinced that it was the End.

In that sense, Nancy was like many of the students I met. Almost all of them seemed anxious about starting a career, getting set in the right job, the right graduate school. While the generation of students a decade before them had wanted to change the system, they wanted just to get into it.

But I was particularly struck by this in young women like Nancy. If choice was the watchword of the middleground, then it was clear to me that an entire generation of women was moving swiftly off that plateau.

Nancy's own mother, Amy, had graduated from college with her MRS. in 1954 and she had established her own life as a wife and mother and helper. She had assumed that everything in her life was settled. Fifteen years and four children later, Nancy had watched her go through a very difficult time of readjusting her life.

"My mother was one of those women who sort of took care of everything so my father wouldn't have to worry. She took care of the books when he first opened the company, and took care of us, and he went on and became a success and she was still just his wife," remembered Nancy.

In fact, Amy sounded like one of the women who felt the sort of despair that Betty Friedan and others wrote about, the sort of despair that motivated the change which had opened options for women.

Ten years ago, when her mother was in her late thirties, she had decided to go back to work. "My mother really had a tough time. She tried lots of things. She tried writing children's books, she tried applying to graduate school. She tried applying for jobs. The only kind of job she could get was as a clerical worker or a saleslady. It was awful for her. Everybody kept telling her she was too old, or she had too little experience." Finally Amy took a job volunteering at a school. This eventually led, five years ago, into a paid job that lasts from grant to grant.

Nancy watched her mother go through this anxious time during her own junior and high school years. "My mother very much regretted that she didn't have a career, you know, before she had kids. She never said that to me, but she told my sister and me to get our careers settled before we ever got married or anything like that."

But what seemed like new possibilities, new options for Amy, seem like conflicts and anxiety for her daughter, Nancy.

A Mrs.? "Are you kidding? Nobody is getting married. The only senior in our dorm who's getting married is sort of a Farrah Fawcett-Majors type. It's considered weird to be getting married now. We're all just worried about our careers."

The interesting thing to me was that Nancy wished that she, like her roommate, wanted to go into medical school, a guaranteed future. "Once you get into medical school," she said, frowning, "then you're set. I mean, you have to work hard and all that, but you're pretty well set. You know what's ahead of you and what you're going to be when you grow up." At the sound of her own words, she smiled.

She shared something with her mother at the same age, a desire to make a permanent commitment, to swallow the future whole. Her mother saw that security in marriage. Nancy and many of her friends saw it in the career. On top of that, she was struggling with a way in which she could plan it all. "Well," she said about her future, "if I knew that I was going to get married and have children, then I'd pick out a career that would be easier, without as much traveling. Say I got married at thirty-one and had kids at thirty-two . . ." Nancy went on, listing alternative life plans. These alternatives were, of course, what her mother envied a bit—choice. But for Nancy they were a source of uncertainty, anxiety, and conflict. Some of her anxiety came from the fear that she wouldn't be able to Do and Have It All. "I just don't see how I could possibly do it," she said, shaking her head. "Work and have kids and have a husband—God, I can hardly just go to school." Some of her anxiety, too, was anxiety about the unknown, about change, about her own capability. "Sure, I think about being a flop, a big failure. I don't think my mother had to think about that at my age. She just got married. That's easy . . . was so eeeaaasssy," she said, and I detected a note of jealousy—nostalgia—even for something she would never choose.

When I left Nancy, I had as many—although different—questions as she.

Is choice merely a convenient word to use during a time of transition? Will her generation really have a flexible set of norms, or is society already moving toward a new norm, even a new single standard? Certainly her peers are convinced of the necessity and inevitability of working women—convinced that a woman's place is not exclusively in the home.

But it is possible that they will continue the trends toward independence, toward egalitarian marriages. It's also possible that they will settle into a modified traditional pattern, or even, after launching a determined career, identify their own growth with time at home. Right now, they see these as their choices, or, as Nancy said, their conflicts. It isn't possible to Have It All, but perhaps they will have a rich sampling.

Finally I thought about Nancy's search for certainties, so like my own when I was her age, and of her fear of personal change.

For all that had occurred between her mother's youth and her own, one thing had remained constant—the anxiety about change itself. She had the desire to replace one certainty with another.

Yet, I knew that she would—if she was to grow, to try to have that rich sampling of life—have to learn about the internal tugs and conflicts that would inevitably come at the turning points of her life. She too would have to understand, in her own time, that she couldn't protect herself from the buffeting of change with a well-written life plan. Rather, she might also find that the most important security in the midst of change comes from understanding—not resisting—the process of change with all its risks and pleasures.

Epilogue

How do you end a story of change? There is never a real sense of completion. It is rather like trying to decide where to stop an autobiography. Even as I was writing this book, I had to fight the continual urge to keep updating and altering the story. The people I met weren't conveniently frozen in time the moment I left their homes. Two who were married have separated. One who was divorced has remated. There have been two births and one death. One of the men has gone into a second career, supported by his wife's first job. Another woman who was poised on a turning point has moved into public office. In a letter that came to my office just the other day, a woman who had struggled out of her traditional role wrote about her anxiety and fear, as her daughter casually left work to be a full-time mother.

I am struck on all sides by both the pervasiveness of change and the iron tenacity of traditions.

To some extent, the momentum for change in sex roles has been defused by its acceptance. Lifestyles which once required the commitment of a radical innovator are now held more easily by people all along the political spectrum.

To be a working mother once automatically entailed the stress of facing social disapproval. That woman was a beleaguered member of a criticized minority. Now it is possible for the working mother to be a "New Conservative."

At the National Women's Conference in Houston in the fall of 1977, I heard Betty Friedan repeat what her daughter had told her: "Mother, I'm not a feminist. I'm a person." There was humanism in that statement, as well as rebellion. But there was also change. Her daughter, after all, was also a medical student.

On a flight home from Minneapolis recently, I talked with a flight attendant who was both married and a mother. She remembered only dimly the time, a decade ago, when women lost their jobs with airlines for either of those facts. When the rules changed, she had been only fifteen.

My own daughter came home from school with a project she'd made in woodworking. I told her that when I was little, girls weren't allowed to take woodworking and boys couldn't take cooking. She listened tolerantly, just as when I'd told her that there was no TV when I was born.

Just a few days ago, I overheard a conversation in the ladies' room at my office. Two clerical workers in their mid-thirties were talking about a third woman who had gone back to work when her baby was six weeks old. They were both disapproving. One said, "I don't understand her. As far as I'm concerned, why have them if you don't want to stay home with them?" The other responded, "You know, I was home with both of mine. I didn't come back until my Johnny was a year and a half. You ought to be there to give them a good start."

As they walked out, I thought how the same traditions cling to vastly different lives. The same philosophy was maintained in circumstances which had been drastically altered. These women shared with so many of us a need for the sense of safety and sameness of traditional thought, even as they changed the traditions. At the same time, new concern has blossomed out of the seeds of this change. Our conflict about the new sex roles has deepened into a national ambivalence about our basic values. In many ways, the women's movement has pushed up to the surface some of the conflicts latent in American society. The ones I see as I write these last pages lie at the core of our history.

Americans have always valued individual rights on the one hand and a sense of community on the other. We believe in the independence of family members and the importance of the family unit. We value both self-realization—the quest for individual growth—and self-sacrifice—the virtue of doing for others. We need the warmth, the safety and security of traditions and roots on the one hand, and desire the excitement of risk, adventure, and exploration on the other. We pursue material values and condemn "materialism." These ambivalences provide the tension in our society which is both dynamic and unsettling.

Traditionally a lot of our conflicting values were dealt with through sex role assignments. Men were encouraged toward self-realization while women were allotted self-sacrifice. Men were the keepers of the adventurous spirit while women were the ones who made and kept homes, families, roots. Men worked in the material world, women were in charge of spiritual values.

Now, as women join men in working outside the home, both, quite naturally, worry more about what is happening to the family. As both change, they simultaneously both reaffirm the values of roots. As both seek self-realization, we all worry more about narcissism and selfishness. This is the shape of our ambivalence now.

People are not suffering so much from what Alvin Toffler called Overchoice as from having to make the tough choices. There are inevitable conflicts even in the most "liberated" lifestyles and psyches. Recently a friend called to tell me about a job offer she had turned down. It would have meant so many nights and weekends away from her family. Hers wasn't the "old conflict," an exclusively female problem. In her shared life, it was one which her husband suffered from as well. This wasn't even a problem imposed upon her by the attitudes of the world or her family, but, rather, by her desires. On the one hand, she would have loved the challenge of the new job, but on the other hand, she wanted the time with her family. There were, there are, limits and choices to be made.

This book has focused on change—how it evolves—and some of the things in society that have changed. Women are no longer exclusively homemakers and men are no longer exclusive breadwinners. The relationship between them is different. What next?

I am more comfortable observing than predicting, but it seems to me that our times contain some direction for the future.

The trends are, I think, firmly set. The place I've called the middleground contains more people every day and inches further along. But I think that the semitraditional life patterns of the middlegrounders will continue to be the dominant ones for some time—although I cannot say whether that "some time" will be a decade or two generations. Unless there is some sudden fait accompli that sends us all again into the unknown, I suspect that the majority of women will either go on carving out a small chunk of their lives for full-time child care, or at least considering their paid jobs secondary to their job of mothering. Many men may go on considering themselves as primary breadwinner, secondary parent.

I don't think we will or can go back to a more traditional lifestyle, with role assignments reinforced. That would entail a change far more disruptive and painful than the one which we have just come through.

The lifestyles we think of as egalitarian are and will be increasingly the social ideal. But they may be a reality for the minority—a growing minority, an elite minority, but still a minority. It may take time and changes in social policy—from child care to flexible work hours—for the majority to move further along this path.

When I began this book, I described it, in part, as a personal quest. Writing it has affected me in ways which I couldn't have predicted. Thinking about the dynamics of change, the internal processes, has helped me focus on other changes—in the world and in my own life.

At one time I was much quicker to make judgments, and to impose my own sense of certainty, like a grid, over someone else's life. I was much less patient with my own conflicts and those of others. I couldn't accept the part of me that resisted what the other part of me labeled "reasonable" rational change.

Now I listen to others and to myself differently. I ask: "What fear of loss makes one person hesitate at a turning point? What conflicting values are inherent in the choices another finds so difficult? What hopes for the future prompt someone else to embark on a risky course? What meaning is invested in the status quo, what meaning is invested in change?"

I have more respect for the individual history—the baggage people carry through change and the personal vehicles which lead them through—and, at the same time, I have a greater sense of the common psychological road they will travel.

I have been made more aware of the scale of change that extends from the lightest adjustments to the heaviest disruptions. I have seen that in a crisis we are often torn by the contradictory desires to take a quick short cut to the future and to retreat to the comfortable familiarity of the past. I have seen how most of us take a trip through a Shuttle Zone of ambivalence and how difficult that journey can be. I am more than ever convinced that change is often an effort to conserve—to conserve meaning.

There will inevitably be turning points in all of our lives, and we will probably always go from one Shuttle Zone of change to another. We can't avoid change by resisting it or leaping ahead of it, but I think that we can go through it with less distress, if we keep open the dialogue between the past and the present, between the arguments we hold in both hands. We can shift our perspective from the fearful hope that things can stay the same to understanding the turning points around which life changes, people change.

ABOUT THE AUTHOR

Ellen Goodman is a national columnist based at the Boston *Globe*. Her column, syndicated by the Washington Post Writers Group, now appears in over 170 newspapers. She is an honors graduate of Radcliffe College and former Nieman Fellow at Harvard University. TURNING POINTS is her first book.